VICIOUS

VOCABULARY

By Professor Snurd

Snurd Press

Santa Monica, CA   90404
E-mail: Snurdpress@aol.com

Snurd Press
1940 Cloverfield Bl Apt C
Santa Monica, CA   90404
E-mail: Snurdpress@aol.com

ISBN 0-9722001-0-X

Library of Congress Control Number: 2002093090

Cover design by Nicole Lomonaco Design
E-mail: Nicolomo@yahoo.com

Print Production by Barbara Garcia
www.printingconsultants.com

The Translavic Font used in the pronunciation keys in this book is
available from Linguist's Software, Inc., P.O. Box 580, Edmonds,
WA 98020-0580, (425) 775-1130 www.linguistsoftware.com.

Acknowledgments

My most heartfelt thanks to my brother Will,
to Stella and her daughter Nicole
to my students at San Fernando Sr. Hi. and LACHSA
to Tom for his advice
to my mother Laura Grace and sisters Christel and Lauralyn
for their support
and to Elise, Mark, Arthur, Alexandra for their prayers.

Table of Contents

Author's Bio

"I'm going to cut you."

It was my first day on the job as a teacher, and I stood face to face with an angry not-quite-sane teen holding a broken bottle up to my neck. I had just broken up a fight and tossed one kid behind a locked door to protect him. Turning, I faced the other only to find a jagged glass pressed against my throat. If I challenged the kid, it would be testosterone city, male toe-to-toe, lock horns time, and the kid would feel he had to follow through on his jugulating promise.

On the other hand, I couldn't let him eviscerate the other kid behind the door either. Besides, the door was locked and the rest of the staff was huddled safe and sound behind it. I was alone, with no safety net, staring down this teenage menace in a school for emotionally troubled youth.

"Well, you can cut me," I offered coolly, "but you still won't get through that door."

The boy looked a tad confused, his eyes shifted back and forth as he weighed his options: I hadn't locked horns with him, but he still wasn't getting what he wanted. He dropped his hands, cursed and walked away. As I strutted through the office, I was slapped on the back many times by other teachers and administrators for this composed diplomacy. Reaching the bathroom, I calmly shut the door.

"They didn't mention this in the teacher manual," I reflected as I spilled my cookies into the bowl.

In one fashion or another, that about sums it up for me. In the years of teaching in the classroom, sometimes dodging bullets, I, like many other teachers, have had to be "creative" when faced with queer circumstances: disinterested students, diminished supplies, and violent and/or chaotic surroundings. The lessons compiled here are those that I conjured up after watching a Monty Python episode, where some bloke accidentally wanders into the Office For Verbal Abuse.

I'd racked my brain to think of a way to teach college level vocabulary to gangsters, students afraid of the gangsters, kids from the barrio, and kids just off the boat. When I saw the Monty Python episode, it hit me: Why not teach them to insult each other? I came up with an initial 20 insults, went over it in class and then promptly forgot about the whole affair until five weeks later when an irate female student plodded in on a bleary Monday morning and plopped her books heatedly on her desk.

"Men," she blurted out trying to stifle the tears trapped up in her throat, "are nothing but lying sycophants!"

Could I believe my ears? Did she correctly use one of the insults I had taught her five weeks before? I hadn't done any review. What was this? My concept worked! And more importantly, no one was shot!!

I began to test my theory and it panned out: people in all walks of life were more prone to remember an insult than to recall random vocabulary. Perhaps this concept works because insults are stored in our primitive brains. This is true of aphasia patients; they can hurl out a cuss word when they can't pronounce the word they want to say. Whatever. The insult seems to stick in our heads.

My hope in writing this book has not been to create more strife than the world already has, but to give students (and others) an alternative to the usual four letter words that fill the scatological vernacular of our "modern" society.

Though the pejoratives may seem to be the unique aspect of this book, it's the quotes that truly set it apart from any other wordbook. Once I began to put the quotes in I noticed people were far more likely to pour over the book and pass it around to their friends. The book had now become both a textbook and a coffee table book.

Now I offer it to you, to the gangsters, secretaries, students, and housewives out there, to bosses and workers, old and young. This book is for all you irate folks who, with repressed rage, grit your teeth searching for that perfect comeback, that salient slur, that ribald retort to give answer to your most ignominious, diabolical foes.

How To Use This Book

There are two major differences between this book and any other wordbook. The first difference is that words are grouped together in a slur, as in mendacious dog or duplicitous cad or traducing pile of tripe. The premise of this is that the reader will more likely remember a phrase than a single word, and, will more likely remember a slur than a random phrase.

Why? When you hear the slur, "mendacious dog" every prevaricating putz you ever deigned to dine with pops into your memory. You now have the word associated with someone you already have in your long-term memory. If you had merely memorized the word mendacious, it would have been forgotten. After all, what is the word mendacious? It's a concept, an abstraction. But if you hear the two words grouped together as in the slur, "mendacious dog," you'll remember that jerk that did you dirty and thereby remember that the definition of mendacious is lying.

Occasionally, words grouped together may sound redundant, as in, "archaic gaffer". This is done to help cement the meaning into the gray matter between your ears. Archaic means ancient or old-fashioned and a gaffer is an old man; hence, gaffer should reinforce the meaning of archaic.

Yes. I know what you're thinking. No argument here. To group archaic with gaffer is redundant, but the next time you'll see the word archaic, you'll more likely remember its definition.

There is a strong emphasis on adjectives in the book, e.g. mendacious dog. Obviously I want you to study the word mendacious, not dog. In almost every case the adjective is the word I want you to emphasize in your study, but sometimes you'll see the second word underlined, as in, lying sycophant. In this case, it is the underlined word that you should learn.

The second unique quality of this book is the quotes. There are plenty of quote books and gobs of wordbooks, but this is the only wordbook that has a quote for virtually every single word. The quotes rarely include the word. Each quote is simply germane to the topic. The purpose of this is to entertain.

The importance of this can't be overstated. What good is it buying a wordbook if you never read it? However, if the book is entertaining, you'll be more apt to thumb through it; furthermore, the more entertaining it is the more likely you'll remember the definition of the words.

As I leafed through the author's intros of the other wordbooks that dotted the shelves of bookstores, many emphasized why their book was superior, better-suited etc. than the other wordbooks on the market. The inference they're making is that you should buy their book and not the others. What a bunch of bumptious, obstipated tripe!! If you want to improve your vocabulary, you should buy all of them. My argument is simply this: if you like sardonic humor, if you like waggish wit, if you're tempted at times to spice up your boss's, or coworker's, or employee's tea with a little arsenic, then you might want buy my book before you drop a dime on the others.

d

The Structure Of The Book

The Intro

Each Grisly List has an intro where I make suggestions on how you should study. If your purpose is to engross yourself in this material, then I suggest you follow my suggestions. If, however, you merely want to breeze through, taking the tests and then scanning the definitions for only the words you miss, that's fine. Use the book as you see fit. If you're the breezy type, you're probably not bothering to read this intro anyway.

The Basic Barbs

With very few exceptions, the words in the Basic List are not words I've culled from vocabulary most likely to be on the SAT or GRE. Many of them are slang words; others are archaic insults. In any case, they are words I felt some might need to learn the definition before going on to study the Brainy List.

The Brainy Barbs

Most of the vernacular in these lists has been culled out from lists of words most likely to be on the SAT or GRE. However, sprinkled throughout the book is arcane verbiage for the word sleuths out there. These are words that might seem new to even the most erudite pedant, e.g. potvaliant, mussitate. It won't kill you to add these to you lexicon of slurs. Remember, most of the words are used as adjectives, but occasionally you'll see a Brainy List word used as a noun, in which case it will be underlined, e.g. lying sycophant.

The Quizzes

Each quiz is divided into two parts: the Brainy List on top and the Basic List on the bottom. I suggest you take each quiz, writing the answer on the left and when you finish the book, go back and take each test again as a review. First, cover the answers on the left and then draw lines from the word to its definition.

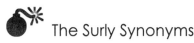 The Surly Synonyms

After each quiz, there are words grouped together loosely into similar slurs. They're not always synonyms; many are merely slurs that might fit a particular dolt in your life, as in, "Men Your Mother Warned You About". You may want to wait till you finish the book before you begin to take the Surly Synonym tests. This is one more way you can review the material. These are made to be easy, but don't sneer. It's in reviewing material in this simple manner that helps it sink into your long-term memory.

Le Mot Quote

For some, this section might be difficult. Don't sweat it. Do your best. Some of the matched quotes and words may seem obvious and others obscure. Pick the best choice possible.

Politically Correct Disclaimer

An effort has been make to make this book as politically correct as possible. Specific racial, sexist and religious slurs were avoided. This was done not out of concern for censorship but out of a sense of direction. The purpose of this book is education, everyone's! A few exceptions were left in where culture or time has extracted the inflammatory value of a particular slur. It is my belief and hope that the book still has its edge. I struggled with the slurs that make fun of the weight-challenged crowd (and this has absolutely nothing to do with my being twenty pounds overweight!) but I've included them in the interest of the perpetuation of knowledge, I, being such a champion of truth. It is my hope that as many people will buy the book as possible so that I can forget work and go to the gym everyday. If you feel I've somehow included a politically incorrect slur that insults your particular clique then I invite you to thumb through the book, cull out insults that you deem would be appropriate to vent at me and spew them out as you shake your fist into the air.

f

Pronunciation Key

ă	rat, scat, splat,		ŏ	rot, lot
ā	no <u>way</u>,		ō	slow, grope, nope
ä	fart, barf, qualms		ô	naughty, raw
â	up <u>there</u>, I don't <u>care</u>		oi	Olive <u>Oil</u>, boil, recoil
			ŏŏ	crook
b	butt, rebut, Hey <u>Bub</u>!		ōō	ooze, booze
			ou	lout, shout
ch	cheat, leach			
			p	putz
d	Duh?, fuddy duddy			
			r	ruck, where
ĕ	red, dead, said			
ē	smelly <u>feet</u>, reek		s	sucks
er	beer, he took one in			
	the <u>rear</u>		sh	<u>Shut</u> up!
f	fiz, flop		t	King Tut, tight ass
			th	thugs, bother, teeth
g	gulp, <u>gag</u> me			
			ŭ	rut, gut
h	hype, hip, hooey		ū	blue, no <u>clue</u>, flu
			û	cur, murmur, slur
ĭ	bit, quit, arm<u>pit</u>			
ī	Yikes!, spite, bite, cry		v	vice, dive
j	jugs, jive		w	wimp, why
k	kook		y	yutz, yo-yo
l	loony, kill		z	daze, zoom
m	mommy, murder		ə	<u>a</u>loof, circ<u>u</u>s,
				The schwa is used for
n	Gun? No! Run!!			a vowel that receives
				very little stress.
ing	wring, ding-a-ling			It often occurs in
				unaccented syllables.

Chapter 1

The first human to hurl an insult
was the founder of civilization. —Freud

Grisly List 1

What is a barb? It's a thorn, something you can prick your finger on, but it's also a slang term for an insult, a slur, a slight. Each Grisly List has been divided into two parts: Basic Barbs and Brainy Barbs. The Brainy Barbs are words I've culled out of lists that were most likely to be in the SAT and GRE tests (the offensive ones, mind you). Usually they're adjectives and I've coupled them with words that are more germane to the average vocabulary. However, occasionally there are words that require a definition or explanation. These I've put in the Basic Barb section for further clarification. It is important to first look over these Basic Barbs before you study the Brainy Barbs.

Basic Barbs

➤ **flop** = a failure
➤ **harridan** = a vicious, scolding woman
➤ **monstrosity** = a monstrous creature
➤ **sourpuss** = one with a sour disposition
➤ **wretch** = a miserable person

Brainy Barbs

1. **abased reject** (ə bāsd´)   To be abased is to be humbled, belittled, humiliated, or lowered. From Latin, *abassare* = to lower, to bring down.

Why do you want to lay there and revel in your abandon?
—Tom Petty

2. **abhorrent monstrosity** (ăb hôr´ ənt)   Instigating fear or disgust, this one is worthy of hate. From Latin, *ab* = away + *horrere* = to shudder.

I captured some of the people who tried to assassinate me.
I ate them before they ate me.
—Idi Amin

3. **abject wretch** (ăb´ jĕkt)   Anyone abject is completely miserable and degraded. From Latin, *abjectus* = to throw away.

It makes no difference whether you win or lose until you lose.
—Unknown

4. **abominable freak** (ə bŏm´ ə nə bəl)   Anything abominable is vile or disgusting. From Latin, *ab homin* = away from man; hence, inhuman.

> *When men are inhuman,*
> *take care not to feel towards them*
> *as they do towards other humans.*
> —Marcus Aurelius

5. **abrasive harridan** (ə brā´ sĭv)   This old shrew is as irritating as they come. From Latin, *ab* = away + *radere* = to scrape.

> *It's like kissing Hitler.*
> —Tony Curtis,
> about Marilyn Monroe

6. **absconding fugitive** (ăb skŏnd´ ing)   To abscond is to run away in a secret manner, especially to avoid capture. From Latin, *ab* = from, away + *candere* = to hide.

> *The thief is sorry that he is to be hanged,*
> *not that he is a thief.*
> —English proverb

7. **abysmal flop** (ə bĭz´ məl)   One is truly wretched to have sunk this low. From Greek, *abyssos* = without bottom.

> *I have a new philosophy.*
> *I'm only going to dread one day at a time.*
> —Charles Shulz

8. **acerbic sourpuss** (ə sûr´ bĭk)   Anyone or anything acerbic is sharp, sour or bitter. From Latin, *acerbus* = bitter.

> *Blame someone else and get on with your life.*
> —Alan Woods

9. **acidulous critic** (ə sĭj´ yə ləs)   Anything acidulous is faintly sour in taste, or like acid, extremely sarcastic. From Latin, *acidus* = sour.

> *Folk whose own behavior is ridiculous are always first to slander others.*
> —Moliere,
> Tartuffe

10. **acquisitive hog** (ə kwĭz´ ə tĭv)   Think acquire, not inquire. This hog is grasping, greedy. From Latin, *ad* = to + *quaerere* = to seek.

> *When all sins are old in us and go upon crutches,*
> *(greed) does but then lie in her cradle.*
> —Decker

Quiz 1

Match the definitions with the words on the left.
Words with similar definitions are lumped together.

Brainy Barbs

__ 1. abased
__ 2. abhorrent
__ 3. abject
__ 4. abominable
__ 5. abrasive
__ 6. abscond
__ 7. abysmal
__ 8. acerbic
__ 9. acidulous
__10. acquisitive

a. disgusting (fits two words)
b. lowered (fits three words)
c. irritating
d. sarcastic, sharp, bitter
   in speech (fits two words)
e. run away in a secretly
   especially to avoid capture
f. greedy

Basic Barbs

__11. sourpuss
__12. harridan
__13. wretch
__14. monstrosity

g. has a sour disposition
h. a miserable creature
i. a monstrous creature
j. a scolding woman

Men Your Mother Warned You About, Part 1

The Surly Synonyms will follow each quiz but the words are rarely from the same chapter. The exercise is meant to be easy. Since the book is in alphabetical order, look up the word if it comes from the Brainy List or check the index if it comes from the Basic List.

(lecher, Peeping Tom, deadbeat, fop)

Unscramble.

1. lrechec = a lustful old man   _____
2. adbedeat = a lazy bum   _____
3. geepinp mot = a voyeur   _____
4. pof = a vain, affected male   _____

The most important way to approach learning these lofty (albeit acerbic) words is to not take it too seriously. After all, everyone hates a bore. No. Think of this as a steam valve, something to help you blow off some hot air. When some abrasive, abhorrent idiot cuts you off on the freeway, these words will help you rise above the situation and sneer with contemptuous conceit. But, to remember these words you must visualize them. And so, I suggest you doodle. Yes, you heard me right. Doodle! First look over the definitions in the Basic Barbs section and then read the Brainy Barbs. Cull out those words you don't know, and draw a cartoon (nothing fancy) of the dolt that depicts the essence of each word. In doing so, you'll more firmly place the definition in your long-term memory.

Basic Barbs

> ➤ **churl** = a peasant, an ill-bred person
> ➤ **fogy** = one who is old fashioned
> ➤ **nit** = a slang term for an idiot
> ➤ **psychopath** (sī´ kə păth´) = one who is mentally ill
> ➤ **rube** = an unsophisticated, country idiot
> ➤ **stuffed shirt** = slang term for a pretentious, pompous person
> ➤ **trull** = a prostitute

Brainy Barbs

1. **acrid slanderer** (ăk´ rĭd) This caustic one speaks words that are sharp and bitter. From Latin, *acris* = sharp.

> *Their throats are open graves....*
> *The poison of vipers is on their lips.*
> *Their mouths are full of cursing and bitterness.*
> —*Romans 3: 13,14*

2. **acrimonious churl** (ăk´ rə mō´ nē əs) This churl's speech is bitter and stinging. From Latin, *acer* = sharp.

> *It is much easier to be critical than to be correct.*
> —*Benjamin Disraeli*

3. **acephales lynchmob** (ā sĕf´ ə ləs) This lynch mob is without a head or without a leader. From Greek, *a* = without + *kephale* = head.

> *A mob has many heads, but no brains.*
> —*Thomas Fuller*

4. **affrontive hatemonger** (ə frŭn´ tĭv) An affront is an insult; hence, to be affrontive is to be openly insulting and purposely offensive. From Old French, *afronter* = to meet face to face.

> *A man who hates men is hated by them.*
> —Ibn Gabirol

5. **agrestic rube** (ə grĕs´ tĭk) This rube is rustic or crude, awkward. From Latin, *ager* = field.

> *A peasant between two lawyers is like a fish between two cats.*
> —Spanish proverb

6. **aloof stuffed shirt** (ə lūf´) A person that is aloof is distant, indifferent or disinterested. From Old English, *aloof* = toward the wind.

> *If a man makes me keep my distance, the comfort is,*
> *he keeps his at the same time.*
> —Jonathan Swift

7. **Amazonian trull** (ăm´ ə zō´ nē ən) The Amazons were a group of women warriors in Ancient Greece. Now it describes a tall or mannish woman. It isn't an insult anymore, but Shakespeare used it as a slur, so I've included it. From Greek, *a* = without + *mazos* = breast.

> *A woman who tries to act like a man lacks ambition.*
> —Graffito

8. **ambivalent nit** (ăm bĭv´ ə lənt) To be ambivalent is to have conflicting feelings: "I love him but I hate him". From Latin, *ambi* = on both sides + *valens* = being strong. Don't confuse ambivalent with ambiguous = having two or more meanings, or vague; as in, "...of ambiguous virtue."

> *What man knows is everywhere at war with what he wants.*
> —Joseph Wood Krutch

9. **amoral psychopath** (ā môr´ əl) This one is without morals or unable of telling the difference between right and wrong. From Latin, *a* = without + *moralis* = customs of behavior.

> *How oft the sight of means to do ill deeds, make deeds ill done!*
> —Shakespeare,
> <u>King John</u>

10. **anachronistic fogy** (ə năk´ rə nĭs´ tĭk) Anything (or anyone) out of its proper time is anachronistic. For example: a Timex watch in a gladiator film. From Greek, *anachronismos* = a wrong time reference.

> *You know you are getting old when you notice*
> *how young the derelicts are getting.*
> —Jeanne Phillips

Quiz 2

Match the definitions with the words on the left.

Brainy Barbs

__ 1. acrid
__ 2. acrimonious
__ 3. acephales
__ 4. affrontive
__ 5. agrestic
__ 6. aloof
__ 7. Amazonian
__ 8. ambivalent
__ 9. amoral
__10. anachronistic

a. a mannish woman
b. insulting
c. bitter and stinging in speech (fits two words)
d. without a head or leader
e. distant, indifferent
f. having conflicting feelings
g. out of its proper time
h. rustic and crude
i. without morals

Basic Barbs

__11. ambiguous
__12. churl
__13. nit
__14. fogy
__15. psychopath
__16. rube
__17. stuffed shirt
__18. trull

j. a peasant, an ill-bred person
k. pretentious, pompous person
l. a prostitute
m. a slang term for an idiot
n. unsophisticated, country idiot
o. having two or more meanings
p. one who is mentally ill
q. one who is old fashioned

Men Your Mother Warned You About, Part 2

(Casanova, Pavlovian dog, priapic, chauvinist,)
(sexist, misogynous, cad, gigolo)

Match.

1. m _ _ _ _ _ _ _ _ _ = one who hates women
2. p _ _ _ _ _ _ _ _ d _ _ = dog trained to salivate
3. c _ _ = a lower class male who behaves disrespectfully to women
4. g _ _ _ _ _ = a male prostitute
5. c _ _ _ _ _ _ _ _ _ _ = one blindly devoted to race or sex
6. p _ _ _ _ _ _ = overly concerned with virility
7. s _ _ _ _ _ = one who discriminates against the opposite sex, or believes the other sex is inferior
8. C _ _ _ _ _ _ _ = any male "stud", rake, or libertine

Grisly List 3

One of the unusual ways this book approaches vocabulary is that it combines an adjective with a noun. Why is that important? Well, if you study the word antediluvian by itself you may or may not remember its meaning. But, if you attach it to a noun making it a slur as in, antediluvian throwback, you are more likely to remember the definition. Therefore, you will keep it in your long-term memory because it is an insult, not some random word. Once again, look over this list, pick out those words you don't know and doodle.

Basic Barbs

- ➤ **gaffer** = an old man, used humorously or contemptuously
- ➤ **highwayman** = a robber
- ➤ **knave** = a servant, a trickster
- ➤ **rustic** = slang term for an old man
- ➤ **outcast** = one cast out of society
- ➤ **throwback** = someone who has reverted back to a former type

Brainy Barbs

1. **anathematic outcast** (ə năth´ ə măt´ ĭk) An anathema is anything accursed, damned, or anyone immensely detested. An anathematic person is disgusting, loathsome, hated and/or hateful. From Greek, anathema = an accursed thing, something dedicated to evil.

> *I wish that for just one time you could stand inside my shoes;*
> *you'd know what a drag it is to see you.*
> —Bob Dylan

2. **antediluvian throwback** (ăn´ tē dĭ lū´ vē ən) Literally, antediluvian means before the flood; as in, the flood in the Bible; Noah's flood?; hence, it means anyone (or anything) very old.

> *Senescence begins*
> *And middle age ends*
> *The day your descendents*
> *Outnumber your friends.*
> —Ogden Nash

3. **anthropocentric pinbrain** (ăn´ thrə pə sĕn´ trĭk) This one views man as the final aim of the universe or interprets life always in terms of human values. From Greek, anthropos = human being + kentron = center.

> *The noblest work of God? Man. Who found it out? Man.*
> —Mark Twain

4. **antipathetic drip** (ăn tĭp´ ə thət´ ĭk)　To have antipathy is to have a strong dislike, aversion or hate towards something. Hence, to be antipathetic is to be filled with aversion and repugnance or to cause that aversion in others. From Greek, *anti* = against + *pathos* = feeling.

> They exchanged the quick, brilliant smile of women
> who dislike each other on sight.
> —Marcus Pugh

5. **antiquated rustic** (ăn´ tə kwā´ tĭd)　This rustic is so old as to be obsolete, useless. From Latin, *antiquus* = ancient, old.

> When I was young, the Dead Sea was still alive.
> —George Burns

6. **apathetic robot** (ăp´ ə thĕt´ ĭk)　An apathetic person is unconcerned, indifferent and/or just plain not interested. From Greek, *a* = without + *pathos* = emotion.

> Scientists announced today that they have discovered
> a cure for apathy. However, they claim no one has shown
> the slightest bit of interest in it.
> —George Carlin

7. **archaic gaffer** (är kā´ ĭk)　Anything or anyone who is archaic is either ancient or old-fashioned. From Greek *archaikos* = old-fashioned.

> My grandfather started walking five miles a day when he was sixty.
> He's ninety-seven now, and we don't know where the hell he is.
> —Ellen DeGeneris

8. **arrant knave** (âr´ ənt)　Arrant means absolute or out and out. So an arrant knave is a complete idiot lacking any social graces. From Middle French, *errer* = to travel.

> Better to keep your mouth shut and to appear stupid,
> than to open it and remove all doubt.
> —Mark Twain

9. **arrogant heartbreaker** (âr´ ə gănt)　This prick has an excessive amount of self-pride. He thinks he's too good, too smart, or too cool for anyone else. From Latin, *arrogare* = to claim.

> The infinitely little have a pride infinitely great.
> —Voltaire

10. **arrogating highwayman** (âr´ ə gāt´ ing)　To arrogate is to seize without right. From Latin, *arrogare* = to claim.

> Thou shall not steal. —Exodus 20:15

Men Your Mother Warned You About, Part 3

(rake, Don Juan, Lothario, satyromaniac, ithyphallic,)
(dandy, philanderer, lecherous)

Match.

1. D _ _ J _ _ _ = a male addicted to the perpetual seduction of women
2. r _ _ _ = a male who is licentious and flits from affair to affair
3. L _ _ _ _ _ _ _ = a seducer of women
4. s _ _ _ _ _ _ _ _ _ _ _ = male addicted to sex
5. p _ _ _ _ _ _ _ _ _ _ _ = one who engages in passing love affairs, makes love insincerely
6. l _ _ _ _ _ _ _ _ = excessively lustful
7. i _ _ _ _ _ _ _ _ _ _ = lustful, obscene
8. d _ _ _ _ = a male who is overly concerned with fashion and appearance; a fop

As you look at the next list, once again pick out the words that are unfamiliar, but this time write down names: names of friends, enemies, politicians or movie characters that fit the words. By doing this you've combined the words with thoughts that are already in you long-term memory. Be my guest and doodle a caricature as well. Make a copy of each drawing with the word underneath and place one on your bathroom mirror. When you feel the word is fixed in your memory, replace it with another.

Basic Barbs

➢ **barker** = one who stands out in front of a theater or side show and with a loud spiel tries to attract an audience to enter in
➢ **dictatress** = a female dictator
➢ **fratrat** = a slang term for a member of a fraternity
➢ **gold digger** = a woman who uses relationships with men to gain money and gifts
➢ **pack rat** = a small rodent that collects garbage in it's tunnel, or one who habitually collects trash and is unwilling to discard useless items
➢ **tyrant** = a cruel, oppressive ruler

Brainy Barbs

1. **asinine annoyance** (ăs´ ə nīn) This jerk behaves like an ass: silly, stupid and obnoxious. From Latin, *asinus* = ass.

> No, Groucho is not my real name.
> I'm breaking it in for a friend.
> —Groucho Marx

2. **aspersive piece of trash** (ə spurs´ sĭv) You may have heard the expression, "to cast aspersions." To cast aspersions is to spread slander or lies about someone. But it works equally well as the adjective, aspersive. From Latin, *aspergere* = to sprinkle.

> Lie lustily, some filth will stick
> —Thomas Hall

3. **astigmatic extremist** (ăs´ tĭg măt´ ĭk) This one has an extremely skewed point of view. From Greek, *a* = without + *stigma* = a mark, puncture.

> Schizophrenia beats dining alone.
> —Unknown

4. **audacious barker** (ô dā´ shəs)   Anyone audacious is extremely bold, recklessly brave or boldly rude. From Latin, *audaci* = daring.

My husband said he needed more space, so I locked him outside.
—Roseanne Barr

5. **Augean pack rat** (ô jē´ ən)   In Greek mythology, the Augean stables were filled with 3000 oxen and hadn't been cleaned for 30 years until Hercules came along; hence, anyone Augean is extremely filthy and degraded.

Dirt parts good company. —Scottish proverb

6. **authoritarian tyrant** (ə thôr´ ĭ târ´ ē ən)   Anyone authoritarian enforces obedience. From Latin, *auctor* = writer.

He who strikes terror into others is himself in continual fear.
—Claudian

7. **autocratic dictatress** (ô´ tō krăt´ ĭk)   This domineering boss loves ruling with absolute power. From Greek, *autokrates* = self-ruling, ruling alone < *auto* = self + *krate* = power.

A friend in power is a friend lost.
—Henry Adams

8. **avaricious gold digger** (ăv´ ə rĭsh´ əs)   What people will do for money -- all because of greed. From Latin, *avarus* = greedy.

I'm a very good housekeeper;
whenever I leave a man,
I keep his house.
—Zsa Zsa Gabor

9. **babbling brook** (băb´ ling)   To babble is to make incoherent sounds, to talk foolishly, excessively or to make the sound a brook makes flowing over rocks. From Latin, *balbutire* = to stammer.

A chattering barber asked Archelaus how he would like his hair cut.
He answered, "In silence."
—Plutarch

10. **bacchanalian fratrat** (băk´ ə nā´ lē ən)   Romping about like a frenzied rabbit in heat, this drunken rake behaves like there's no tomorrow. The word comes from Bacchanalia, a drunken, orgiastic festival given in honor of Bacchus, the Greek god of wine.

Alcohol is like love: the first kiss is magic,
the second is intimate, the third is routine.
After that, you just take the girl's clothes off.
—Raymond Chandler

Often in the Quiz section, I will switch an adjective to its verb counterpart, e.g. babble and badger. This is to help you from getting locked into using the word only as an adjective.

Quiz 4

Match the definitions with the words on the left.

Brainy Barbs

__ 1. asinine		a.	spreading slander
__ 2. aspersive		b.	ruling with absolute power
__ 3. astigmatic		c.	drunken, orgiastic
__ 4. audacious		d.	enforces obedience
__ 5. Augean		e.	extremely filthy, degraded
__ 6. authoritarian		f.	like an ass: silly, stupid
__ 7. autocratic		g.	with an extremely skewed view of life
__ 8. avaricious		h.	recklessly brave; boldly rude
__ 9. babble		i.	greedy
__10. bacchanalian		j.	to talk foolishly

Basic Barbs

__11. barker		k.	lady who uses men for money
__12. tyrant		l.	a cruel, oppressive ruler
__13. gold digger		m.	stands in front of a theater and attracts an audience to enter

Women Your Mother Warned You About, Part 1

(virago, trollop, tart, Circean, strumpet, lamia)

Match.

1. t _ _ _ = a small pie or a loose woman
2. t _ _ _ _ _ _ = a shabby, loose woman
3. v _ _ _ _ _ = a shrewish or manlike woman
4. C _ _ _ _ _ _ = like a dangerously or fatally attractive woman
5. l _ _ _ _ = a half-snake/half-woman monster who sucked the blood of infants; a female vampire
6. s _ _ _ _ _ _ _ = a prostitute

Grisly List 5

If you're methodically plowing through this book like some lifeless automaton you may be missing the point. I believe the more fun (and less repetitious) you make the process, the more likely you'll remember the words. When you get bored thumbing through the text, challenge yourself with a list and quiz, and vice versa. If you wander through the text in this fashion, it will seem less like studying. Then, later, go through the book again in a methodical manner. Now you'll be reviewing the information and it will seem much, much easier.

Basic Barbs

➤ **frump** = a dowdy, unattractive woman
➤ **loon** = a crazy person
➤ **pushover** = one easily tricked or influenced
➤ **wise guy** = an offensively conceited person, a smart aleck

Brainy Barbs

1. **badgering bore** (băj ər ing) To badger is to nag or bother. From Medieval English, *bagge* = badge, because of the mark on the badger's face, but use of it as a slur comes from the badger's feisty personality.

Lady Astor:
Winston, if I were married to you, I'd put poison in your coffee.

Sir Winston Churchill:
Nancy, if you were my wife -- I'd drink it!

2. **baleful assailant** (bāl´ fəl) This assailant is harmful, threatening harm, deadly, or ominous. From Old English, *bealu* = calamity + *ful* = full.

A serpent will still bite, even though it's been kept
and tended a long time.
—Panchatantra

3. **banal pushover** (bān´ əl, bə näl´) Anyone who is banal is ordinary, common. From Old French, *banal* referred to objects belonging to feudal serfs; hence, common, ordinary.

Just remember, so long as you don't hurt anybody,
or talk badly about them, or take advantage of them,
you'll always be disappointingly dull.
—Eric Idle

4. **baneful backstabber** (băn´ fəl)   Beware! This backstabber is deadly. From Old English, *bana* = to strike, wound.

> *If called by a panther, don't anther.* —Ogden Nash

5. **Barmecidal host** (bär´ mĭ sīd´ əl)   In *Arabian Nights*, Barmecide was a noble who gave a beggar a pretended feast with empty dishes; hence, barmecidal fits anyone who pretends hospitality.

> *With affection beaming in one eye, and calculation out of the other.*
> —Charles Dickens

6. **bathetic wise guy** (bə thĕt´ ĭk)   Bathos is a false pathos, an abrupt change from the lofty to the trivial, the anti-climax.   Hence, bathetic means one is insincerely sentimental. From Greek, *bathos* = depth.

> *The ring of the false coin is not more recognizable*
> *than that of a rhyme setting forth a false sorrow.*
> —Thomas Bailey Aldrich

7. **bawdy frump** (bô´ dē)   This one is humorously coarse and lewd.   A bawd is a prostitute or a keeper of a house of prostitutes.   So you could have frumpy bawd or a bawdy frump. Then, there's bawdry, which has the same gist as bawdy. From Middle English, *bawde* = a lewd person.

> *I used to be Snow White, but I drifted.*
> —Mae West

8. **bedraggled loon** (bĭ drăg´ əld)   This loon is wet, dirty and disheveled. From Middle Low German, *be* = make + *draggen* = to dredge.

> *(W. H.) Auden's face looks like a wedding cake*
> *that was left out in the rain.*
> —Stephen Spender

9. **beetling bully** (bēt´ ling)   Besides the bug called beetle (which means 'the little biter') another use of the word comes from Middle English, *bitel* = projecting. To say one is beetling implies one is menacing because his/her eyebrows stick out like an overhanging cliff.

> *Gold rope wearer, neighborhood terror,*
> *can't hang around my mother*
> *'cause she says I scare her.*
> —Ice - T, Rhyme Pays.

10. **begrudging giver** (bĭ grŭj´ ing)   A begrudging person gives but doesn't want to give. From Medieval English, *be* + *gruchen* = to grumble.

> *He gives only the worthless gold who gives from a sense of duty.*
> —James Russell Lowell

Quiz 5

Match the definitions with the words on the left.

Brainy Barbs

__ 1. badger	a.	nag
__ 2. baleful	b.	deadly (fits two words)
__ 3. banal	c.	give but don't want to give
__ 4. baneful	d.	humorously coarse and lewd
__ 5. Barmecidal	e.	insincerely sentimental
__ 6. bathetic	f.	boring, dull, common, ordinary
__ 7. bawdy	g.	menacing
__ 8. bedraggled	h.	pretending hospitality
__ 9. beetling	i.	wet and dirty
__10. begrudge		

Basic Barbs

__11. frump	j.	a crazy person
__12. loon	k.	a dowdy, ugly woman
__13. pushover	l.	a smart aleck
__14. wise guy	m.	one easily tricked

Women Your Mother Warned You About, Part 2

(harpy, shrew, fury, Jezebel, femme fatale,)
(malapert, siren, nymphomaniac)

Unscramble and match.

1. wresh = a scolding woman _____

2. yurf = violent anger or a vengeful person,
   especially a woman _____

3. zejeleb = a shameless, wicked woman _____

4. n _ _ _ _ _ _ _ _ _ _ _ = a woman with an wild sex drive

5. h _ _ _ _ = a half-bird, half-woman creature; a greedy, grasping
   person or a shrewish woman

6. f _ _ _ _ f _ _ _ _ _ = an attractive woman who leads men into
   dangerous situations

7. s _ _ _ _ = a sea nymph, half bird and half woman, who lured
   sailors to their death by their seductive singing;
   any woman who uses her charms to entice men

8. m _ _ _ _ _ _ _ = an impudent, saucy person

Try to match each word with a quote that most closely resembles its meaning. Le Mot Quote is a humorous reference to *le mot juste*, a phrase used by the novelist, Gustave Flaubert, meaning that search to find just the right word to fit in a sentence.

LE MOT QUOTE 1

Match each quote with the appropriate word.

1. The deadliest sin
    were the consciousness of no sin. —Carlyle

2. By keeping men off you keep them on.
    —John Gay

3. Off with her head!! —the Red Queen, Lewis Carroll,
    Alice's Adventures in Wonderland

4. When the world has once begun to use us ill,
    it afterwards continues the same treatment
    with less scruple or ceremony,
    as men do to a whore.
    —Jonathan Swift

    _ a. autocratic

    _ b. aloof

    _ c. amoral

    _ d. abject

LE MOT QUOTE 2

Match each quote with the appropriate word.

1. One may have good eyes and see nothing.
   —Italian proverb

2. I don't care about Jesus. I don't care about Allah
   All I care about is the almighty dollah. —D.J. Quik

3. He rolled the executions on his tongue like berries
   —Osip Mandelstam,
   speaking of Stalin

___ a. astigmatic

___ b. baneful

___ c. avaricious

LE MOT QUOTE 3

Match each quote with the appropriate word.

1. A false friend and a shadow attend
   only while the sun shines. —Benjamin Franklin

2. Rich gifts wax poor when givers prove unkind.
   —Shakespeare

3. By ignorance is pride increased;
   those most assume who know the least. —Gay

___ a. begrudging

___ b. arrogant

___ c. bathetic

Chapter 2

Insults should be well avenged
or well endured. —Spanish proverb

Grisly List 6

As you go through this book you're bound to come across words that fit a drawing you have already made. That's okay. Just add that word to the other word next to the picture, and presto! You have a more vicious slur as in, "that belittling, acerbic pile of pus!" Get a dartboard. Take the picture and center it on the board. Toss darts at it. By the time the picture crumbles, the words will be permanently fixed inside your head.

Basic Barbs

> **insurrectionist** = one seeking to overthrow the government
> **loathsome** = excites hate and fear
> **scoffer** = one who mocks and treats others derisively
> **scourge** = a whip used to punish; any cause of extensive affliction

Brainy Barbs

1. **belittling scoffer** (bĭ lĭt´ əl ing) Jefferson invented this word in 1780. To belittle is to make something small, to insult, to put down.

> *He can see a louse as far away as China*
> *but is unconscious of an elephant on his nose.*
> *—Malay proverb*

2. **bellicose insurrectionist** (bĕl´ ə kōs´) If you're bellicose then you like to fight or argue. From the Latin, *bellum* = war.

> *Those who in quarrels interpose,*
> *must often wipe a bloody nose.*
> *—John Gay, Fables*

3. **belligerent rival** (bə lĭj´ ər ənt) This bloke is warlike, ready to fight, aggressively hostile. It's derived from Latin, *belliger* = waging war.

> *To fight is a radical instinct; if men have nothing else to fight over*
> *they will fight over words, fancies or women,*
> *or they will fight because they do not like each other's looks,*
> *or because they have met walking in opposite directions.*
> *—George Santayana*

4. benighted scourge (bĭ nī´ tĭd)   A benighted person is surrounded by darkness; or this one is intellectually, culturally, or morally in the dark. [be + night from Gothic, *nahts* = night]

In the country of the blind the one-eyed man is king.
—*Erasmus*

5. berating broad (bĭ rāt´ ing)   To berate someone is to severely scold him or her. Be + Old French, *reter* = to blame, accuse.

Taking to pieces is the trade of those who cannot construct.
—*Ralph Waldo Emerson*

6. bestial brawler (bĕs´ chəl)   This brawler is like a beast: brutal, savage and vile. From Latin, *bestialis*.

At worst, is not this an unjust world,
full of nothing but beasts of prey,
four-footed or two-footed?
—*Thomas Carlyle*

7. loathsome bête noire (bĕt nwär´)   Literally in French, it means black beast. Your bête noire is the person that you most hate or fear.

If a pit bull romances your leg, fake an orgasm.
—*Hut Landon*

8. bibulous boozer (bĭb´ yə ləs)   This one has a predilection to drink too much booze. From Latin, *bibere* = to drink, akin to imbibe.

I was so drunk last night I fell down and missed the floor.
—*Dean Martin*

9. biddable gofer (bĭd´ ə bəl)   A biddable person is willing to do whatever is asked of him. It's a combination of bid and able. Bid comes from Old English, *biddan* = to beg, ask.

He who humbles himself too much gets trampled upon.
—*Yugoslavian proverb*

10. bilious brute (bĭl´ yəs)   To be bilious is to be cross, bad-tempered. The word is based on bile that is secreted by the liver. Once it was believed that black bile caused depression and yellow bile caused one to be angry.

When angry, count to four; when very angry, swear.
—*Mark Twain*

Quiz 6

Match the definitions with the words on the left.

Brainy Barbs

__ 1. belligerent
__ 2. benighted
__ 3. berate
__ 4. bestial
__ 5. bête noire

__ 6. bibulous
__ 7. biddable
__ 8. bilious
__ 9. belittling
__10. bellicose

a. to severely scold
b. drunken
c. intellectually backwards
d. like a beast: brutal, savage
e. given to fighting
   (fits two words)
f. willing to do what is asked
g. your most feared enemy
h. to be cross, bad-tempered
i. insulting

Basic Barbs

__11. scoffer
__12. scourge
__13. loathsome

j. excites hate and fear
k. a mocker
l. any cause of pervasive
   affliction

Women Your Mother Warned You About, Part 3

(wench, harridan, battle-ax, Delilah, prima donna,)
(hussy, skank, coquette, beldam)

Match.

1. w _ _ _ _ = a young woman, or a sexually loose girl
2. c _ _ _ _ _ _ _ = one who flirts just for the attention
3. p _ _ _ _ d _ _ _ _ = principal female singer, or one arrogant,
   vain and/or temperamental
4. D _ _ _ _ _ _ = the seductress that seduced Samson;
   any evil seductress
5. b _ _ _ _ _ - _ _ = a heavy ax used as a weapon;
   a domineering woman
6. h _ _ _ _ _ _ _ = a vicious, scolding woman
7. s _ _ _ _ = slang term for an unattractive woman or a woman
   with a bad reputation
8. h _ _ _ _ = a saucy or immoral woman
9. b _ _ _ _ _ = a hag

By now you might be saying, "Isn't this book just a tad too pessimistic?" Duh. So is one third of the dictionary. I've actually received a great deal of flak for writing this book. What I don't see are people throwing away dictionaries because of those unpleasant words. I didn't invent them. In any event, any student will probably feel more positive about these words when he/she sees them on a test and is able to answer the question. So, if anyone comes up to you and says, "Hey, isn't that book just a tad too pessimistic, too caustic, too testy?" Say this, "Aren't you?"

Basic Barbs

➤ **bellyacher** = a complainer
➤ **big wig** = an important person, dignitary
➤ **bum** = an irresponsible person; a homeless person, a beggar
➤ **hooligan** = a crook, a young rowdy hoodlum
➤ **shcmo** = a fool, from Yiddish
➤ **slacker** = one who shirks his work or duty

Brainy Barbs

1. **bland hole-in-the-wall** (blănd) Bland can mean something is mild or that something is dull, tasteless, and insipid. From Latin, *blandus* = mild.

Television: the bland leading the bland. —Unknown

2. **blatant bellyacher** (blāt´ ənt) Anything blatant is either offensively noisy or so conspicuous it draws excessive attention. Coined from Spencer's play, The Blatant Beast = a bellowing beast, perhaps derived from Latin, *blatire* = to babble.

The nail that sticks up gets hammered down.
—Japanese proverb

3. **blithering idiot** (blĭth´ ər ing) This one who speaks nonsensically. From Old Norse, *blaor* = nonsense.

A fool is known by his babbling. —English proverb

4. **blowsy bimbo** (blou´ zē) Fat and coarse looking, this one is untidy. The derivation is obscure but it might come from Medieval English, *blowze* = beggar, wench.

My girlfriend was fat. How fat was she? She sweats gravy.
—Ben Creed

5. **blusterous hothead** (blŭs´ tər ing)   A blusterous person is a blowhard, swaggering in like a storm off the coast of Florida. From Latin, *blustern* = to blow violently.

> His rash fierce blaze of riot cannot last,
> for violent fires soon burn out themselves;
> small showers last long,
> but sudden storms are short.
>
> —Shakespeare,
> Richard II

6. **Boeotian bum** (bē ō´ shən)   Way down yonder in Athens, Greece, way back in them Alexander days, there was this hick-town called Boeotia where the folk got a reputation for being kind of dull—without the cultural refinement like them city slickers down in Athens or up in Thebes. And to their credit—or to their discredit as the case may be—we still use their name as a fancy way of calling somebody stupid.

> Never attribute to malice what can be
> adequately explained by stupidity.
>
> —Nick Diamos

7. **bombastic big wig** (bŏm băs´ tĭk)   This one speaks or writes with high-sounding but meaningless words. From Latin, *bambax* = cotton.

> Every ass loves to hear himself bray.
>
> —English proverb

8. **boondoggling slacker** (bōōn´ dŏg ling)   This slacker minces about doing pointless work (paper shuffling etc.) to avoid doing any real work.

> Some folks can look so busy doing nothin'
> that they seem indispensable.
>
> —F. M. Hubbard

9. **boorish hooligan** (bŏŏr´ ĭsh)   Anyone boorish is extremely rude. From Dutch, *boer* = a farmer.

> Rudeness is the weak man's imitation of strength.
>
> —Eric Hoffer

10. **bootless schmo** (bōōt´ ləs)   Anyone bootless is either useless or without success. From Old English, *bot* = advantage + less.

> Even the most useless person can serve as a bad example.
>
> —Unknown

Women Your Mother Warned You About, Part 4

(termagant, trull, gold digger, vixen)
(Circe, Xanthippe, minx, spitfire, demirep)

Unscramble and match.

1. veinx = a female fox or a shrewish woman   _____

2. tertnamag = a bad-tempered woman   _____

3. rullt = a prostitute   _____

4. dlog gidger = a woman who uses relationships
with men to gain money   _____

5. X _ _ _ _ _ _ _ _ = a quarrelsome, nagging wife
6. s _ _ _ _ _ _ _ = a highly excitable person, especially a woman
7. m _ _ _ = an impudent or flirtatious girl; or a promiscuous woman
8. d _ _ _ _ _ _ = a kept woman; prostitute
9. C _ _ _ _ = an enchantress who turned men into pigs;
a seducer of men

I once was stuck listening to this lawyer babble on about his tenacity in business. He didn't to have much respect for me until I said, "You know what they say, 'For every back there is a knife'." This made him stop and spread a wide grin of admiration. The rest of the conversation went much better. Try this. Browse through the text looking at the quotes that interest you. Use them to spice up your conversation.

Basic Barbs

➤ **gloat** = to look at with excessive satisfaction

➤ **harpy** = In Greek Mythology, a hideous half-bird, half-woman creature, now a greedy, grasping person or a shrewish woman

➤ **hussy** = a saucy or immoral woman

➤ **Jezebel** = a pagan queen of Israel who pursued the prophet Elijah; any shameless, wicked woman

➤ **mooncalf** = a fool because of birth, a freak said because people believed the moon had a harmful effect on birth

➤ **toad (or toady)** = Once, quacks foisted their cure-alls on a naive public. An accomplice planted in the crowd would take the potion (i.e. lick the toad) and be healed of an illness. Thus, a toad became akin to a sycophant, brownnoser or bootlicker.

Brainy Barbs

1. **bootlicking toad** (bōōt' lĭk' ing)   To bootlick is to brownnose, to flatter to gain advantage. Figuratively, to lick another's boot.

> *Just as foods produce disgust for the palate,*
> *so perfumed and gallant words make our ears belch.*
> — *Pietro Aretino*

2. **borborygmic bozo** (bôr' bə rĭg' mĭk)   A borborygmic person is troubled by stomach rumblings. From Greek, *borborygmos* = stomach rumblings.

> *An empty stomach can't tolerate anything.*
> —*Yiddish proverb*

3. **bourgeois materialist** (boor zhwô')   The bourgeois is the middle class. In Marxist theory, anyone bourgeois is above the working class; hence, materialistic and in favor of the status quo. It can also be used to describe anyone conventional and unrefined. From Late Latin, *burgus* = castle.

> *The bourgeois prefers comfort to pleasure, convenience to liberty,*
> *and a pleasant temperature to that deathly inner consuming fire.*
> —*Hermann Hesse*

4. **gloating bovarist** (bō´ və rĭst)   A bovarist sees himself/herself with a glamorized, exaggerated view.   It is derived from Flaubert's novel, *Madame Bovary*.

> *When they came to shoe the horses,*
> *the beetle stretched out his leg.*
> —English proverb

5. **bovine mooncalf** (bō´ vīn)   This one looks, acts or has a mind like a cow. From Latin, *bos* = ox.

> *A cow is of a bovine ilk*
> *One end is moo, the other, milk.*
> —Ogdan Nash

6. **brabbling harpy** (brăb´ ling)   To brabble is to quarrel over nothing. From Dutch, *brabbelen* = to quarrel, jabber.

> *Quarreling is like cutting water with a sword.*
> —Chinese proverb

7. **brackish sailor** (brăk´ ĭsh)   Move over Captain Ahab; this salty sailor is ready to sail. From Middle Dutch, *brak* = salty.

> <u>Likely comment:</u>
> *Shiver me timbers.*
>
> <u>Your response:</u>
> *I never shiver anyone else's timbers.*

8. **braggadocian loudmouth** (brăg´ ə dō´ shē ən)   This is the adjective form of braggadocio. A braggadocio is either a braggart or empty bragging in concert with an air of overconfident self-enhancement. Spencer invented this word by combining brag with an Italian ending.

> *Brag's a good dog but dares not bite.*
> —English proverb

9. **brash Jezebel** (brăsh)   This one is offensively or foolishly bold. It may be a blend of bold and rash, or possibly a blend of brassy and rash.

> *The rash call the brave cowards.*
> —Professor Snurd

10. **brazen hussy** (brā´ zən)   Shamelessly bold, and boldly shameless, this tart flaunts what others would hide. Brazen probably is influenced by the derivative sense of brassy. From Old English, *braes* = brass.

> *Losing my virginity was a career move.*
> —Madonna

Quiz 8

Match the definitions with the words on the left.

Brainy Barbs

___ 1. bovarist   a. boldly shameless
___ 2. bovine   b. braggart
___ 3. brabble   c. salty
___ 4. brackish   d. to quarrel over nothing
___ 5. braggadocian   e. an exaggerated view of self
___ 6. brash   f. like a cow
___ 7. brazen   g. offensively bold
___ 8. bourgeois   h. with stomach rumblings
___ 9. bombastic   i. speak high-sounding words
___10. borborygmic   j. middle class

Basic Barbs

___11. sea wolf   k. a fool because of birth
___12. hussy   l. a wicked woman
___13. Jezebel   m. a saucy woman
___14. mooncalf   n. an experienced sailor
___15. harpy   o. look with extreme pleasure
___16. gloat   p. half-bird, half-woman being
___17. toad   q. a brownnoser

If You Don't Have Something Nice To Say, Part 1

(acerbic, acidulous, sarcastic, sardonic, grizzle)
(scabrous, scathing, maundering)

Unscramble .

1. cerabic = sharp or bitter in temper   _____
2. aciludous = like acid; sarcastic   _____
3. castginh = harsh, mean-spirited   _____
4. casborus = indecent, shocking   _____
5. sacdonir = disdainfully sneering   _____
6. sracicast = typified by sneering remarks
            that mean the opposite of what
            they seem to say   _____
7. rilgzze = grumble   _____
8. amingunder = grumble incoherently   _____

Grisly List 9

They say if you want to remember someone's name, practice it at every opportunity. They also say that if you want to learn a foreign language you must speak it if you want to retain it. That holds true for vocabulary as well. Take time to look at the pronunciation at the end of each word and sound it out. But don't stop there. Look for every opportunity to use it throughout the day—within reason! Use discretion, but use it.

Basic Barbs

- ➢ **braggart** = one who brags
- ➢ **lily-livered** = cowardly, timid
- ➢ **neophyte** = a recent convert; a beginner
- ➢ **poseurs** = one who poses merely for its effect on others
- ➢ **scurvy** = a disease caused by the lack of vitamin C; a contemptible person or persons
- ➢ **syndicate** = an alliance of people for enterprise; also, a slang term for the Mafia

Brainy Barbs

1. **brusque roughneck** (brŭsk)   Anyone brusque is rough and abrupt. From Latin, *ruscum* = butcher's broom.

> O, to what purpose dost thou hoard thy words,
> that thou returnest no greeting to thy friends?
> —William Shakespeare,
> *Richard II*

2. **bumptious braggart** (bŭmp´ shəs)   As if being conceited wasn't enough, he is disagreeably conceited. Bumptious is possibly a blend of bump and presumptuous.

> He was like a cock who thought the sun had risen to hear him crow.
> —George Eliot

3. **Byzantine syndicate** (bĭz´ ən tēn´)   Anything Byzantine is like the Byzantine Empire, fraught with complexity, deviousness and intrigue.

> Government is an association of men who do violence to the rest of us.
> —Leo Tolstoy

4. **cachinnating kook** (kăk´ ə nāt´ ing)   This lunatic laughs too loud and/or too much. From Latin, *cachinnatus* = laughed immoderately.

> No one is more profoundly sad than he who laughs too much.
> —Jean Paul Richter

5. **cacopygian eyesore** (kăk´ ə pĭj ē ən)   This eyesore has an ugly butt. Callipygian, on the other hand, means one has a well-shaped, or beautiful rear. From Greek, *kakos* = bad + *pyge* = rump.

> *I got hit by a Volkswagen*
> *and had to go to the hospital to have it removed.*
> —*Pat McCormick*

6. **cadaverous poseurs** (kə dăv´ ər əs)   Anything cadaverous is like a cadaver. Which seems to be the latest fashion – to look like a dead body, pale and ghastly. From Latin, *cadaveros* = like a corpse.

> *The worst evil of all*
> *is to leave the ranks of the living before one dies.*
> —*Seneca*

7. **lily-livered caitiff** (kā´ tĭf)   Caitiff comes from the Latin word, *captivus*, meaning captive, and now signifies a mean or cowardly person.

> *There is enough for the needy*
> *but not for the greedy.*
> —*Mohandas Gandhi*

8. **calculating crook** (kăl´ kyə lā´ ting)   This crook is cunning in a selfish way, devising plots to further him/herself. From Latin, *calculus* = pebble, small stone used in arithmetic.

> *It is the masterpiece of villainy*
> *to smooth the brow,*
> *and so outface suspicion.*
> —*Howard*

9. **callous scurvy** (kăl´ əs)   This uncaring and unfeeling lout won't lift a finger to help a needy soul. From Latin, *callum* = hard skin.

> *It is nothing.*
> *They are only thrashing my husband.*
> —*Portuguese proverb*

10. **callow neophyte** (kăl´ ō)   To be callow is to still lack one's feathers; hence, to be immature. From Old English, *calu* = bare, bald.

> *When I grow up I want to be a little boy.*
> —*Andy Warhol*

Quiz 9

Match the words with the definitions on the right.

Brainy Barbs

__ 1. brusque
__ 2. bumptious
__ 3. Byzantine
__ 4. cachinnate
__ 5. cacopygian

__ 6. cadaverous
__ 7. caitiff
__ 8. calculating
__ 9. callous
__10. callow

a. a mean or cowardly person.
b. an ugly butt
c. devising plots
d. disagreeably conceited
e. fraught with complexity, deviousness and intrigue
f. immature
g. laugh too loud or too much
h. like a dead body, pale
i. rough and abrupt
j. uncaring and unfeeling

Basic Barbs

__11. braggart
__12. callipygian

__13. lily-livered
__14. neophyte
__15. poseur
__16. scurvy
__17. syndicate

k. a recent convert; a beginner
l. a disease caused by the lack of vitamin C
m. cowardly, timid
n. poses for its effect on others
o. enterprise alliance of people
p. one who brags
q. having a well-shaped butt.

If You Don't Have Something Nice To Say, Part 2

(objurgate, derogatory, deprecate, disparage, chastise, belittle,)

(badger, berate, censorious, deride, Momus)

Match.

1. d _ _ _ _ _ _ _ _ _ = to put down, disparage
2. c _ _ _ _ _ _ _ _ _ = harshly critical
3. d _ _ _ _ _ = laugh at with contempt
4. d _ p _ _ _ _ _ _ = express disapproval
5. d _ _ _ _ _ _ _ _ = speak slightingly of
6. c _ _ _ _ _ _ _ _ = punish by beating; scold
7. o _ _ _ _ _ _ _ _ _ = to criticize severely
8. b _ _ _ _ _ _ _ _ = to put down in speech
9. b _ _ _ _ _ = nag
10. b _ _ _ _ _ = scold severely
11. m _ _ _ _ = the Greek god of ridicule

If you have followed all the advice I've given (doodling pictures, etc.) my guess is you're probably the exception. Most people start projects, then stop, then try to start again, then stop when they feel discouraged. No problem. After all, this book is part textbook and part coffee table book. Don't get discouraged if your study habits are haphazard. Simply keep at it. Use it. Every time you start and stop, start again. If you view this as part and parcel of the process you'll be less likely to drop out from disappointment.

Basic Barbs

➤ **Casanova** = a renowned ladies' man known for his sexual exploits; hence, it is used today to describe any male stud.
➤ **cuss** = 1. to curse 2. a person or animal
➤ **dilettante** = a dabbler in the arts
➤ **taskmaster** = a demanding person who assigns tasks for others
➤ **wench** = a young or sexually loose woman
➤ **whiner** = one who whines and complains

Brainy Barbs

1. **calumnious pack of lies** (kə lŭm´ nē əs)   Calumny is a false, malicious insult that blackens someone's reputation.   Thus, anyone calumnious is slanderous. From Latin, *calumnios* = full of tricks, deception.

> *At every word a reputation dies.*
> —Alexander Pope

2. **cantankerous old fart** (kă tang´ kər əs)   This one is bad-tempered. From Medieval English, *contakour* = a troublemaker, or possibly a blend of contentious and rancorous.

> TOMBSTONE EPITAPH
> *Finally, in his last hour*
> *He had a real reason to be sour.*

3. **cantish little cuss** (kănt´ ĭsh)   To be cantish is to be insincerely sentimental, hypocritically conveying kindness or religious devotion. Cant can also refer to the special jargon of thieves, beggars etc.
From Latin, *cantus* = song.

> *An open foe may prove a curse,*
> *But a pretended friend is worse.*
> —John Gay

4. capricious dilettante (kə prĭsh´ əs) To be capricious is to be erratic and flighty. From Italian, *capriccio* = a shivering, whim.

> *A woman talks to one man,*
> *looks at a second,*
> *and thinks of a third.*
> —Bhartrihari

5. captious wench (kăp´ shəs) She's too quick to find fault, or she's prone to try to ensnare or perplex others in an argument. From Latin, *captios* = sophistical.

> *Most women set out to try to change a man,*
> *and when they have changed them*
> *they do not like him.*
> —Marlene Dietrich

6. carking whiner (kärk´ ing) To cark is to worry and fret. From Medieval English, *cark* = to be anxious.

> *Why torture yourself when life will do it for you?*
> —Laura Walker

7. carnal Casanova (kär´ nəl) This Casanova is completely obsessed with flesh and sexual desire. From Latin, *caro* = flesh.

> *Beds are the poor man's opera.*
> —Italian proverb

8. carping crab (kärp´ ing) This crab will complain and complain. From Latin, *carpere* = to pluck, harass.

> *It is the growling man who lives a dog's life.*
> —Fenelon

9. cashiering taskmaster (kă shər´ ing) To cashier is to dismiss in dishonor. From Middle French, *casser* = to break, discharge.

> WARNING TO ALL PERSONNEL
> *Firings will continue until morale improves*
> —Unknown

10. castigating combatant (kăs´ tĭ gāt´ ing) To castigate is to punish or rebuke severely. From Latin, *castigare* = to purify, chastise.

> *I don't believe in nagging at a man.*
> *You can accomplish so much more by hitting him with something.*
> —N. Hoifjeld

Quiz 10

Match the words with the definitions on the right.

Brainy Barbs

__ 1. calumnious	a. anxious
__ 2. cantankerous	b. bad-tempered
__ 3. cantish	c. complaining
__ 4. capricious	d. erratic and flighty
__ 5. captious	e. fleshly and worldly desire
__ 6. carking	f. insincerely sentimental
__ 7. carnal	g. slanderous
__ 8. carping	h. to dismiss in dishonor
__ 9. cashier	i. to punish or rebuke severely
__10. castigate	j. too quick to find fault

Basic Barbs

__11. Casanova	k. a dabbler in the arts
__12. whiner	l. a demanding person who assigns tasks for others
__13. cuss	m. a renowned ladies' man
__14. dilettante	n. young or loose woman
__15. taskmaster	o. a complainer
__16. wench	p. slang for a person or animal

If You Don't Have Something Nice To Say, Part 3

(recriminate, pejorative, malign, derisive, grouse,)

(denigrate, lambaste, querulous, defamatory, vituperative)

Match.

1. r _ _ _ _ _ _ _ _ _ _ = answer an accusation by accusing back
2. l _ _ _ _ _ _ _ = beat soundly; scold severely
3. q _ _ _ _ _ _ _ _ = complaining, faultfinding
4. d _ _ _ _ _ _ _ _ _ = slanderous
5. v _ _ _ _ _ _ _ _ _ _ _ = speaking abusively
6. p _ _ _ _ _ _ _ _ _ = disparaging
7. m _ _ _ _ _ = to speak harmful untruths of another
8. d _ _ _ _ _ _ _ = ridiculing
9. g _ _ _ _ _ = complain
10. d _ _ _ _ _ _ _ _ = blacken; disparage someone's reputation

LE MOT QUOTE 4

Match each quote with the appropriate word.

1. Every man has a wild animal inside him.
   —Frederick the Great

2. Man is his own worst enemy. —Cicero

3. A man's venom poisons himself more than his victim.
   —Charles Buxton

4. He has the greatest blind side
   who thinks he has none. —Dutch proverb

___ a. bête noire

___ b. bilious

___ c. bestial

___ d. benighted

LE MOT QUOTE 5

Match each quote with the appropriate word.

1. I was shadow boxing the other day,
   figured I was ready for Cassius Clay.
   —Bob Dylan

2. A useless life is an early death. —Goeth

3. Remember, you're fighting for this woman's honor,
   which is probably more than she ever did. —Kalmar

4. Some so speak in exaggerations and superlatives
   that we need to make a large discount from their
   statements before we can come at their real
   meaning. —Tyron Edwards

___ a. bombastic

___ b. carnal

___ c. bootless

___ d. belligerent

LE MOT QUOTE 6

Match each quote with the appropriate word.

1. Most quarrels amplify a misunderstanding.
   —Andre Gide

2. I never wonder to see men wicked,
   but I often wonder to see them not ashamed.
   —Swift

3. Being in a ship is being in a jail,
   with the chance of being drowned.
   —Samuel Johnson

4. Wind puffs up empty bladders; opinion, fools.
   —Socrates

5. Just as you are pleased at finding faults,
   you are displeased at finding perfections.
   —Lavater

6. Violent delights have violent ends.
   —Shakespeare

___ a. brazen
___ b. brabble
___ c. brackish
___ d. bovarist
___ e. bellicose
___ f. carp

Chapter 3

Words are, of course, the most powerful drug
used by mankind. —Rudyard Kipling

Grisly List 11

If your main interest in this book is to improve your SAT or your
GRE scores, take another look at the quizzes. After each quiz
you've written the answers, a, b, c, etc. before each word.
Don't stop there. When you need to review, go back to each
quiz and draw a line from the definition to the correct answer.

Basic Barbs

➢ **contemptible** = worthy of hate
➢ **kakistocrasy** = a government run by the worst part of society
➢ **kvetch** = a chronic complainer, from Yiddish, *kvetchen* < from
   German, *quetschen*, to squeeze
➢ **laughingstock** = one who is the object of other's laughter

Brainy Barbs

1. **castrating witch** (kăs´ trāt ing)   To castrate is to remove someone's
testicles. From Latin, *castratus* = gelded, emasculated.

> *Women just want men who'll share your hopes and dreams.*
> *If you don't, we'll bitch at you until you die.*
> —Stephanie Hodge

2. **casuistic evader** (kăzh´ ū ĭs´ tĭk)   Casuistry is solving problems of
right and wrong by using universal laws of ethics, but it also applies to
using subtly false logic about moral issues. From Latin, *cadere* = to fall.

> *Likely comment:*
> *Now what if you had to have sex with a hundred gorgeous pinups just
> to save your wife's life. Would you do it then? Uh? Uh?*
>
> *Your response:*
> *Well, if you were my wife, it would be a tough decision.*

3. **categorical liar** (kăt´ ə gôr´ ĭ kəl)   Categorical means completely,
without qualifications, absolute. Thus, a categorical liar is a complete liar.
From Greek, *kategorein* = to accuse.

> *He occasionally stumbled over the truth,*
> *but hastily picked himself up and hurried on as if nothing had happened.*
> —Winston Churchill

4. **caustic scold** (kŏs´ tĭk)   This one is bitter, critical, sarcastic, corroding and/or acidic. From Greek, *kaustikos* = burning.

> TOMBSTONE EPITAPH:
> *This caustic scold*
> *got a little old.*

5. **cavalier playboy** (kăv´ ə lēr´)   He/she is casually or arrogantly indifferent to important issues. From Late Latin, *caballarius* = horseman.

> *Nothing is more conducive to peace of mind*
> *than not having any opinion at all.*
> —G. C. Lightenberg

6. **caviling kvetch** (kăv´ ə ling) This one complains with little cause, or raises irritating objections. From Latin, *cavillari* = to jeer, scoff, quibble.

> *It is in disputes as in armies, where the weaker side sets up false lights,*
> *and makes a great noise, to make the enemy believe them*
> *more numerous and strong than they really are.*
> —Jonathon Swift

7. **censorious kakistocrasy** (sĕn sōr´ ē əs)   A censorious person (or government) is severely critical and faultfinding. From Latin, *censere* = to tax, value, judge.

> *Whatever you condemn, you have done yourself.*
> —Groddeck

8. **chagrined laughingstock** (shə grĭn´)   This one's humiliated and embarrassed. The expression "much to his chagrin" depicts the irritation of being humiliated or disappointed. From French, *chagrin* = distressed.

> *George Bush will lead us out of this recovery.*
> —Dan Quayle

9. **contemptible changeling** (chānj´ ling)   A changeling is an ugly mischievous baby elf switched by elves for a real baby. It now can mean an elf, a turncoat, or an idiot. From Latin, *cambire* = to trade + ling, a suffix of nouns used usually pejoratively; e.g. underling.

> *All children are essentially criminal.*
> —Denis Diderot

10. **sly charlatan** (shär´ lə tən)   A fake who pretends to be an expert. From Italian, *ciarlare* = to chatter + *(cerre)tano* = hawker, quack.

> *A thing worth having is a thing worth cheating for.*
> —W. C. Fields

Quiz 11

Match the words with the definitions on the right.

Brainy Barbs

___ 1. castrate   a. an elf, a turncoat, or an idiot.

___ 2. casuistic   b. bitter, critical, sarcastic, corroding and/or acidic

___ 3. categorical   c. casually indifferent

___ 4. caustic   d. complaining with little cause

___ 5. cavalier   e. humiliated and embarrassed

___ 6. caviling   f. pretends to be an expert

___ 7. censorious   g. critical and faultfinding

___ 8. chagrined   h. remove someone's testicles

___ 9. changeling   i. using subtle but misleading reasoning

___10. charlatan   j. absolute

Basic Barbs

___11. kakistocrasy   k. a chronic complainer

___12. kvetch   l. government run by the worst element in society

Them's Fightin' Words, Part 1

(beetling, martial, bilious, fistic, bellicose, belligerent)
(bestial, dentigerous, litigious, pugilistic, defenestrate, jingo)

Unscramble.

1. gnltieeb = menacing   _____

2. llcsioebe = of a hostile nature, eager to fight   _____

3. bllgrnteeie = warlike   _____

4. suoilib = of the bile; bad-tempered   _____

5. iictfs = characterized by boxing, inclined to fight with fists   _____

6. tialmar = eager to fight, warlike   _____

7. tinedgesour = bearing teeth   _____

8. sebliat = like a beast   _____

9. gipuliscit = ready to box, fight   _____

10. itigilosu = always ready to sue   _____

11. nijgo = one who is warlike or extremely patriotic   _____

12. fedenesetrat = to throw out the window   _____

Some of the Basic Barbs are obscure. You won't hear these words used at the local pub. Nor will they be on the SAT or GRE test. However, knowing them still enhances your command of the English language. Moreover, drop these words into your banter to stump nerdy types that hang out at the physics lab. They'll be too embarrassed to admit they don't know the word.

Basic Barbs

➤ **Banshee** = a female spirit that cries of foreboding death
➤ **coot** = a web toed bird; an eccentric old man
➤ **firebrand** = slang for one easily angered
➤ **machinator** = one who plans devious plots
➤ **skinflint** = a miser, a stingy person
➤ **stooge** = an actor who feeds lines to a comedian and serves as the butt of the jokes; an underling or assistant, used scornfully

Brainy Barbs

1. **chary money-grubber** (châr´ ē) Chary can either connote one being careful or one being stingy. From Old English, *cearu* = care.

> *Money isn't everything: Usually it isn't even enough.*
> —Anonymous

2. **chastising banshee** (chăs tīz´ ing) To chastise is to punish with a stick, or scold severely. From Latin, *castigatas* = driven to be faultless.

> *The man who acts the least, upbraids the most.* —Homer

3. **chauvinist pig** (shō´ və nĭst) Nicholas Chauvin was famous for his unrealistic blind devotion to Napoleon Bonaparte: hence, this jerk has a blind devotion to his cause, race (or more recently common) his sex. Coined by early feminists (chauvinist pig) to decry men who repress women, it's still a favorite slam for any man who resists change.

> *The husband is the head, the wife is the neck;*
> *she can turn him whichever way she wants.*
> —Russian proverb

4. **cheeseparing skinflint** (chēz´ pâr ing) Anything cheeseparing is as worthless as the rind cut from cheese, but it also describes one who is stingy, miserly. From Latin, *case* = cheese + Latin, *parare* = to prepare.

> *A miser is like a pig, useful only when dead.*
> —Czechoslovakian proverb

5. **chimerical dreamer** (kǐ mer´ ǐ kəl)   A chimera was a Greek mythological fire-breathing monster. Now, it's any amazing monster, or an unreal, imaginary creature or notion; hence, to be chimerical is to indulge in imaginary fancies or to be unrealistic. From Greek, *chimaira* = a fantastic monster, but originally, it was a goat which had survived winter.

The loss of our illusions is the only loss from which we never recover.
—Ouida

6. **choleric old coot** (kŏl´ ər ĭk)   A long time ago, it was believed the body was made up of four humors. The yellow humor, choler, was the humor that caused anger and irritability. Hence, to be choleric is to be bad-tempered. From Greek, *cholera* = a name of several intestinal diseases.

Anger begins in madness, and ends in regret.
—Hasdai

7. **churlish firebrand** (chûr´ lish)   One who is churlish is surly, stingy, peasant-like, and hard to manage. A churl being a boor the word is derived from Old English, *ceorl* = a freeman of lowest rank.

We've upped our standards. Up yours.
—Pat Paulsen

8. **Cimmerian stooge** (sǐ mēr´ ē ən)   In Greek mythology, Cimmerians referred to a western people who lived in perpetual darkness. Now anything Cimmerian is gloomy and engulfed in darkness.

Men loved darkness rather than light, because their deeds were evil.
—John 3:19

9. **Circean charmer** (sər sē´ ən)   In Greek mythology, Circe was the enchantress who turned the companions of Odysseus into pigs by means of a magic potion. Now it means any woman who is dangerously or fatally attractive. Of course, a lot of women believe you don't need a woman to turn men into pigs.

(God) gave women intuition and femininity. And, used properly,
that combination easily jumbles the brain of any man I've ever met.
—Farrah Fawcett

10. **circuitous machinator** (sər kyū´ ǐ təs)   Anyone circuitous uses roundabout evasions to be untruthful. From Latin, *circuire* = to go around.

A lie can run around the world six times
while the truth is still trying to put on its pants.
—Mark Twain

Quiz 12

Match the words with the definitions on the right.

Brainy Barbs

__ 1. chary   a. any woman who is fatally or dangerously attractive

__ 2. chastising   b. bad-tempered

__ 3. chauvinist   c. careful; stingy

__ 4. cheeseparing   d. indulging in imaginary fancies

__ 5. chimerical   e. living in perpetual darkness

__ 6. choleric   f. punishing; severely scolding

__ 7. churlish   g. blindly devoted to a cause, sexist

__ 8. Cimmerian   h. stingy

__ 9. Circe   i. surly, stingy, peasant-like

__10. circuitous   j. using roundabout evasions

Basic Barbs

__11. stooge   k. slang for one easily angered

__12. skinflint   l. a web toed bird

__13. coot   m. a miser, a stingy person

__14. firebrand   n. an underling or assistant

__15. machinate   o. a wailing female spirit

__16. banshee   p. to plan devious plots

Them's Fightin' Words, Part 2

(predatory, fustigate, oppugnant,)
(minatory, pugnacious, truculent, jugulate, militant)

Unscramble and match.

1. ustiftage = to beat with a club, to criticize severely   _____

2. popungant = hostile, antagonistic   _____

3. dapertory = living by exploiting, plundering, or robbing others   _____

4. t _ _ _ _ _ _ _ _ = savage

5. p _ _ _ _ _ _ _ _ _ = ready to fight

6. j _ _ _ _ _ _ _ = to cut the throat, kill

7. m _ _ _ _ _ _ _ = threatening

8. m _ _ _ _ _ _ t = willing to fight

Grisly List 13

In Chapter 10 I mentioned that I see people browse through the book, laugh at a particular word or quote and then share it with someone else. This shouldn't be underestimated in the learning process. By sharing it with another, you end up more firmly planting it in your own memory. It's like practicing a dance step with someone else. When you go to the dance, you'll have a better chance of remembering it when you dance with your partner. It also makes the effort more of a community experience. And, when you then use the word, at least there will be one bloke who knows what you're saying.

Basic Barbs

➤ **bantling** (bănt´ ling) = a brat
➤ **blue bloods** = nobility, said because with the nobility's easy life one could see the blue veins beneath the soft, white skin.
➤ **clique** (klĭk) = a small, exclusive group, often snobbish
➤ **rat race** = the mad scramble in the business world to survive, or to achieve status

Brainy Barbs

1. **cloying footlicker** (kloi´ ing)   Anything cloying causes disgust because it's in excess, as in food, sentimentality or flattery.   From Old French, *encloyer* = to drive-in a nail; hence, to stop up, to glut.

The best of things, beyond their measure, cloy. —Homer

2. **cockered bantling** (kŏk´ ərd)   From the Old English word *cocer*, cocker was a sheath; hence, cocker means to protect too much or to pamper.

He who spares the rod hates the child. —Proverbs 13:24

3. **coercive gangster** (kō ur´ sĭv)   To coerce is to force someone to do something; hence, anyone who is coercive is forcing others to do something against their will. From Latin, *coercere* = to surround, restrain.

Force is all conquering but its victories are short-lived. —Lincoln

4. **collusive clique** (kə lū´ sĭv)   To be collusive is to connive with others, to plot schemes in secret, to agree to deceive.   From Latin, *colludere* = to play.

There are some frauds so well conducted
that it would be stupidity not to be deceived by them.
—Charles Caleb Colton

5. **complacent layabout** (kəm plā´ sənt)   This one is self-satisfied, and smug. Don't confuse it with compliant, meaning yielding, or complaisant, meaning willing to please. From Latin, *complacere* = to be very pleasing.

> We cannot really learn anything
> until we rid ourselves of complacency.
>
> —Mao Tse-Tung

6. **concupiscent skirt-chaser** (kŏn kyū´ pĭ sənt)   This womanizer has an abnormal sexual desire. From Latin, *concupiscere* = to desire greatly.

> I have an intense desire to return to the womb. Anybody's.
>
> —Woody Allen

7. **condescending blue bloods** (kŏn´ dĭ sĕn´ ding)   To condescend is to stoop down to deal with others lower in status.   From Late Latin, *condescendere* = to let oneself down.

> The richer your friends, the more they will cost you.
>
> —Elizabeth Marbury

8. **confabulating screwball** (kən făb´ yə lā´ ting)   To confabulate is to chat, but the other connotation is to replace fact with fantasy in memory. From Latin, *confabulari* = to talk together.

> <u>Likely comment:</u>
>
> As I remember it, I was a benchwarmer—I mean quarterback—yeah, that's it! I was quarterback for the high school, I mean, college—wait! No! It was the Green Bay Packers and, and, and—
>
> <u>Your response:</u>
>
> Then you woke up.

9. **conniving con artist** (kə nīv´ ing)   To connive is to either feign ignorance of another's wrongdoing or cooperate secretly in some evil scheme. From Latin, *conivere* = to wink.

> Who makes the fairest show means most deceit.
>
> —Shakespeare

10. **constricting rat race** (kən strĭk´ ting)   As we climb into our little cars to race to our insignificant jobs only to fight our way back to the tiny cubicles we dismally call our homes, it's easy to feel like we're growing smaller as society squeezes us out of existence. From Latin, *constringere* = to draw together.

> The trouble with the rat race is that even if you win you're still a rat.
>
> —Lily Tomlin

Has It Come To This? Part 1

(debased, abased, debilitated, demeaned, ignominious,)
(moribund, mortified, recidivistic, retrogressive, freeloader, peon)

Match.

1. a _ _ _ _ _ = humiliated, lowered in rank
2. m _ _ _ _ _ _ _ _ = humiliated
3. i _ _ _ _ _ _ _ _ _ _ = shameful
4. m _ _ _ _ _ _ _ = dying
5. r _ _ _ _ _ _ _ _ _ _ _ _ = moving back to a worse condition
6. r _ _ _ _ _ _ _ _ _ _ _ = prone to relapse to past criminal deeds
7. d _ _ _ _ _ _ _ = to be debased in dignity
8. d _ _ _ _ _ _ _ _ _ _ = weakened or feeble
9. d _ _ _ _ _ _ = to be lowered in value or character
10. p _ _ _ = one forced into servitude to work off a debt;
            an exploited laborer
11. f _ _ _ _ _ _ _ _ _ = habitually imposes on others for food

Grisly List 14

Although many of these words are derived from lists of vocabulary most likely to be on the SAT or GRE, I felt that it was important that this book be a bit more erudite, and I have searched the dictionary to find words that would appeal to you word sleuths out there. Hence, you'll come across words like potvaliant, umbrageous and contumacious, that once you know their meaning, are awfully fun to use to spice up your conversation. You may not see them on a test, but that doesn't mean they aren't good to know.

Basic Barbs

➤ **coy** = shy or artfully and affectedly shy
➤ **lush** = very full or abundant; an alcoholic
➤ **peon** = one forced into servitude to work off a debt; an unskilled or exploited laborer, peasant; a foot soldier
➤ **rapscallion** = a rascal
➤ **rebel** = one who resists authority; a confederate soldier

Brainy Barbs

1. **contentious old-timer** (kən tĕn´ shəs)   Argue, fuss and fight: that's all this one wants to do. From Medieval English, *contenden* = to compete.

> *In quarreling the truth is always lost.*
> —*Syrus*

2. **contumacious rebel** (kŏn´ tŏŏ mā´ shəs)   This one obstinately resists authority. From Latin, *contumax* = haughty, stubborn.

> *There are three sides to every question:*
> *your side, his side, and to hell with it.*
> —*Unknown*

3. **coy coquette** (kō kĕt´)   A coquette teases but doesn't please, she flirts just for the attention. From French, *coqueter* = to flirt; literally, to strut like a rooster.

> *A coquette is woman*
> *without any heart,*
> *who makes a fool of a man*
> *that hasn't got any head.*
> —*Mad. Deluzy*

4. **corpulent tank** (kôr´ pyə lənt)   This one is fat. Of course, there are always those who prefer a more rounded figure. From Latin, *corpulentus* = well bodied.

> She was so big she could kick-start a 747.
> —George "Goober" Lindsey

5. **cosseted mama's boy** (kŏs´ ĭt əd)   To cosset means to treat like a pet. From Old English, *cossetung* = kissing.

> A real dog, pampered by his mistress, is a lamentable spectacle.
> He suffers from fatty degeneration of his moral being.
> —Agnes Repplier

6. **cowering peon** (kou´ ər ing)   To cower is to crouch or shrink from fear. From Swedish, *kura* = to squat.

> Tell the truth and run.
> —Yugoslavian proverb

7. **crabbed complainer** (krăb´ ĭd)   Anyone crabbed is always in a bad temper. From Medieval English, *crabbe* = crustacean.

> Start every day off with a smile and get it over with.
> —W. C. Fields

8. **crapulous lush** (krăp´ yū ləs)   Lacking any moderation, a crapulous lush is a drunken sot drenched in booze. From Latin, *crapula* = drunkenness.

> TOMBSTONE EPITAPH:
> Ashes to ashes,
> dust to dust
> If the women don't get you,
> then the whiskey must

9. **crass rapscallion** (krăs)   One who is crass is crude, without sensitivity, and extremely gross. From Latin, *crasses* = thick, gross, fat.

> Likely comment:
> Hey buddy, so how's the bladder infection?!
>
> Your response:
> Check your soup.

10. **craven dog** (krā´ vən)   One who is craven is a coward through and through. From Latin, *crepare* = to crack, rattle.

> It is better to be a coward for a minute,
> than to be dead the rest of your life.
> —Irish proverb

Quiz 14

Match the words with the definitions on the right.

Brainy Barbs

__ 1. contentious
__ 2. contumacious
__ 3. coquette
__ 4. corpulent
__ 5. cosset
__ 6. cower
__ 7. crabbed
__ 8. crapulous
__ 9. crass
__10. craven

a. cowardly
b. crude, without sensitivity
c. drunken
d. fat
e. given to arguing
f. in a bad temper
g. obstinately resists authority
h. flirts just for the attention
i. treat like a pet
j. to crouch or shrink from fear

Basic Barbs

__11. rapscallion
__12. lush
__13. peon
__14. coy
__15. rebel

k. a rascal
l. one who resists authority
m. peasant; a foot soldier
n. shy or artfully, affectedly shy
o. very full or abundant; a drunk

Has It Come To This? Part 2

(derelict, destitute, impecunious, impoverished, indigent)

Unscramble.

1. pomivederish = poor   _____
2. dinitgen = poor, lacking   _____
3. pemicusunio = poor   _____
4. sedetutit = lacking the necessities of life   _____
5. relidect = one without a home   _____

(abject, pathetic, leech, opprobrious, pariah, wretch)

Match.

6. l _ _ _ _ = to cling to another to get what one can from them
7. o _ _ _ _ _ _ _ _ _ _ = disgraceful
8. a _ _ _ _ _ = miserable; degraded
9. p _ _ _ _ _ _ _ = pitiful
10. p _ _ _ _ _ = an outcast
11. w _ _ _ _ _ = a miserable person

Grisly List 15

There was a man who had grown up as an army brat, moving from place to place, always having to make new friends. He became a priest and traveled to Asia to do missionary work. His bishop was a bit surprised to receive a letter from the priest announcing his upcoming marriage to one of the village natives and joining her tribe. Concerned, he intervened and convinced the priest he had become a "cultural marginal." In essence, never having been firmly planted in his own world, he had become lost between the two cultures. I've included the term in this book because I believe in our world of clashing cultures, we're likely to see more and more of those lost between two cultures.

Basic Barbs

> ➤ **codger** = an eccentric old man
> ➤ **crone** = an ugly, withered old woman
> ➤ **goldbricker** = one who tries to avoid work
> ➤ **gruntling** = a small or baby pig
> ➤ **ornery** = stubborn or bad tempered
> ➤ **quack** = a fake doctor

Brainy Barbs

1. **credulous sucker** (krĕj´ ə ləs)   This sucker believes too easily, is too easily convinced.   From Latin, *credere* = to believe.

> *I'm not saying this woman is stupid,*
> *but when the wind blows, her forehead buckles.*
> —*Brett Butler*

2. **cringing scaredy-cat** (crĭnj´ ing)   To cringee is to shrink back in fear. From Old English, *cringean* = to yield or fall in battle.

> *Many would be cowards if they had courage enough.*
> —*Thomas Fuller*

3. **crotchety old codger** (krŏch´ ĭ tē)   A crotchet is an odd idea; hence, one who is crotchety is full of stubborn notions, twisted, and eccentric. From Medieval English, *crotchet* = hook.

> *I wouldn't want to belong to any club*
> *that would have me as a member.*
> —*Groucho Marx*

4. crusty crone (krŭs´ tē)   Crusty is anything like crust, the hard shell surrounding bread; hence, a crusty person is hard —harsh and rude. From Latin, *crusta* = shell, crust.

> *I am free of all prejudices. I hate everyone equally.*
> —W. C. Fields

5. culpable suspect (kŭl´ pə bəl)   To be culpable is to be deserving blame. From Latin, *culpa* = blame.

> **TOMBSTONE EPITAPH:**
> *Though he said it was a frame*
> *His alibi was lame.*

6. cultural marginal (kŭl´ chər əl mär´ jə nəl)   To be a cultural marginal is to be someone who is lost between two cultures.

> *Human life is reduced to real suffering, to hell,*
> *only when two ages, two cultures and religions overlap.*
> —Hermann Hesse,
> *Steppenwolf*

7. cunctative goldbricker (kŭngk´ tə tĭv)   Get used to waiting, since this one procrastinates. From Latin, *cunctari* = to linger, hesitate.

> *My mother said, "You won't amount to anything*
> *because you procrastinate." I said, "Just wait."*
> —Judy Tenuta

8. cunning quack (kŭn´ ing)   One who is cunning is skillful in cheating, dishonesty. From Medieval English, *cunnen* = to know.

> *"Will you walk into my parlor?" Said a spider to the fly;*
> *"Tis the prettiest little parlor that ever you did spy."*
> —Mary Howitt

9. cupidinous gruntling (kyoo pĭd´ ə nəs)   This is a greedy, avaricious, rapacious little pig. From *cupidus* = eager, desirous.

> *The avaricious man is like the barren sandy ground of the desert*
> *which sucks in all the rain and dew with greediness,*
> *but yields no fruitful herbs or plants for the benefit of others.*
> —Zeno

10. ornery curmudgeon (kər mŭj´ ən)   A curmudgeon is a surly, stubborn and bad-tempered person. The origin is uncertain. Perhaps from Scottish, *curmurring* = a low rumbling in the stomach, or from French, *coeur mechant* = an irritable heart.

> *Success didn't spoil me. I've always been insufferable.*
> —Fran Lebowitz

Quiz 15

Match the definitions with the words on the left.

Brainy Barbs

__ 1. credulous
__ 2. cringe
__ 3. crotchety

__ 4. crusty
__ 5. culpable
__ 6. cultural marginal
__ 7. cunctative
__ 8. cunning
__ 9. cupidinous
__10. curmudgeon

a. greedy, avaricious, rapacious
b. believes too easily
c. full of stubborn notions, twisted, and eccentric
d. harsh and rude
e. lost between two cultures
f. is surly, bad-tempered
g. procrastinating
h. skillful in deception
i. to be deserving blame
j. to shrink back in fear

Basic Barbs

__11. codger
__12. crone
__13. felon
__14. goldbricker
__15. gruntling
__16. ornery
__17. quack

k. a fake doctor
l. an eccentric old man
m. an ugly, withered old woman
n. one guilty of a crime
o. one who tries to avoid work
p. slang for a small or baby pig
q. stubborn or bad tempered

Has It Come To This? Part 3

(insolvent, mendicant, pauper, squander, serf,)
(vagabond, vagrant, wastrel, recluse)

Match and unscramble.

1. p _ _ _ _ _ = one who lives on charity
2. s _ _ _ = one bound to his master's land
3. r _ _ _ _ _ _ = shut away from the world
4. w _ _ _ _ _ _ = a wasteful person
5. v _ _ _ _ _ _ = wanders from place to place

6. dabgavon = one who moves from place to place _____
7. derqnauns = spend wastefully _____
8. dimcanent = a beggar _____
9. sotinlven = unable to pay their debts _____

LE MOT QUOTE 7

Match each quote with the appropriate word.

1. Strong and bitter words indicate a weak cause.
   —Victor Hugo

2. Quacks are gamesters and they play
   With craft and skill to ruin and betray;
   With monstrous promise they delude the mind,
   And thrive on all that tortures humankind.
   —George Crabbe

3. Golden dreams make men awake hungry.
   —English proverb

4. When you get home, throw your mom a bone.
   —Dorothy Parker

___ a. calumnious

___ b. charlatan

___ c. chimerical

___ d. caustic

LE MOT QUOTE 8

Match each quote with the appropriate word.

1. A surfeit of the sweetest things
   the deepest loathing to the stomach brings.
   —Shakespeare

2. Plots, true or false, are necessary things,
   To raise up commonwealths, and ruin kings. —Dryden

3. Who draws his sword against the prince
   must throw away the scabbard. —James Howell

4. The most insignificant people
   are the most apt to sneer at others. —Hazlit

5. The fear of ill exceeds the ill we fear. —Mad. Sevigne

___ a. condescend

___ b. cower

___ c. contumacious

___ d. cloy

___ e. collusive

LE MOT QUOTE 9

Match each quote with the appropriate word.

1. Many would be cowards,
   if they had enough courage. —English proverb

2. When once a man is determined to believe,
   the very absurdity of the doctrine
   confirms him in his faith. —Junius

3. One of these days is none of these days.
   —H. G. Bohn

4. Of all the bad things by which mankind is curst
   their own bad tempers surely are the worst.
   —Cumberland

___ a. credulous

___ b. craven

___ c. curmudgeon

___ d. cunctative

Chapter 4

The qualities necessary to a demagogue are these:
to be foul-mouthed, base-born, a low, mean fellow.
—Aristophanes

Grisly List 16

This book focuses on adjectives, but that doesn't mean you *have* to use them as adjectives. Many of these words can also be used as nouns and verbs. After all, you might run into a dastard that dawdles about debasing himself. The less stuck you are with a word the better you are at using it at the appropriate time.

Basic Barbs

- ➤ **bookworm** = one who is always reading books
- ➤ **dataholic** = addicted to dating
- ➤ **deadbeat** = one who avoids paying his bills
- ➤ **deviant** = (adj.) turned from what is normal; (noun) one who has turned from normal behavior
- ➤ **duffer** = an inept, stupid person
- ➤ **turncoat** = one who changes to the opposite party or group
- ➤ **weasel** = Besides the animal, a weasel is slang for a despicable person, especially one who tries to shirk out of responsibilities. Weasel can work as a verb as well.

Brainy Barbs

1. **curt bookworm** (kûrt) This character is brief and to the point—to the point of rudeness, that is. From Latin, *curtus* = short.

> *Many a man's tongue broke his nose.*
> —*Seumas MacManus*

2. **daft driveler** (dăft) Think of Daffy Duck; this one is silly, foolish, and/or crazy. From Medieval English, *dafte* = awkward.

> *One hundred thousand lemmings can't be wrong.*
> —*Graffito*

3. **dastardly turncoat** (dăs´ tərd lē) A dastard is a mean, cowardly, sneaking person; hence, dastardly should be used when someone is both vicious and cowardly. From Old Norwegian, *dasask* = to get tired.

> *Ever will a coward show no mercy.* —*Thomas Mallory*

4. dawdling slowpoke (dôd´ ling) A dawdling person is a laggard, a slowpoke, piddling about, finding little things to do to waste time. From Medieval English, *dadel* = chattering (of birds).

> *I've been on a calendar but never on time.*
> —Marilyn Monroe

5. debased deadbeat (dĭ bāsd´) To debase is to lower or cheapen the value or dignity of something. From Late Latin, *de* = down, utterly + *bassus* = low.

> *He that is down need fear no fall.*
> —Bunyan

6. debauched dataholic (dĭ bôcht´) This one has succumbed to immoral living and excessive lusts. From Old French, *desbaucher* = to seduce, originally to separate the branches from the trunk.

> *Debauchery is perhaps an act of despair in the face of infinity.*
> —Edmond
> and Jules De Goncourt

7. debilitated addict (dĭ bĭl´ ĭ tāt´ ĕd) To debilitate means to make weak or feeble. From French, *debilite* = to render weak.

> *Show him death and he'll be content with fever.*
> —Persian proverb

8. decadent deviant (dĕk´ ə dənt) Anyone decadent is in a state of decline or decay. From Vulgar Latin, *decadere* = to fall away.

> *Man was not born wicked;*
> *he becomes so, as he becomes sick.*
> —Voltaire

9. deceptive weasel (dĭ sĕp´ tĭv) To be deceptive is to be deceitful and dishonest. From Latin, *decipere* = to ensnare.

> *O, what a tangled web we weave,*
> *when first we practice to deceive.*
> —Walter Scott

10. decrepit duffer (dĭ krĕp´ ĭt) The poor dear! He's either broken down or worn out by old age. From Latin, *decrepitus* = broken down.

> *It's hard to be nostalgic when you can't remember anything.*
> —Unknown

Quiz 16

Match the definitions with the words on the right.

Brainy Barbs

___ 1. curt
___ 2. daft
___ 3. dastardly
___ 4. dawdle
___ 5. debased
___ 6. debauched
___ 7. debilitated
___ 8. decadent
___ 9. deceptive
___10. decrepit

a. worn out by old age
b. deceitful and dishonest
c. given over to excessive lusts
d. in a state of decline or decay
e. lowered, or cheapened
f. rudely brief
g. silly, foolish, and/or crazy
h. to waste time
i. vicious and cowardly
j. weakened or feeble

Basic Barbs

___11. duffer
___12. weasel
___13. deviant
___14. turncoat
___15. deadbeat

k. turned from normal behavior
l. avoids paying bills
m. an inept, stupid person
n. switches to opposite party
o. to shirk out of responsibilities

Has It Come To This? Part 4

(degrade, importune, disenfranchised, abysmal, nugatory,)
(woebegone, cadge, scrimp, hapless, necessitous)

Unscramble.

1. pcsrmi = try to make ends meet   _____
2. dgreade = corrupting morally;
   bringing dishonor or contempt   _____
3. isedendfrancish = deprived of rights   _____
4. pimoretun = to annoy with insistent requests   _____
5. cenesosistu = needy   _____
6. shalpes = without luck   _____
7. bayalsm = bottomless; wretched   _____
8. ebewogeeno = wretched   _____
9. gunyator = worthless   _____
10. cdega = to obtain by imposing
    on another's generosity   _____

I could have used a quote for *every* word in the book, but I felt it was important that you also imagine what an idiot might say. So I've included the "Likely comment" and "Your response" occasionally throughout the book. I wouldn't dismiss these too quickly. If you can picture what a person might say, you'll get a stronger image of them in your mind. If there is a word that you continually miss, even if I haven't mentioned what their "Likely comment" might be, try to imagine your own. It is one more way to fix a word into your long-term memory.

Basic Barbs

➤ **deplorable** = worthy of reproach; lamentable or wretched. From Latin, *deplorare* = to weep
➤ **drudge** = one who does menial, tedious labor
➤ **hedonist** = one devoted to pleasure as the chief aim in life
➤ **lunatic**, adj. or n. = insane or utterly foolish, people once thought the moon's influence (*luna* = Latin for moon) made you crazy
➤ **ragamuffin** = a poor, ragged child or person
➤ **windbag** = slang for a person who talks too much but says little

Brainy Barbs

1. **defalcating employee** (dĭ făl´ kāt ing) To defalcate is to steal funds entrusted to one's care. From Latin, *defalcare* = to cut off.

TOMBSTONE EPITAPH:
This priest fled to Vegas with embezzled funds
Unaware he was stealing from militant nuns

2. **defamatory dirtbag** (dĭ făm´ ə tor ē) This one is slanderous, likely to damage your reputation. From Latin, *diffamare* = take away another's reputation.

I hate the man who builds his name
on ruins of another's fame.
—Gay

3. **defenestrating ruffian** (dē fĕn´ ĭ strā´ ting) To defenestrate means to throw out the window. Avoid this goon, especially if you're near any windows. From Latin, *fenestra* = window.

We're gonna make him an offer he can't refuse.
—Marlon Brando,
The Godfather

4. degenerate hedonist (n. and adj., dǐ jěn´ ər ǐt; verb, dǐ jěn´ ə rāt)   This one is morally corrupt and depraved. From Latin, *degenerare* = to become unlike one's race.

> *Whenever I'm caught between two evils,*
> *I take the one I've never tried.*
> —Mae West

5. degraded drudge (dǐ grā´ dǐd)   This one is lowered, debased, or corrupted morally. From Latin, *de* = down + *gradus* = a step, degree.

> *By working faithfully eight hours a day, you may eventually*
> *get to be a boss and work twelve hours a day.*
> —Robert Frost

6. dejected ragamuffin (dǐ jěk´ tǐd)   In low spirits, this poor child will break your heart. From Latin, *de* = down + *jacere* = to throw.

> *He's turned his life around. He used to be depressed and miserable.*
> *Now he's miserable and depressed.* —David Frost

7. deleterious carrier (děl´ ǐ tēr´ ē əs)   Anything deleterious is harmful to your health. From Greek, *deleter* = a destroyer.

> <u>Likely comment:</u>
> *Hey, a little nuclear waste in the water won't hurt anybody.*
>
> <u>Your response:</u>
> *Would you stand by my chair*
> *so I can read by the glow off your face?*

8. deplorable <u>demagogue</u> (děm´ ə gäg)   A demagogue is a leader who, to gain power, stirs up mobs by appealing to their prejudice. From Greek, *demos* = the people + *agogos* = leader.

> *The demagogue is one who preaches doctrines*
> *he knows to be untrue to men he knows to be idiots.*
> —H. L. Mencken

9. demeaning mudslinger (dǐ mēn´ ing)   To demean another is to lower his/her dignity. The root word is *mean* = inferior, low in station.

> *Do not use a hatchet to remove a fly from your friend's forehead.*
> —Chinese proverb

10. demented lunatic (dǐ měn´ tǐd)   This one's insane. Twisted. Out of one's gourd. From Latin, *demens* = mad, out of one's mind.

> **TOMBSTONE EPITAPH:**
> *We knew he was one crazy fella'*
> *When he tried to get fresh with a gorilla*

Quiz 17

Match the words with the definitions on the right.

Brainy Barbs

___ 1. defalcate
___ 2. defamatory
___ 3. defenestrate
___ 4. degenerate
___ 5. degraded
___ 6. dejected
___ 7. deleterious
___ 8. demagogue

___ 9. demean
___10. demented

a. a leader who stirs up mobs
b. harmful
c. in low spirits
d. insane
e. lowered, (fits two words)
f. morally corrupt and depraved
g. slanderous
h. steal funds entrusted to one's care
i. to throw out the window

Basic Barb

___11. lunatic
___12. deplorable
___13. dung
___14. ragamuffin
___15. drudge
___16. hedonist
___17. brigand

k. a bandit
l. worthy of reproach
m. a poor, ragged child or person
n. crap
o. insane or utterly foolish
p. one devoted to pleasure
q. does menial, tedious labor

Pride Comes Before The Fall, Part 1

(Adonis, arrogant, audacious, preen, temerarious, narcissistic)

(bumptious, egocentric, egotist, flaunty, brash)

Match.

1. a _ _ _ _ _ = very handsome young man
2. t _ _ _ _ _ _ _ _ _ _ _ = foolish boldness
3. a _ _ _ _ _ _ _ _ _ = rudely bold
4. a _ _ _ _ _ _ _ _ = excessive self-pride
5. p _ _ _ _ = to excessively groom of oneself
6. n _ _ _ _ _ _ _ _ _ _ _ = excessive self-love
7. e _ _ _ _ _ _ = self-centered
8. e _ _ _ _ _ _ _ _ _ = self-centered
9. f _ _ _ _ _ _ = showing off proudly
10. b _ _ _ _ _ _ _ _ _ = disagreeably conceited
11. b _ _ _ _ = offensively bold

Grisly List 18

We've thought about what some of these characters might say, but what about what they might do? Or eat? Or what might we say about them on their tombstone? If you're having trouble with remembering some of the words, take the time to write down what you think their profession might be, or their favorite sandwich. It is just one more creative way to improve your vocabulary without the tedious task of memorization.

Basic Barbs

➢ **brigand** = a bandit
➢ **detractor** = one who belittles others
➢ **dimwit** = a stupid person
➢ **Momus** = the Greek god of blame and ridicule
➢ **schmuck** = a despicable, foolish jerk
➢ **strumpet** = a prostitute

Brainy Barbs

1. **denigrating backbiter** (dĕn´ ə grāt´ ing)   This one disparages another's reputation by blackening it. From Latin, *denigrare* = to blacken.

> *Slanderers are like flies,*
> *that pass all over a man's good parts*
> *to light only on his sores.*
> —*Rule of Life*

2. **dentigerous adversary** (dĕn tĭj ər əs)   Anyone dentigerous is bearing his teeth. From Latin, *dens* = tooth + gerous.

> *I loathe people who keep dogs. They are cowards*
> *who haven't got the guts to bite people themselves.*
> —*August Strindberg*

3. **depraved strumpet** (dĭ prăvd´)   Anyone depraved is morally corrupted. From Latin, *depravare* = to make crooked.

> *This is my last year to fool around.*
> *Then I'm going to settle down and marry a rock star.*
> —*from the movie Modern Girls*

4. **deprecating schmuck** (dĕp´ rə kāt´ ing)   To deprecate is to express disapproval, to belittle or to argue against. From Latin, *deprecatuss,* = to ward off by prayer.

> *Evil report, like the Italian stiletto, is an assassin's weapon.*
> —*Mad. de Maintenon*

5. **depredatory brigand** (dĭ prĕd´ ə tôr´ ē)   This one will rob and strip you of goods. From Late Latin, *depraedatus* = plundered.

> *The rich rob the poor and the poor rob one another.*
> —*Sojourner Truth*

6. **deranged dimwit** (dĭ rānjd´)   To put it mildly, this one's brain is off kilter, insane, loony, daffy, half-baked etc. From Old French, *des* = apart + *rengier* = to put in a row.

> *The madman thinks the rest of the world crazy.*
> —*Publilius Syrus*

7. **God-forsaken <u>derelict</u>** (der´ ə lĭkt)   Derelict has several meanings: as an adjective it can signify someone is neglectful, or that something is abandoned; as a noun it can signify an abandoned ship or a bum. From Latin, *derelictus* = abandoned.

> *Were all of us sentenced*
> *to solitary confinement*
> *inside our own skins,*
> *for life.*
> —*Tennessee Williams*

8. **deriding Momus** (dĭ rīd´ ing)   To deride is to laugh with contempt, or ridicule another. From Latin, *de* = down + *ridere* = to laugh.

> *The more I see of men,*
> *the more I like my dogs.*
> —*Madame de Stael*

9. **derisive detractor** (dĭ rī´ sĭv)   Derisive remarks are comments that ridicule. From Latin, *de* = down + *ridere* = to laugh.

> *Why don't you put your face in dough and make jackass cookies?*
> —*Soupy Sales*

10. **derogatory gossip** (dĭ rŏg´ ə tôr´ ē)   To be derogatory is to put others down, to speak slightingly of them. From Latin, *derogare* = detract from.

> *In judging others, folks will work overtime for no pay.*
> —*Charles Carruthers*

Quiz 18

Match the words with the definitions on the right.

Brainy Barbs

__ 1. denigrating
__ 2. dentigerous
__ 3. depraved
__ 4. deprecate
__ 5. depredatory
__ 6. deranged
__ 7. derelict
__ 8. deriding
__ 9. derisive
__10. derogatory

a. bearing teeth
b. given to robbing
c. insane
d. morally corrupted
e. neglectful, or abandoned
f. ridiculing (fits two words)
g. slandering (fits two words)
h. to express disapproval

Basic Barbs

__11. detractor
__12. Momus
__13. brigand
__14. schmuck
__15. strumpet
__16. dimwit

i. a despicable, foolish jerk
j. a prostitute
k. a stupid person
l. one who belittles others
m. Greek god of blame, ridicule
n. a bandit

Pride Comes Before The Fall, Part 2

(impertinent, cavalier, clique, flaunt, flounce, malapert,)
(peevish, aloof, pert, petulant, presumptuous)

Match and unscramble.

1. vhsipee = hard to please, impatient   _____
2. palamert = a saucy person   _____
3. tnualf = show off proudly   _____
4. trep = bold, saucy, forward   _____

5. c _ _ _ _ _ = a snobbish exclusive group
6. p _ _ _ _ _ _ _ _ _ _ _ = take too much for granted
7. c _ _ _ _ _ _ _ = casually indifferent
8. f _ _ _ _ _ _ = move the body with quick flinging motions, as in anger or impatience
9. p _ _ _ _ _ _ _ = peevish, froward, impatient
10. i _ _ _ _ _ _ _ _ _ _ = disrespectful, saucy
11. a _ _ _ _ = distant in interest

Grisly List 19

If you're in school browsing through this book, you have probably made some friends and some enemies. Take a look around you, your enemies, for example, and think of what you might say about them in your yearbook. On a separate paper, write down their names next to the words in this list. Perhaps Luis, the ruthless despoiler, might be voted most likely to end up at Folsom prison. Or, Betty, the destitute twit, is most likely to end up homeless. When you finish I suggest you toss the paper, or shred it, so it doesn't fall into the wrong hands. In the end, you'll now remember the vocabulary whenever you see them.

Basic Barbs

➤ **despot** = an absolute ruler, tyrant
➤ **double-crosser** = one who betrays by intentionally not doing what they promised
➤ **dweeb** = a nerd
➤ **ruthless** = cruel, without pity
➤ **schoolmarm** = a female schoolteacher; hence, anyone who's old-fashioned and pedantic
➤ **washout** = a slang term for one who is a complete failure

Brainy Barbs

1. **despicable little devil** (dĕs´ pĭ kə bəl)   To be despicable is to be contemptible, deserving hate. From Latin, *despicari* = to despise.

> *No one can have a higher opinion of him than I have,*
> *and I think he's a dirty little beast.*
> —W. S. Gilbert

2. **ruthless despoiler** (dĭ spoil´ ər)   To despoil is to rob, to plunder everything of value. From Latin, *spoliare* = to spoil, rob.

> *Thieves respect property;*
> *they merely wish the property to become their property*
> *that they may more perfectly respect it.*
> —G. K. Chesterton

3. **despondent hardluck case** (dĭ spŏn´ dənt)   This poor soul has lost all courage and hope. From Latin, *despondere* = to lose courage.

> *You are free, and that is why you are lost.*
> —Franz Kafka

4. **destitute washout** (dĕs´ tĭ tūt´) To be destitute is to lack even the bare necessities of life, to be poverty-stricken. From Latin, *destitutus* = put away, abandoned. It can be used as a noun or an adjective.

> *The destitute does not live, but dies by inches.*
> —Russian proverb

5. **desultory dweeb** (dĕs´ əl tor´ ē) This dweeb is disconnected, random and aimless. From Latin, *desilire* = to leap down.

> *The less men think, the more they talk.*
> —Montesquieu

6. **twisted deviate** (noun, dē´ vē ĭt; adjective, dē´ vē āt) This one turns away from what is normal or right, especially if it involves anything sexual. As an adjective, deviate means to turn aside from the path you're on. From Latin, *deviatus* = turned from the straight road.

> *I believe that sex is the most beautiful,*
> *natural, and wholesome thing*
> *that money can buy.*
> —Steve Martin

7. **devious double-crosser** (dē´ vē əs) Anything devious is winding or deceiving. From Latin, *devius* = off the road.

> *One may smile, and smile and be a villain.*
> —Shakespeare,
> Hamlet

8. **diabolical despot** (dī´ ə bŏl´ ĭ kăl) To be diabolical is to have the attributes of the devil. From Greek, *diabol* = devil.

> *No doubt Jack the Ripper excused himself*
> *on the grounds that it was his human nature.*
> —A. A. Milne

9. **dictatorial bigshot** (dĭk tə´ tōr ē əl) This bigshot is tyrannical, bossy domineering. From Latin, *dictator* = chief magistrate.

> *Dictators always look good until the last minutes.*
> —Thomas Masaryk

10. **didactic schoolmarm** (dī dăk´ tĭk) Didactic can mean instructive, or intended to give moral instruction, or one who is too inclined to teach, excessively instructing to the annoyance of others.   From Greek, *didaktikos* = apt at teaching, instructive.

> *Education is a state-controlled manufactory of echoes.*
> —N. Douglas

Liar, Liar, Pants On Fire, Part 1

(changeling, charlatan, equivocal, fabulist, mountebank,)
(pettifogger, pseudologist, Janus-faced,)

Match and unscramble.

1. c _ _ _ _ _ _ _ _ _ = elf; turncoat; idiot
2. c _ _ _ _ _ _ _ _ = a pretended expert, fake
3. m _ _ _ _ _ _ _ _ _ = charlatan, quack
4. f _ _ _ _ _ _ _ = a liar, one who tells fables, tall tales
5. p _ _ _ _ _ _ _ _ _ _ _ = a liar
6. voqecaiul = purposely vague, give answers that can be interpreted in more than one way   _____
7. fopttiegger = a lawyer who handles petty cases using unethical methods;   _____
8. decaf-sunaJ = t wo-faced, deceiving   _____

Has anyone recently really ticked you off? Stabbed you in the back? Run off and left you high and dry? Then write them a letter. Fill the letter with as many aspersions as you can and then go back and add some more. Write the letter in blood if you have to. Just kidding. My point is this: get the anger out of you. Then take the letter, seal it and burn it, or nail it to something. I wouldn't mail it. Someone might mail one back.

Basic Barbs

➢ **hag** = an old shrewish woman
➢ **highbrow** = one excessively pretentious about his so-called intellectual or cultural height
➢ **John Doe** = Originally John and Jane Doe were legal names used for unknown plaintiffs, now it is used to signify the average person, unknown corpses, or faceless individuals in a crowd.
➢ **pulpit drone** = a boring preacher
➢ **wall flower** = a woman who stands at the side of a party
➢ **whiffler** (hwĭf´ lər) = one who frequently shifts his opinion

Brainy Barbs

1. **diffident wall flower** (dĭf´ ĭ dənt)   This shy lamb lacks self-confidence. From Latin, *diffidens* = mistrust, despairing.

> *What is more mortifying than to feel*
> *that you have missed the plum*
> *for want of courage to shake the tree?*
> —*Logan Pearsall Smith*

2. **digressive pulpit drone** (dī grĕs´ ĭv)   A digressive person wanders from the main point. From Latin, *digressus* = having departed or gone aside.

> *He's a wonderful talker*
> *who has the art of telling you nothing*
> *in a great harangue.*
> —*Moliere*

3. **dilatory goof-off** (dĭl´ ə tôr ē)   Anything dilatory tends to cause delay. From Latin, *dilator* = dilatory person.

> *Saturday afternoon,*
> *although occurring at regular and well-foreseen intervals,*
> *always takes this railway by surprise.*
> —*W. S. Gilbert*

4. **discombobulated whiffler** (dĭs´ kəm bäb´ yū lāt əd)   This one is completely perplexed, and/or frustrated. It's possibly an alteration of discomfit.

I'm in a phone booth at the corner of Walk and Don't Walk.
—Unknown

5. **disconsolate John Doe** (dĭs kŏn´ sə lĭt)   This unhappy soul is so dejected he's beyond any comfort. From Latin, *dis* = cause to be the opposite + *com* = with + *solari* = to solace, comfort.

TOMBSTONE EPITAPH:
Before we could tell him of the sweepstakes he'd won
He solved all his woes with point of a gun.

6. **discursive speechifier** (dĭ skûr´ sĭv)   This orator wanders from one topic to another. From Latin, *discurrere* = to run to and fro.

Wise men talk because they have something to say;
fools talk because they have to say something.
—Plato (427—347)

7. **disdainful highbrow** (dĭs dān´ fəl)   This highbrow looks down on others with aloof contempt. From Latin, *dedignari* = to think unworthy.

The higher the monkey climbs, the more you see of his ass.
—"Vinegar Joe" Stilwell

8. **disenfranchised herd** (dĭs´ ĕn frăn´chīzd)   These slaves have been deprived of the rights of citizenship or of the hope of those rights. From Old French, *dis* = not + *franc* = free.

I feel a lot better since I gave up hope.
—Unknown

9. **disgruntled hag** (dĭs grŭn´ təld)   This hag has been made peevishly unhappy and cross. From Latin, *dis* = apart + an out of date, idiomatic English expression, *gruntle* = to grunt often. Grunt comes from Latin, *grunnire* = to grunt.

I told my mother-in-law that my house was her house,
and she said, "Get the hell off my property."
—Joan Rivers

10. **disingenuous rake** (dĭs´ ĭn jĕn´ yū əs)   To be disingenuous is to not be straight forward, not candid or insincere. From Latin, *dis* = to be the opposite of + *ingenuus* = native, inborn, freeborn, noble.

A little truth helps the lie go down.
—Italian proverb

Quiz 20

Match the words with the definitions on the right.

Brainy Barbs

__ 1. diffident
__ 2. digressive
__ 3. dilatory
__ 4. discombobulated
__ 5. disconsolate
__ 6. discursive
__ 7. disdainful
__ 8. disenfranchised
__ 9. disingenuous
__10. disgruntled

a. beyond any comfort
b. completely perplexed
c. deprived of the rights of citizenship
d. lack self-confidence
e. look down with aloof scorn
f. peevishly unhappy and cross
g. to cause delay
h. to not be straight forward
i. wander from the main point (fits two words)

Basic Barbs

__11. pulpit drone
__12. hag
__13. wall flower
__14. highbrow
__15. John Doe
__16. whiffle

j. an old shrewish woman
k. a boring preacher
l. woman standing at the side of a party
m. an excessively pretentious intellectual
n. frequently shifts his opinion
o. the average person; unknown corpses

Liar, Liar, Pants On Fire, Part 2

(prevaricate, dissemble, sophistical, mendacious,)
(fabricate, renege, perjure)

Match.

1. r _ _ _ _ _ = back out of a promise
2. f _ _ _ _ _ _ _ _ = to make up stories
3. m _ _ _ _ _ _ _ _ _ = lying
4. d _ _ _ _ _ _ _ _ = to conceal under a false appearance
5. p _ _ _ _ _ _ = lie under oath
6. p _ _ _ _ _ _ _ _ _ _ _ = to lie
7. s _ _ _ _ _ _ _ _ _ _ = clever and believable but unsound

LE MOT QUOTE 10

Match each quote with the appropriate word.

1. A wise fellow who is worthless
   always charms the rabble. —Euripides

2. Cutting honest throats by whispers.
   —Sir Walter Scott

3. It is a bitter dose to be taught obedience
   after you have learned to rule. —Publilius Syrus

4. We said nonsense, but it was important nonsense.
   —Nora Astorga

__ a. demagogue

__ b. debased

__ c. daft

__ d. demean

LE MOT QUOTE 11

Match each quote with the appropriate word.

1. War makes thieves; peace hangs them.
   —George Herbert

2. Take care of the children of the poor,
   for they will be the ones who advance knowledge.
   —Talmud

3. A clean glove often hides a dirty hand.
   —English proverb

4. Every dog is entitled to one bite. —Anonymous

5. Ordinarily, he's insane, but he has lucid moments
   when he's merely stupid. —Henrich Heine

__ a. deranged

__ b. depredatory

__ c. devious

__ d. destitute

__ e. dentigerous

LE MOT QUOTE 12
Match each quote with the appropriate word.

1. No sooner is a temple built to God,
   but the devil builds a chapel hard by. —Herbert

2. It is the old practice of despots to use a part
   of the people to keep the rest in order. —Jefferson

3. Pedantry crams our heads with learned lumber,
   and takes out our brains to make room for it.
   —Colton

4. If you are too hesitant to ask the way,
   you will be lost. —Malay proverb

5. The lie indirect is often as bad, and always meaner
   and more cowardly than the lie direct. —H. Ballou

___ a. disingenuous
___ b. diffident
___ c. didactic
___ d. dictatorial
___ e. diabolical

Chapter 5

Words ought to be a little wild for they are the
assault of thoughts on the unthinking.
—John Keynes

The more you improve your vocabulary; the more you'll hear
words others use you had never heard. News reporters, radio
announcers are dropping in little erudite morsels into their
banter. You never heard them before because your brain tuned
them out and made sense of the word in the context of the
sentence. Now that you understand them, relish the moment.

Basic Barbs

➤ **dipsomaniac** = an alcoholic
➤ **fascist** = a member of a rigid dictatorship characterized by
belligerent nationalism
➤ **impostor** = one who pretends to be another to deceive or cheat
➤ **pig-headed** = stubborn

Brainy Barbs

1. **disheveled drifter** (dǐ shěv´ əld)   This one is uncombed and untidy.
From Old French, *descheveler* = to tousle < dis + *chevel* = hair.

> She was a large woman who seemed
> not so much dressed as upholstered.
> —James Barrie

2. **dismal failure** (dǐz´ məl)   Anything dismal is either very dreary or
completely inept or boring. From Old French, *dis mal* = unlucky days.

> Great souls have wills; feeble ones have only wishes.
> —Chinese proverb

3. **disparaging accuser** (dǐ spâr´ ǐj ing)   To disparage is to put
someone down, to speak slightingly of others.   From Old French,
desparagier = to marry one of inferior rank.

> There are different ways of assassinating a man:
> by pistol, sword, poison, or moral assassination.
> They are the same in their results
> except that the last is more cruel.
> —Napoleon I.

4. **dispiteous fascist** (dĭs pĭt′ ē əs)   This one is ruthless, cruel, and without pity. From Latin, *despicere* = to look down on.

Any excuse will serve a tyrant. —Aesop

5. **disputatious grump** (dĭs′ pyə tā′ shəs)   This one's always ready to argue. From Latin, *disputare* = to discuss; hence, to argue.

He that blows coals in quarrels he has nothing to do with
has no right to complain if the sparks fly in his face.
—Benjamin Franklin

6. **dissembling deceiver** (dĭ sĕm′ bling)   This one conceals something under a false appearance, to disguise. From Latin, *dissimulare* = to feign, altered by *semble*, (an obsolete English word) = to resemble.

To know how to dissemble is the knowledge of kings.
—Richelieu

7. **pig-headed dissident** (dĭs′ ĭ dənt, adj. and noun)   To be dissident is to disagree. From Latin, *dissidere* = to disagree.

If, by ill luck, people understood each other, they would never agree.
—Baudelaire

8. **dissimulating impostor** (dĭ sĭm′ yə lāt′ ing)   To dissimulate is to dissemble, to hide one's true feelings. From Latin, *dissimulare* = to feign.

The United States brags about its political system,
but the president says one thing during the election,
something else when he takes office,
something else during midterm,
and something else when he leaves.
—Deng Xiaoping

9. **dissipated drunk** (dĭs′ ə pā′ tĭd)   To be dissipated is to have wasted time indulging in drinking, gambling etc. until one has withered away. From Latin, *dissipare* = to scatter < *dis* = apart + *supare* = to throw.

Drunkenness is voluntary madness. —Seneca

10. **dissolute dipsomaniac** (dĭs′ ə lūt)   This one is immoral and/or dissipated, having wasted away from excess and debauchery. From Latin, *dissolucioun* = loosened, unrestrained.

Everybody should believe in something;
I believe I'll have another drink.
—Unknown

Quiz 21

Match the words with the definitions on the right

Brainy Barbs

__ 1. disheveled   a. conceal under a false
                              appearance (fits two words)
__ 2. dismal   b. gloomy; inept
__ 3. disparage   c. wasted from immoral living
                              (fits two words)
__ 4. dispiteous   d. ready to argue
__ 5. disputatious   e. ruthless, cruel, without pity
__ 6. dissemble   f. speak slightingly of others
__ 7. dissident   g. to disagree
__ 8. dissimulate   h. uncombed and untidy
__ 9. dissipated
__10. dissolute

Basic Barbs

__11. dipsomaniac   i. member of a rigid dictatorship
__12. fascist   j. an alcoholic
__13. pig-headed   k. stubborn
__14. impostor   l. pretends to be someone else

Liar, Liar, Pants On Fire, Part 3

(disingenuous, dissimulate, fallacious, farcical,)
(welsher, quibble)

Unscramble.

1. calciarf = absurd   _____
2. laflacious = false, misleading, or deceptive   _____
3. imudilatess = hide one's feelings or motives,
                  dissemble   _____
4. uounegnisid = not straightforward, insincere   _____
5. erhslew =   one who cheats
               by failing to pay a debt   _____
6. qibelbu =   evade the main point
               by emphasizing some petty detail_____

Grisly List 22

In Chapter 21 I talked about how you are hearing words now that you had never heard before. This is power. Now that you have a stronger command of language you are less likely to be fooled by it. We live in a society where lawyers and politicians mince words about what the word "is' means. The value in this society has shot up not only for those who can communicate with others with skilled rhetoric but also for those who, with craft and subtlety, obscure information. This might be a painful truth, but it is truth nonetheless. Whether you want to communicate or obscure information, you will benefit from improving your vocabulary.

Basic Barbs

➤ **agitator** = one who stirs up the crowd for a political cause, an activist

➤ **denizen** = a resident, inhabitant

➤ **diehard** = one who vigorously defends a hopeless case, one who is tenaciously stubborn

➤ **ditz** = a silly, eccentric idiot

➤ **dotard** = one weak, child-like due to old age

➤ **dunderpate** = an idiot

➤ **dupe** = one who is easily fooled or unwittingly serves the cause of another. It's descended from the French phrase, *tete d'uppe*, head of a hoopoe, i.e. a bird considered especially stupid.

➤ **nebbish** = from Yiddish, an inept, shy, dull person, usually ignored

Brainy Barbs

1. **distrait screw-up** (dĭs trā´)   To be distrait is to be absent-minded and/or inattentive. From Latin, *distrahere* = to draw apart.

   It's nice to be here in Iowa. —Gerald Ford in Ohio

2. **distraught denizens** (dĭ strôt´)   Hand them a hanky. Anyone distraught could be anxious, upset or even crazed. From Latin, *distrahere* = to pull apart.

   Fate finds for every man his share of misery.
   —Euripides

3. **dithering ditz** (dĭth´ ər ing)   To dither is to tremble in a nervously excited, confused or timid way. From Middle English, *didderen* = tremble.

   Favorite drink:
   Double shot of espresso with a PCP twist.

4. divisive agitator (dĭ vī´ sĭv)   One who is divisive divides, causing factions or disagreements between others. From Latin, *divisivus* = divisive < *dis* = apart + *vidua* = widow.

> *The quarrels of friends are the opportunities of foes.*
> —*Aesop*

5. docile dupe (dŏs´ əl)   A docile person is easy to manipulate, control and not likely to create problems. From *docilis* = easily taught.

> *Mongo merely pawn in chess game of life.*
> —*Mel Brooks*
> *Blazing Saddles*

6. stiff-necked <u>doctrinaire</u> (dŏk´ trə nâr´)   A doctrinaire is stuck holding to a belief system in an unyielding, dogmatic way. It can be used as an adjective or a noun. From Latin, *docere* = to teach.

> *Stiff in opinion, always in the wrong.*
> —*John Dryden*

7. doddering dotard (dŏd´ ər ing)   To dodder is to tremble from old age, ready to fall down. From Old English, *dyderian* = to baffle, delude.

> *Old age comes at a bad time.*
> —*Sue Banducci*

8. dogged diehard (dô´ gĭd)   To be dogged is to be stubborn or determined, resolute. From Medieval English, *dogge* = dog.

> *The foolish and the dead never change opinion.*
> —*Lowell*

9. dogmatic dunderpate (dŏg măt´ ĭk)   This one is arrogantly opinionated or pushes a specific dogma. From Greek, *dogma* = opinion, judgment.

> *His bedroom window is made out of bricks.*
> —*Bob Dylan*

10. dolorous nebbish (dŏl´ ər əs, dō´ lər)   Anything or anyone dolorous exhibits, brings about or entails sorrow or pain. This one is sad. From Latin, *dolere* = to suffer.

> *Even when the gates of Heaven*
> *are closed to prayer,*
> *they are open to tears.*
> —*Talmud*

Quiz 22

Match the words with the definitions on the right.

Brainy Barbs

__ 1. distrait   a. absent-minded
__ 2. distraught   b. arrogantly opinionated
                          (fits two words)
__ 3. dithering   c. cause factions or quarrels
__ 4. divisive   d. easy to manage
__ 5. docile   e. nervously excited or confused
__ 6. doctrinaire   f. sad
__ 7. doddering   g. stubborn
__ 8. dogged   h. trembling from old age
__ 9. dogmatic   i. upset
__10. dolorous

Basic Barbs

__11. diehard   j. one who vigorously defends a
                          hopeless case
__12. agitator   k. an inept, shy and dull person
__13. dunderpate   l. an idiot
__14. ditz   m. one weak, due to old age
__15. dupe   n. one who is easily fooled
__16. denizen   o. a resident, inhabitant
__17. dotard   p. a silly, eccentric person
__18. nebbish   q. one who stirs up the crowd
                          for a political cause

Something Wicked This Way Comes, Part 1

(facinorous, flagitious, deleterious, deplorable, despicable,)
(diabolical, execrable, execrative)

Match.

1. fa _ _ _ _ _ _ _ _ = extremely wicked
2. fl _ _ _ _ _ _ _ _ _ = shamefully wicked
3. d _ p _ _ _ _ _ _ _ = worthy of our hate
4. d _ _ _ _ _ _ _ _ _ _ = harmful, injurious
5. d _ _ _ i _ _ _ _ _ = worthy of scorn, hate
6. e _ _ _ _ _ _ _ _ _ = denouncing; loathsome
7. e _ _ _ _ _ _ _ _ _ = deserving hate, very bad
8. d _ _ _ _ _ _ _ _ _ = devilish

In this book, I've coupled one noun with one adjective to create a slur you might use to describe the irritants you have to deal with day in and day out. But why limit yourself? There is no reason why you can't describe an idiot with ten adjectives and a noun. It can have a tremendous impact when you do. For example, you might say of some dunderpate: "This dummkopf is a driveling, doting dingbat with dubious intellectual talent because his ductile spine is made of feathers. This, at first, might seem a bit too much blather on your part. However, "If you don't use it, you'll lose it," or so the saying goes. So I encourage you, for the sake of your "education" to practice this technique.

Basic Barbs

➢ **buttinski** = a meddler, one prone to butt in
➢ **cad** = Originally meaning a servant boy, the word changed to signify any lower class man who acts disrespectfully to women
➢ **dingbat** = an idiot
➢ **dummkopf** = idiot, in German
➢ **overlord** = one who is lord over other lords
➢ **party-pooper** = one who's attitude is so dismal that it ruins the party for others

Brainy Barbs

1. **doting dummy** (dōt´ ing) This dummy is either feeble-minded because of old age or foolishly and excessively expressing fondness for someone. From Icelandic, *dotta* = to doze.

> *I did but see her passing by*
> *And yet I love her till I die.*
> —Thomas Ford

2. **doughty dummkopf** (dou´ tē) Literally, doughty means brave, but it is now used humorously, often questioning the validity of the compliment. From Old English, *dohtig* = worthy.

> *It is easy to be brave from a safe distance.*
> —Aesop

3. **dour party-pooper** (dour) A dour person is too serious and/or too gloomy. From Latin, *duras* = hard.

> *We are growing serious, and, let me tell you,*
> *that's the very next step to being dull.*
> —Addison

4. dowdy dame (dou´ dē) This dame is distastefully ordinary, shabby. From Early Modern English, *dowd* = an ill-dressed or slovenly woman.

> *She wears her clothes as if they were thrown on with a pitchfork.*
> —Jonathan Swift

5. Draconian overlord (drā kō´ nē ən) Draco was a 7th-century statesmen who set up a code of laws known for their extreme severity. Anything Draconian is then extremely harsh.

> *Use an accordion. Go to jail! That's the law.*
> —Bumper sticker

6. driveling dingbat (drĭv´ əl ing) To drivel is to let saliva drip from one's mouth or nose, to slaver, to talk childishly or foolishly: hence, to speak like a congenital idiot. From Old English, *dreflian* = to slobber.

> *He mouths a sentence as curs mouth a bone.*
> —Charles Churchill

7. dubious intellectual (dū´ bē əs) If it's dubious it's doubtful, uncertain or morally questionable. From Latin, *dubare* = to be of two minds.

> *My father had silicone shots in his head to enlarge his brain.*
> *It worked. Now he has to wear a bra to keep his eyes in.*
> —Jack Graiman

8. ductile yes man (dŭk´ təl) Like putty, he is easily molded or led. From Latin, *ductus* = a leading.

> *Last week I told my wife a man is like wine;*
> *he gets better with age. She locked me in the cellar.*
> —Rodney Dangerfield

9. duplicitous cad (dū plĭs´ ĭ təs) This one is hypocritically cunning, double-dealing and deceitful. From Latin, *duplicare* = to double.

> *For I have sworn thee fair, and thought the bright,*
> *Who art as black as hell, as dark as night.*
> —Shakespeare

10. dyspeptic buttinski (dĭs pĕp´ tĭk) If you're dyspeptic then you either have impaired digestion or you're grouchy. Or maybe you're grouchy because your digestion is impaired. From Greek, *dys* = bad + *pepsis* = digestion.

> *The next pleasantest feeling in the world*
> *to being perfectly happy is being perfectly cross.*
> —Finley Peter Dunne

Quiz 23

Match the words with the definitions on the right

Brainy Barbs

__ 1. doting   a. brave
__ 2. doughty   b. doubtful
__ 3. dour   c. easily molded or led
__ 4. dowdy   d. extremely harsh
__ 5. Draconian   e. feeble-minded from old age
__ 6. drivel   f. have impaired digestion or grouchy
__ 7. dubious   g. hypocritically cunning, double-dealing
__ 8. ductile   h. shabby, ill-dressed or slovenly
__ 9. duplicitous   i. too serious and/or too gloomy
__10. dyspeptic   j. to slaver, to talk foolishly

Basic Barbs

__11. cad   k. lord over other lords
__12. dummkopf   l. a meddler, prone to butt in
__13. buttinski   m. disrespectful to women
__14. overlord   n. idiot, in German

Something Wicked This Way Comes, Part 2

(malevolent, miscreant, egregious, vile, malignant,)
(perfidious, malefactor, nefarious)

Unscramble.

1. levi = evil, repulsive   _____
2. gesuoireg = extremely bad   _____
3. suoidifrep = treacherous   _____
4. tenlovelam = wishing evil or harm to others   _____

Match.

5. n _ _ _ _ _ _ _ _ = wicked
6. m _ _ _ _ _ _ _ _ = evil, criminal
7. m _ _ _ _ _ _ _ _ _ = having an evil influence
8. m _ _ _ _ _ _ _ _ _ _ = evildoer

The nouns and adjectives I've coupled together don't have to stay coupled. There's no reason you can't have an effete fatalist or a dystopian society. In fact, these coupled insults are to be remembered and forgotten. They are to be remembered when they help you remember the meaning of the word and they are to be forgotten when you move beyond the mere definition of words and begin to use this vocabulary in your daily life. This first goal is to help you do better on a test. The second is to help you do better in life.

Basic Barbs

➢ **fatalist** = one who believes life is controlled by inevitable fate
➢ **glutton** = one who greedily eats too much
➢ **ill-conceived** = not thought out, poorly planned
➢ **preppy** = student from a preparatory school, upper class and snobbish
➢ **privilegentsia** = the upper class; those, because of their status, that enjoy privileges others can't
➢ **runt** = a small fry
➢ **turpitude** = extreme wickedness, depravity

Brainy Barbs

1. **dystopian fatalist** (dĭs tō´ pē ən)   Dystopia is a fictitious place where life is dreadful, which is the opposite of Utopia, an imaginary place where everyone enjoys the perfect community.

> *Maybe this world is another planet's hell.* —Aldous Huxley

2. **edacious glutton** (ĭ dā´ shəs)   Anyone edacious is consuming and devouring. From Latin, *edacitas* = gluttonous.

> *The lust of avarice has so totally seized upon mankind*
> *that their wealth seems rather to possess them*
> *than they possess their wealth.*
> —Pliny

3. **effete snob** (ĭ fēt ')   It comes from the Latin word, *effetus*, which means worn out by childbearing; hence, its present definition is infertile or unable to produce. However, it has also taken on the meaning of weakness caused by self-indulgence and decadence.

> *They remind me of a very tired rich man who said to his chauffeur,*
> *"Drive off that cliff, James, I want to commit suicide."*
> —Adlai Stevenson

4. **ill-conceived effrontery** (ĭ frŭn' tə rē) Effrontery is shameless boldness, impudence. From Latin, *effrons* = barefaced <*ex* = from + *frons* = forehead.

In skating over thin ice, our safety is in our speed. —Emerson

5. **egocentric preppy** (ē' gō sĕn' trĭk) To be egocentric is to be self-centered, totally engrossed in oneself. From Latin, *ego* = I.

That man that lives for self alone,
lives for the meanest mortal known.
—Joaquin Miller

6. **egregious turpitude** (ĭ grē' jəs) Until the movie Bill and Ted's Excellent Adventure, one rarely heard this word. It means extremely bad or shocking and is now used in high school classrooms, "Like, most egregious!" or in aristocratic society, "an egregious error in judgment." From Latin, *egregius* = separated from the herd.

Kill one and you are a murderer.
Kill millions and you are a conqueror.
Kill all and you are a God.
—Jean Rostand

7. **eldritch wacko** (ĕl' drĭch) This strange wacko is a little too weird and eerie. From Medieval English, *elve* = elf.

Ordinarily he is insane, but he has lucid moments
when he is merely stupid.
—Heinrich Heine

8. **elitist privilegentsia** (ĭ lēt' ĭst, ā lēt' ĭst) An elitist believes government should be controlled by the richest, smartest or most powerful. From Latin, *eligere* = to set apart.

Even on the highest throne, we are still sitting on our ass.
—Michel de Montaigne

9. **emaciated stick** (ĭ mā' shē ā' tĭd) Someone feed this poor stick. This one is abnormally lean. From Latin, *emaciare* = to make lean.

She was built like a boy arrow. —E. M. Ashcraft, III

10. **emasculated runt** (ĭ măs' kyə lāt əd) This one's testes have been cut off, either physically or emotionally. From Latin, *e* = out + *masculus* = male.

Married men live longer than single men.
But married men are a lot more willing to die.
—Johnny Carson

Quiz 24

Match the definitions with the words on the left.

Brainy Barbs

___ 1. dystopian

___ 2. edacious

___ 3. effete

___ 4. effrontery

___ 5. egocentric

___ 6. egregious

___ 7. eldritch

___ 8. elitist

___ 9. emaciated

___10. emasculated

a. abnormally lean

b. believes government should be controlled by the best

c. castrated

d. consuming and devouring

e. extremely bad or shocking

f. self-centered

g. shameless boldness

h. weakness caused by self-indulgence

i. weird and eerie

j. where life is dreadful

Basic Barbs

___11. runt

___12. turpitude

___13. ill-conceived

___14. preppy

___15. glutton

___16. fatalist

k. a small fry

l. believes life is controlled by inevitable fate

m. extreme wickedness

n. greedily eats too much

o. not thought out

p. upper class and snobbish

Something Wicked This Way Comes, Part 3

(blaspheme, hypocrite, impenitent, iniquitous,)
(peccable, profane, sacrilegious, sanctimonious, simoniac)

Match.

1. p _ _ _ _ _ _ = disrespectful to sacred things

2. h _ _ _ _ _ _ _ _ = one who pretends to be virtuous when he/she is not

3. s _ _ _ _ _ _ _ = one who buys or sells sacred items for corrupt reasons

4. s _ _ _ _ _ _ _ _ _ _ _ _ = having a hypocritical show of piety

5. i _ _ _ _ _ _ _ _ _ = wicked, sinful

6. i _ _ _ _ _ _ _ _ _ = without shame or regret

7. b _ _ _ _ _ _ _ _ = speak of God irreverently

8. s _ _ _ _ _ _ _ _ _ _ _ = profane

9. p _ _ _ _ _ _ _ = liable to sin

In Chapter 16 I suggested you go beyond using these words as adjectives and use them as nouns or verbs. One should never embezzle or equivocate. And, one should not be filled with ennui when dealing with an enigma. You see; these words are just as powerful and expressive in whatever form you use them. Consequently, what I'd like you to do is review these words by going back and identifying the words that can be used as nouns or verbs. It will remind you of the definition and give you a stronger command of language.

Basic Barbs

➤ **fair-weather friend** = a friend who deserts when times get tough
➤ **parvenu** = a person who has recently acquired wealth but lacks the status of that social class
➤ **trendoid** = one who is overly concerned with trends

Brainy Barbs

1. **embezzling fat cats** (ĕm bĕz´ ling) To embezzle is to steal money entrusted to one's care. From Old French, en = into + besillier = to destroy.

> Public money is like holy water: everyone helps himself to it.
> —Italian proverb

2. **enervated drop-out** (ĕn´ ər vā´ tĭd) This one is without strength, weakened. From Latin, enervis = nerveless, weak.

> Nothing of worth or weight can be achieved with half a mind,
> with a faint heart, and with a lame endeavor.
> —Barrow

3. **enigmatic nut** (ĕn´ ĭg măt´ ĭk) This puzzling one is filled with riddles. From Greek, ainissesthai = to speak in riddles.

> What does a woman want? —Freud

4. **ennoye parvenu** (än´ nwē yā´) Ennui is fatigue due to boredom or inactivity. However, if you truly want to sound erudite and shrewdly elite, use the adjective (which is French) ennoye for anyone male or ennoyee for anyone female. From Old French, enui = displeasure.

> She, while her lover pants upon her breast,
> Can mark the carvings in an Indian chest.
> —Alexander Pope

5. epicene trendoid (ĕp´ ĭ sēn´) Epicene is a grammar term describing a word that denotes either sex and hence, it has come to mean someone who is effeminate. From Greek, *epikoines* = common.

> *He is every woman's man and every man's woman.*
> —Gaius Scribonius Curio
> of Julius Caesar

6. ephemeral fair-weather friend (ĭ fĕm´ ər əl) Anything ephemeral is fleeting, transitory, short-lived. From Greek *ephemeros* = short-lived.

> *Your love is like the morning mist*
> *that leaves quickly with the dawn.*
> —Hosea 6:4

7. freewheeling epicurean (ĕp´ ĭ kyū rē ən) Epicurus was a Greek philosopher who preached the objective of life is the pursuit of pleasure moderated by morals, self-control, and cultural edification. An epicurean, then, is a seeker of sensuous pleasure and luxury. It is not necessarily a pejorative but it might be if you're a Marxist or a puritan.

> *Who loves not women, wine and song*
> *remains a fool his whole life long.*
> —Martin Luther

8. equivocal wheeler-dealer (ĭ kwĭv´ ə kəl) To be equivocal is to give purposely vague answers, or give answers that can be interpreted in more than one way. From Late Latin, *aequivocari* = to have the same sound.

> *A sudden lie may sometimes be only manslaughter upon truth;*
> *but by a carefully constructed equivocation truth is always,*
> *with malice aforethought, deliberately murdered.*
> —Shakespeare

9. eristic pain (ĭ rĭs´ tĭk) This twit is argumentative, controversial or given to specious reasoning. From Greek, *erizein* = to dispute.

> *In arguing of the shadow, we forgo the substance.*
> —John Lyly

10. erratic weirdo (ĭ răt´ ĭk) This nut is irregular, inconsistent, or wandering. From Latin, *erraticus* = wandering.

> *He who begins many things finishes nothing.*
> —C. Simmons

Yiddish Schmidish

(kvetch, nebbish, nudnik, schlep, schmuck,)
(schnook, schlemiel, yenta)

Match.

1. n _ _ _ _ _ _ = an inept, shy and dull person
2. s _ _ _ _ _ _ _ _ = a habitual bungler
3. schn _ _ _ = one easily cheated
4. s _ _ _ _ _ = an ineffectual person
5. s _ _ _ _ _ _ = a despicable, foolish jerk
6. k _ _ _ _ _ = a chronic complainer
7. y _ _ _ _ = an annoying, gossipy woman
8. n _ _ _ _ _ = a pest, a stupid annoying person

LE MOT QUOTE 13
Circle the word that best fits the quote.

We are so accustomed to disguise ourselves to others, that in the end we become disguised to ourselves.

—La Rochefoucauld

a. diffident   b. dissemble   c. disdainful

LE MOT QUOTE 14
Match each quote with the appropriate word.

1. But then, that's what young men are there for.
   —Adolf Hitler,
   remarking on the heavy casualty lists

2. How strange it is to see with how much passion
   People see things only in their own fashion!
   —Moliere

3. Life is a sexually transmitted disease. —Anonymous

__ a. doctrinaire

__ b. dystopia

__ c. dispiteous

LE MOT QUOTE 15

Match each quote with the appropriate word.

1. ...That wretched disease that rivets a man so firmly to his own belief that he becomes incapable of conceiving other men may believe otherwise.
   —Montaigne

2. A yawn is a silent shout. —G. K. Chesterton

3. Severities should be dealt out all at once, that by their suddenness they may give less offence; benefits should be handed out drop by drop, that they may be relished the more. —Machiavelli

4. [Men] are all but stomachs and we all but food; they eat us hungrily, and when they are full, they belch us. —Shakespeare

___ a. draconian

___ b. edacious

___ c. dogmatism

___ d. ennui

LE MOT QUOTE 16

Match each quote with the appropriate word.

1. Show me the man who would go to heaven alone, and I will show you
   one who will never be admitted there. —Feltham

2. With pleasure drugged, he almost longed for woe.
   —Byron

3. Everything by starts, and nothing long. —Dryden

4. We'll show you too some elders of the town whose only joy is to put joy down. —A. P. Herbert

___ a. erratic

___ b. egocentric

___ c. dour

___ d. epicurean

Chapter 6

Fate never wounds more deeply the generous heart,
than when a blockhead's insult points the dart.
—Johnson

Grisly List 26

I've matched some adjectives with a simplistic word; as in, exasperating pest. I've coupled other words with obscure words; as in: eructating grobian. The simple word will help you remember the definition of the adjective. The more obscure word will stick in your head simply because it is just that—obscure and unusual.

Basic Barbs

➢ **beldam** = a hag
➢ **blow-hard** = slang for braggart, one who talks big but does little
➢ **bumpkin** = a country idiot
➢ **chowhound** = slang term for a glutton
➢ **grobian** = the patron saint of idiots
➢ **louse** = a sucking insect; a contemptible person

Brainy Barbs

1. **eructating grobian** (ĭ rŭk´ tāt ing) To eructate is to burp, to belch. From Latin, *e* = out + *ructare* = to belch.

TOMBSTONE EPITAPH:
He burped and belched like prodigious thunder
Till an avalanche took him six feet under

2. **esurient chowhound** (ĭ sŏŏr´ ē ənt) This one is hungry and/or greedy. From Latin, *esurire* = hungering.

Treat debtors like your family; exploit them!
—Ferengi acquisition rule #111
Deep Space 9

3. **ethnocentric bumpkin** (ĕth´ nō sĕn´ trĭk) This one is blind from seeing another culture's viewpoint, insisting his/her own culture is superior to others. From Greek, *ethnos* = race, culture + centric.

Few people can be happy
unless they hate some other person, nation or creed.
—Bertrand Russell

4. **euphuistic blow-hard** (yū´ fyū ĭs´ tĭk)   With an affected and bombastic style of writing or speaking popular in the 16th century, this airbag blows like St. Helens. From Greek, *euphyes* = graceful, shapely.

God is silent, now if we could only get man to shut up.
—Woody Allen

5. **exacerbating nuisance** (ĭg zăs´ ər bāt´ ing)   To exacerbate is to make worse, irritate or annoy. From Latin, *exacerbare* = to make angry.

Too many creatures, both insects and humans,
estimate their own value by the amount of minor irritation
they are able to cause to greater personalities than themselves.
—Don Marquis

6. **exacting beldam** (ĭg zăk´ ting)   Anyone or anything exacting is demanding, entailing grueling effort or rigorous attention to detail. From Latin, *exigere* = to drive out.

I don't want any yes-men around me.
I want everybody to tell me the truth,
even if it costs them their jobs.
—Samuel Goldwyn

7. **exasperating pest** (ĭg zăs´ pə rā ting)   To exasperate is to irritate, annoy, or make angry. Form the Latin, *exasperare* = to roughen.

Jesus loves you, but everybody else thinks you're a jerk.
—Anonymous

8. **excrementitious slob** (ĕks´ krə mĕn tĭsh´ əs)   This one is of or like excrement, feces, and crap. From Latin, *excrementum* = that which is sifted out, refuse.

Always look out for Number One
and be careful not to step in Number Two.
—Rodney Dangerfield

9. **execrable louse** (ĕk´ sə krə bəl)   Anyone execrable is revolting, detestable, and utterly hated. From Latin, *ex(s)ecrabil* = accursed.

You're a good reason why some animals eat their young.
—Jim Samuels

10. **execrative big mouth** (ĕk´ sə krā´ tĭv)   This creep is either denouncing, or detestable and loathsome. From Latin, *ex(s)ecrabil* = accursed.

TOMBSTONE EPITAPH:
Opened his big mouth once too often
Now he lays here in a wooden coffin

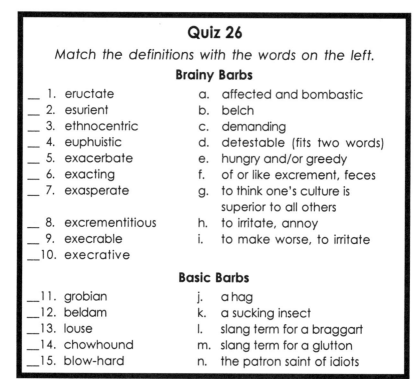

Quiz 26

Match the definitions with the words on the left.

Brainy Barbs

__ 1. eructate

__ 2. esurient

__ 3. ethnocentric

__ 4. euphuistic

__ 5. exacerbate

__ 6. exacting

__ 7. exasperate

__ 8. excrementitious

__ 9. execrable

__10. execrative

a. affected and bombastic

b. belch

c. demanding

d. detestable (fits two words)

e. hungry and/or greedy

f. of or like excrement, feces

g. to think one's culture is superior to all others

h. to irritate, annoy

i. to make worse, to irritate

Basic Barbs

__11. grobian

__12. beldam

__13. louse

__14. chowhound

__15. blow-hard

j. a hag

k. a sucking insect

l. slang term for a braggart

m. slang term for a glutton

n. the patron saint of idiots

It Takes A Sneak, Part 1

(collusive, circuitous, devious, Machiavellian, calculating, wily,)
(serpentine, sinister, sinuous, surreptitious, cabal)

Unscramble.

1. yiwl = crafty, sly _____

2. caginlcutla = cunning in a selfish way _____

3. malachinaveli = full of plots and intrigue _____

4. dsuoive = roundabout; shifty; veering from the correct course _____

5. csouitucir = taking a roundabout course; deceitful _____

6. cusillveo = cooperating secretly in misconduct _____

7. tiperurtiosus = acting in a secret, stealthy way _____

8. retsinis = devious, wicked _____

9. snunious = winding; devious _____

10. serenipent = like a serpent _____

11. claba = a conspiratorial group of plotters _____

Grisly List 27

This is a vocabulary book, but it is also a quote book. If you want to improve your writing, you'll study the quotes as you do the vocabulary. You'll surprise yourself with the wisdom you'll gain. We don't value wisdom much anymore. Being shrewd and conniving is more popular—and rewarding. However, wisdom comes with its own gifts. If you peruse these pearls of wisdom, you'll find that it can come in handy at the most opportune moments.

Basic Barbs

➤ **far-fetched** = unbelievable, from an unlikely time or place
➤ **fibber** = one who lies about unimportant things
➤ **fink** = a hired strikebreaker; an informer; an undesirable person
➤ **gangrel** = a lanky beggar
➤ **ilk** = type or kind, as in "don't marry one of his ilk"
➤ **kingpin** = the foremost bowling pin; the main person or thing holding power, often used in relation to a major crime figure
➤ **logomachist** = one who is disputatious about words or argumentative with words
➤ **rabble-rouser** = one who stirs up the crowd

Brainy Barbs

1. **exigent kingpin** (ĕk´ sĭ jənt)   If something is exigent it requires immediate action; it is urgent or demanding. It can also mean something (or someone) requires more than is reasonable. From Latin, *exigere* = to drive out.

> *He who demands, does not command.*
> —Italian proverb

2. **extraneous blathermouth** (ĭk strā´ nē əs)   Anything extraneous is not essential or is irrelevant. From Latin, *extraneus* = external, foreign.

> *But far more numerous was the herd of such*
> *who talk too little and who talk too much.*
> —John Dryden

3. **fabricating fink** (făb´ rə kāt´ ing)   To fabricate is to make up stories. From Latin, *fabricatus* = to construct, build.

> *A half-truth is a whole lie.*
> —Swedish proverb

4. **far-fetched fabulist** (făb´ yə lĭst)   A fabulist tells fables, tall tales; hence, a he/she's a liar. From Latin, *fabula* = a story.

> *It is always the best policy to tell the truth,*
> *unless, of course, you are an exceptionally good liar.*
> —Jerome K. Jerome

5. **facinorous ilk** (fă sĭn´ ər əs)   Anyone facinorous is enormously wicked. From Latin, *facinoros* = criminal.

> *It is easier to denature plutonium*
> *than to denature the evil spirit of man.*
> —Albert Einstein

6. **factious rabble-rouser** (făk´ shəs)   To be factious is to stir up strife between unsuspecting clans. It's related to the word faction, a group working in a common cause against other groups. Don't confuse this word with factitious which means something is not genuine or that something is fake. From Latin, *factio* = action, or mode of making.

> *There are fearful excitements on any side. Any side can accuse*
> *the other and feel virtuous without the hardships of virtue.*
> —Christopher Fry

7. **faineant good-for-nothing** (fā´ nē ənt)   One more lazy good-for-nothing. Literally from French, *fait-nient*, which means "he does nothing."

> *I like work; it fascinates me. I can sit and look at it for hours.*
> —Jerome K. Jerome

8. **fallacious logomachist** (fə lā´ shəs)   If something is fallacious it contains an error, or is misleading and deceptive, or perhaps delusive. From Latin, *fallacia* = deception, artifice.

> *Truth is the safest lie.*
> —Unknown

9. **farcical fibber** (fär´ sĭ cəl)   This fibber lies to absurd, ludicrous proportions. From Latin, *farcire* = to stuff: the farce was used to fill (stuff) interludes between acts.

> *Everybody lies, but it doesn't matter because nobody listens.*
> —Nick Diamos

10. **farouche gangrel** (fä rōōsh´)   This one is not a social sort, for to be farouche is to be shy, perhaps even fierce from lack of breeding. It's not actually an English word but you'll find it in some unabridged dictionaries. It's French and literally means neglected children.

> *Men are bears with furniture.*
> —Elaine Boosely

Quiz 27

Match the definitions with the words on the left.

Brainy Barbs

___ 1. exigent   a. absurd, ludicrous
___ 2. extraneous   b. extremely wicked
___ 3. fabricate   c. lazy
___ 4. fabulist   d. misleading and deceptive
___ 5. facinorous   e. not essential or irrelevant
___ 6. factious   f. one who tells tall tales
___ 7. faineant   g. to make up stories
___ 8. fallacious   h. to stir up strife
___ 9. farcical   i. urgent or demanding
___10. farouche   j. wild

Basic Barbs

___11. gangrel   k. an informer
___12. kingpin   l. a lanky beggar
___13. fib   m. lie about unimportant things
___14. rabble-rouser   n. one who stirs up the crowd
___15. ilk   o. the main person holding power
___16. fink   p. type or kind
___17. far-fetched   q. unbelievable, from an unlikely time or place

It Takes A Sneak, Part 2

(Byzantine, cagey, conniving, deceptive, guileful,)
(duplicitous, casuistic, tergiversate, cunning, fob)

Match.

1. d _ _ _ _ _ _ _ _ = deceitful, cheating, false
2. g _ _ _ _ _ _ _ = sneaky
3. B _ _ _ _ _ _ _ _ = devious intrigue
4. c _ _ _ _ _ _ _ _ = typified by making secret deals for sly reasons
5. c _ _ _ _ = sly, careful not to get caught
6. t _ _ _ _ _ _ _ _ _ _ _ = desert a cause or party; use evasions; equivocate
7. c _ _ _ _ _ _ _ _ = subtle but misleading reasoning
8. c _ _ _ _ _ _ = skillful in deception
9. d _ _ _ _ _ _ _ _ _ _ _ = deceitful, cheating
10. f _ _ = steal by substituting an inferior object

In Chapter 27, I suggested you look at the quotes. Let me take that one step further. Why don't you write your own quotes? You can take a quote like: Inside every fat person is a thin person waiting to get out. And then switch it around: Inside every thin person is a fat person etc. Or, inside every French man is a Napoleon waiting to bust out. Or whatever. In the process of doing this you'll be working on something that will help you in your speech and in your writing.

Basic Barbs

- ➤ **fanatic** = one who is overly devoted to a cause
- ➤ **feline** = a cat, of or like the cat family
- ➤ **miscreation** = a monster, a mutant
- ➤ **prude** = one who is overly modest or proper
- ➤ **snoot** = a nose or one whose nose is arrogantly stuck up in the air

Brainy Barbs

1. **fastidious prude** (fă stĭd´ ē əs)   Not easy to please and too refined, this prude is easily disgusted. From Latin, *fastus* = disdain, contempt.

> *People who get shocked easily*
> *should be shocked a little more often.*
> —Mae West

2. **fastuous snoot** (făs´ chū əs)   This one looks down on everyone with a haughty, scornful contempt. From Latin, *fastus* = scornful contempt.

> *With their snoots in the air, they would sniff and they'd snort,*
> *"We'll have nothing to do with the Plain-Belly sort!"*
> —Dr. Seuss,
> The Sneeches

3. **fatuous fool** (făch´ ū əs)   Oblivious, this one is not only stupid, but happy and contented to stay stupid. It comes from the Latin word, *fatuus*, where we also derive the word, infatuation. Scary!

> *Nothing in the world is more dangerous*
> *than sincere ignorance and conscientious stupidity.*
> —Martin Luther King, Jr.

4. fawning flatterer (fôn´ ing) To fawn is to slavishly flatter. From Medieval English, *fawnen* = to rejoice; and later, to welcome, flatter.

> *A flatterer is a friend who is your inferior, or pretends to be so.*
> —Aristotle

5. febrile fanatic (fē´ brəl) One who is febrile is feverish. From Latin, *febris* = fever.

> *Fanatic: the false fire of an overheated mind.*
> —Cowper

6. feckless weakling (fĕk lĭs) This weakling is reluctant or not able to do something worthwhile. A feckless person is either too ineffective or negligent to succeed. From Medieval English, Scottish, *fek* = effect + less.

> *He that is good for making excuses,*
> *is seldom good for anything else.*
> —Franklin

7. feculent spectacle (fĕk´ yə lənt) Gross! This filthy, foul spectacle has the nature of feces. From Latin, *faex* = dregs, lees.

> *There is no odor so bad as that which arises from goodness tainted.*
> —Thoreau

8. fell miscreation (fĕl) This fierce one is cruel and horrifying, with an ominous potential for killing and destruction. From Old French, *felon* = wicked.

> *There was a laughing devil in his sneer*
> *which raised emotions both of rage and fear;*
> *and where his frown of hatred darkly fell,*
> *hope withering fled, and mercy sighted farewell.*
> —Byron

9. felonious mobster (fə lō´ nē əs) This one is wicked and criminal. From Latin, *fello* = treacherous.

> *Fear the boisterous savage of passion less*
> *than the sedately grinning villain.*
> —Lavater

10. feral feline (fĕr´ əl, fēr´ əl) If you like your cats wild, you can't get any wilder than this cat. From Latin, *fera* = wild beast.

> *When a woman really loves a man,*
> *he can make her do anything she wants to.*
> —Anonymous

Quiz 28

Match the definitions with the words on the left.

Brainy Barbs

___ 1. fastidious   a. cruel and horrifying
___ 2. fastuous   b. contented to stay stupid
___ 3. fatuous   c. feverish
___ 4. fawn   d. scornfully contemptuous
___ 5. febrile   e. having the nature of feces
___ 6. feckless   f. ineffective and irresponsible
___ 7. feculent   g. not easy to please
                        and too refined
___ 8. fell   h. to slavishly flatter
___ 9. felonious   i. wicked and criminal
___10. feral   j. wild

Basic Barbs

___11. prude   k. a cat, of or like the cat family
___12. snoot   l. a monster, a mutant
___13. fanatic   m. nose
___14. miscreation   n. overly devoted to a cause
___15. feline   o. this one is overly proper

Say What?

(splutter, maunder, babble, blither, brabble, drivel,)
(gibber, inarticulate, incoherent, jabber, gabble, garble)

Unscramble.

1. balebb = speak incoherently or foolishly _____
2. libtehr = speak incoherently or foolishly _____
3. elbbarb = quarrel over nothing _____
4. levrid = speak incoherently while drooling _____
5. bagble = speak incoherently or foolishly _____
6. ragleb = to mix up part of a story _____
7. bergib = speak incoherently or foolishly _____
8. nrtclteiaiua = unintelligible _____
9. teninhocer = not sticking together _____
10. rbbjae = speak foolishly, meaninglessly _____
11. rettulps = speak incoherently while spitting _____
12. mndauer = act aimlessly, speak incoherently _____

Grisly List 29

We have a lot of homophones in the F's. Fey and fay. Or words that almost sound alike: fastuous and fatuous; factious and fractious. This can be very confusing. It's worthwhile to look over these words and note how they are alike and in what ways they are different. Factious and fractious have similar meanings and yet on a test, knowing just how they are different can make the difference between passing or failing. More importantly, using one word when you mean another is the ultimate social blunder. Literature is filled with comic characters that make such malapropisms. Therefore, it is really worth your while to study the nuances of words and how they are different from each other.

Basic Barbs

> **aberration** = deviance or abnormality
> **boor** = a rude, clownish peasant
> **crassitude** = extreme stupidity
> **felon** = one guilty of a crime
> **fleecer** = one who steals
> **glitterati** = the fashionably elite; glitzy celebrities
> **spastic** = one who has spasms, often used in slang to describe one who is uncoordinated

Brainy Barbs

1. **festering rot** (fĕs´ tər ing) Anything festering is filled with pus or bitterness. From Latin, *festula* = ulcer.

> *The best things, corrupted, become the worst.*
> —Latin proverb

2. **fetid pile of dung** (fĕt´ ĭd, fē´ tĭd) Anyone fetid stinks in a way that is rank from decay. From Latin, *foetere* = to stink.

> *Every man loves the smell of his own farts.*
> —Graffiti
> on a cave wall from Ancient Greece

3. **fey aberration** (fā) One in a fey mood is extremely excited and perhaps unusually so. It was once thought extreme excitement might foreshadow impending death and fey still carries that connotation. From Icelandic, *feigr* = doomed.

> *How oft when men are at the point of death have they been merry,*
> *which their keepers call a lightening before death.*
> —Shakespeare

4. filching fleecer (fĭlch´ ing)   To filch is to steal; hence, a filching person is given to stealing. From Medieval English, *filchen* = to attack, take as plunder.

Every rascal is not a thief, but every thief is a rascal.
—Aristotle

5. fistic boor (fĭs´ tĭk)   He (or she) likes to box and/or fight. From Old High German, *fust* = fist + *ic.*

I was shadow boxing the other day,
figured I was ready for Cassius Clay.
—Bob Dylan

6. flagitious felon (flə jĭsh´ əs)   This one is wicked, shamefully wicked. From Latin, *flagiti* = shame, scandal.

His lack of education is more than compensated for
by his keenly developed moral bankruptcy.
—Woody Allen

7. flagrant crassitude (flā´ grənt)   Anything flagrant is glaringly bad. From Latin, *flagrans* = burning.

The nail that sticks up gets hammered down.
—Japanese proverb

8. flatulent spastic (flăch´ ə lənt)   This spastic farts. But the question is: What kind of farts are they? Is it the noisy but harmless sort that makes all the kiddies giggle? Or is it the silent but deadly one, quietly sneaking up on you and melting the lining of your nose? From Latin, *flare* = to blow.

TOMBSTONE EPITAPH:
He finally met his doom
When his last fart went boom

9. flaunty flirt (flŏnt´ ē)   One who is flaunty is showy, vain, gaudy. From Norwegian, *flanta* = to gad about.

She wore a low but futile décolletage.
—Dorothy Parker

10. fleering glitterati (fler´ ing)   To fleer is to laugh or smile contemptuously. From Norwegian, *flire* = to snicker, laugh.

Men more gladly recall what they deride than what they esteem.
—Horace

Quiz 29

Match the definitions with the words on the left.

Brainy Barbs

___ 1. festering
___ 2. fetid
___ 3. fey
___ 4. filch
___ 5. fistic
___ 6. flagitious
___ 7. flagrant
___ 8. flatulent
___ 9. flaunty
___10. fleer

a. extremely excited
b. farting
c. filled with pus or bitterness
d. glaringly bad
e. laugh derisively
f. likes to box and/or fight
g. shamefully wicked
h. showy, vain, gaudy or flashy
i. steal
j. stinking

Basic Barbs

___11. crassitude
___12. fleece
___13. boor
___14. felon
___15. spastic
___16. glitterati
___17. aberration

k. fashionably elite; celebrities
l. a rude, clownish peasant
m. deviation, something unnatural
n. extreme stupidity
o. has spasms, is uncoordinated
p. one guilty of a crime
q. to steal

You're Such An Animal

(feline, bovine, hircine, limacine, lupine, ophidian, ovine,)

(piscine, porcine, simian, taurine, vulpine)

Match.

1. l _ _ _ _ _ _ _ = like a slug
2. b _ _ _ _ _ = like a cow
3. h _ _ _ _ _ _ = like a goat, lustful
4. p _ _ _ _ _ _ = like a fish
5. l _ _ _ _ _ = like a wolf
6. t _ _ _ _ _ _ = like a bull
7. p _ _ _ _ _ _ = like a pig
8. s _ _ _ _ _ = like an ape
9. o _ _ _ _ = like sheep
10. o _ _ _ _ _ _ _ = like a snake
11. v _ _ _ _ _ _ = like a fox
12. f _ _ _ _ _ = like a cat

Grisly List 30

Wit, at one time, was considered a sign of intelligence. Nowadays, we both reward and punish those who are witty. Actors and comedians can make beaucoup bucks for their quick-witted quips and cuts. But the kid sitting in the back of the class whose repartee outshines his teacher is usually sent with a referral slip off to the dean. This is unfortunate. Not that I want to encourage disrespect for one's elders. But it is unfortunate in that we are missing an opportunity. If we can't channel this child's wit in some positive way, I'm afraid we end up crushing and truncating this child's chance of success. If you can encourage yourself in studying these words and quotes, you may end up awakening that witty wag inside you that has been lying dormant for years.

Basic Barbs

➤ **activist** = one who takes direct political action
➤ **alarmist** = one frightened easily who always believes the worst
➤ **biddy** = a fussbudget or fussy old women
➤ **butterfingers** = a clumsy person whose fingers drop things
➤ **fop** = a vain, affected male who pays too much attention to his clothes, appearance etc.
➤ **social climber** = one who attempts to move up the social ladder to be in a higher social strata.

Brainy Barbs

1. **flippant old biddy** (flĭp´ ənt)   To be flippant is to improperly talk with a lack of gravity for the topic. From Icelandic, *fleipa* = to babble.

> *When the snake is old, the frog will tease him.*
> —*Persian proverb*

2. **flouncing fop** (floun´ sing)   To flounce is to move the body with quick flinging motions in anger or impatience. From Scandinavian, *flunsa* = to hurry.

> *A tart temper never mellows with age.*
> —*Washington Irving*

3. **floundering butterfingers** (floun´ dər ing)   To flounder is to move, speak or act in a awkward and confused way. The origin of this word is unknown. It may be a blend of flounce and founder.

> *A drowning man takes hold of his own hair.*
> —*Greek proverb*

4. flouting social climber (flout´ ing)   To flout is to mock, jeer and show contempt. From Medieval English, *flouten* = to play the flute; hence, to whistle at.

When the mouse laughs at the cat, there is a hole nearby.
—Nigerian proverb

5. flummoxed space cadet (flŭm´ əkst)   This poor soul is bewildered and confused. The origin of this word is unknown.

I had a terrible education.
I attended a school for emotionally disturbed teachers.
—Woody Allen

6. fobbing thief (fäb´ ing)   This thief replaces an inferior item for what he steals. From Medieval English, *fobben* = to cheat.

The faults of a burglar are the qualities of a financier.
—George Bernard Shaw

7. fomenting hell-raiser (fō´ mĕnt ing)   To foment is to stir up trouble. From Latin, *fomentum* = a warm application.

Thinkers prepare for revolution; bandits carry it out.
—Mariano Azuela,
The Flies

8. foul piece of filth (foul)   A foul person can be offensive to your senses: dirty, ugly, smelly; or to your morals: mean, obscene, and/or dishonorable. Foul can also refer to wet and stormy weather. From Greek, *faul* = rotten, lazy.

You are not worth the dust, which the rude wind blows in your face.
—Shakespeare,
King Lear

9. fractious activist (frăk´ shəs)   This rebellious activist is difficult to control. This word shares the same etymology as fraction. From Latin, *frangere* = to break.

No one can go on being a rebel too long
without turning into an autocrat.
—Lawrance Durrell

10. frenetic alarmist (frə nĕt´ ĭk)   To be frenetic is to be frantic, feverishly moving about. From Greek, *phrenitis* = a brain disease.

The bow too tensely strung is easily broken.
—Publilius Syrus

Quiz 30

Match the definitions with the words on the left.

Brainy Barbs

___ 1. flippant
___ 2. flounce
___ 3. flounder
___ 4. flout
___ 5. flummoxed
___ 6. fob

___ 7. foment
___ 8. foul

___ 9. fractious
___10. frenetic

a. confused and bewildered
b. difficult to control
c. disrespectful in speech
d. frantic, moving excitedly
e. mock, jeer, show contempt
f. move the body with quick flinging motions in anger
g. offensive, mean, and obscene
h. replace an inferior item for what one steals
i. stir up trouble
j. to move, speak or act in a awkward and confused way

Basic Barbs

___11. biddy
___12. fop
___13. social climber
___14. butterfingers

___15. activist

___16. alarmist

k. a fussy old women
l. a clumsy person
m. a vain, affected male
n. one frightened easily who always believes the worst
o. one who attempts to move up the social ladder
p. takes direct political action

Nothing Succeeds Like Excess

(cachinnate, cloy, extraneous, fulsome,)
(saccharine, superfluous, treacly)

Match.

1. s _ _ _ _ _ _ _ _ _ _ = more than needed
2. c _ _ _ = to weary or disgust because of excess of food, sweetness or pleasure
3. s _ _ _ _ _ _ _ _ _ = too sweet
4. f _ _ _ _ _ _ = disgustingly excessive
5. c _ _ _ _ _ _ _ _ _ = laugh too loud or too much
6. e _ _ _ _ _ _ _ _ _ = not essential, irrelevant
7. t _ _ _ _ _ _ = given to overly sweet talk or sentiment

LE MOT QUOTE 17

Match each quote with the appropriate word.

1. You gotta say this for the white race—its self-confidence knows no bounds. Who else could go to a small island in the south Pacific where there's no poverty, no crime, no unemployment, no war and no worry—and call it a 'primitive society'?
   —Dick Gregory

2. Where speech is corrupted, the mind is also.
   —Seneca

3. When the state is weak, the army rules. —Napoleon

4. White lies are but the ushers to black ones. —Marryat

__ a. fabulist

__ b. ethnocentric

__ c. execrative

__ d. fractious

LE MOT QUOTE 18

Match each quote with the appropriate word.

1. Put a knife to thy throat
   if thou be a man given to appetite. —Proverbs 23: 2

2. The most contemptible are the most contemptuous.
   —Fielding

3. Flatterers are the worst kind of enemy. —Tacitus

4. Affectation is a greater enemy to the face
   than the smallpox. —St. Evremond

5. A fool takes a bath and forgets to wash his face.
   —Yiddish proverb

__ a. foppish

__ b. fawn

__ c. esurient

__ d. fastuous

__ e. fatuous

LE MOT QUOTE 19

Match each quote with the appropriate word.

1. Why babble about brutality and be indignant about tortures? The masses want that. They need something that will give them a thrill of horror.
   —Adolf Hitler

2. With all his tumid boasts, he's like the swordfish, who only wears his weapon in his mouth. —Madden

3. What luck for rulers that men do not think.
   —Adolf Hitler

4. A cat pent up becomes a lion. —Italian proverb

5. When women kiss, it always reminds one of prizefighters shaking hands. —H. L. Mencken

___ a. fistic
___ b. euphuistic
___ c. crassitude
___ d. flagitious
___ e. feral

Chapter 7

The tongue is but three inches long,
yet it can kill a man six feet high.
—Japanese proverb

Grisly List 31

One way to review these words is to cull out the words with similar definitions and place them together as I've done at the end of each chapter. Each word then, reminds you of the definition of the other. In your mind you will see words in the context of other words with similar meanings. Cloy will be seen with fulsome, fretful with feckless and tremulous. It may not give you the exact definition but you'll at least have a close enough idea to help your ability on any test.

Basic Barbs

➢ **culprit** = one who is arraigned for an offense,
From Latin, *culpa* = blame.
➢ **femme fatale** (fĕm´ fə tăl) = an irresistibly attractive woman who leads men into dangerous situations
➢ **heifer** = a young cow, or an obese person
➢ **Pollyanna** = an overly optimistic person
➢ **spoilsport** = a killjoy, spoils the fun of others

Brainy Barbs

1. **fretful worrywart** (frĕt´ fəl) Wringing his/her hands, this wart worries too much. From Old English, *fretan* = to eat up, consume.

How much pain has cost us the evils, which have never happened.
—Thomas Jefferson

2. **frothy Pollyanna** (frô´ thē) Frothy literally means foamy, light, or worthless. From Indo-European, *preu-th* = slavering, snorting.

Errors, like straws, upon the surface flow,
He who would search for pearls must dive below.
—John Dryden

3. **froward femme fatale** (frō wərd) Anyone froward is not easily controlled. From Old Norse, *fram* = forward.

Favorite motto:
Men are just desserts.

4. **frowzy heifer** (frou´ zē) This shabby one is knee-deep in stink and dirt. From Early Modern English, around 1500, *frowy* = rank-smelling.

She had a wart on the left side of her chin,
with one long black hair growing out of it.
When she sneezed, it cracked like a whip;
and if she caught cold, she flogged her cheek raw.
— *Pinky Thompson*

5. **fulsome porker** (fŏŏl´ səm) Anything fulsome is disgustingly excessive. From Medieval English, *fulsom* = disgustingly excessive. This word may be a blend of meaning of full and foul + some.

In everything the middle course is best; all things in excess bring trouble.
—*Plautus*

6. **braindead functionary** (fŭngk´ shə nər´ ē) One more cog in the wheel, this bureaucrat, this stagnating official knows the tyranny of red tape. From Latin, *functio* = to perform.

The only thing that saves us from the bureaucracy is its inefficiency.
—*Eugene McCarthy*

7. **funereal spoilsport** (fyū ner´ ē əl) Always dark and gloomy, this one is like a funeral. From Latin, *funus* = a funeral.

I was going to buy a copy of "The Power of Positive Thinking,"
and then I thought: What the hell good would that do?
—*Ronnie Shakes*

8. **furtive culprit** (fur´ tĭv) This culprit is secretive and goes about in a sneaky, sly way. From Latin, *frutum* = theft.

Let wickedness escape as it may at the bar, it never fails of doing justice
upon itself; for every guilty person is his own hangman.
—*Seneca*

9. **fustian fuddy-duddy** (fŭs´ chən) Fustian is a stout cotton fabric, but it may also be one who is bombastic and pompous. This bore hasn't realized he only has an audience of one—himself. No one else is listening.

When there's a wind, garbage flies high. —*Jewish proverb*

10. **fustigating hellcat** (fŭs´ tə gāt ing) To fustigate is to punish, beat or criticize severely. From Latin, *fustigatus,* = to cudgel to death (a cudgel is a short, thick stick used as a weapon).

I've got a good mind to join a club and beat you over the head with it.
—*Groucho Marx*

Quiz 31

Match the definitions with the words on the left.

Brainy Barbs

__ 1. fretful   a. a bureaucrat, a stagnating official

__ 2. frothy   b. bombastic and pompous

__ 3. froward   c. dark and gloomy

__ 4. frowzy   d. disgustingly excessive

__ 5. fulsome   e. foamy, light, or worthless

__ 6. functionary   f. not easily controlled

__ 7. funereal   g. done in a sneaky, sly way

__ 8. furtive   h. stinky and dirty

__ 9. fustian   i. beat severely; criticize harshly

__10. fustigate   j. worried

Basic Barbs

__11. culprit   k. an overly optimistic person

__12. Pollyanna   l. is arraigned for an offense

__13. femme fatale   m. an irresistibly attractive yet dangerous woman

Get A Spine, part 1

(emasculated, cower, feckless, fretful, poltroon, repine,)
(milquetoast, snivel, tremulous, wince, xenophobic, patsy)

Match.

1. w _ _ _ _ = shrink back
2. p _ _ _ _ _ _ _ = coward, chicken
3. r _ _ _ _ _ = complain
4. f _ _ _ _ _ _ = worried, peevish
5. s _ _ _ _ _ = to run at the nose; cry
6. c _ _ _ _ = shrink from fear
7. f _ _ _ _ _ _ _ = weak; careless
8. x _ _ _ _ _ _ _ _ _ = fear of strangers or foreigners
9. t _ _ _ _ _ _ _ _ = shaking from fear
10. p _ _ _ _ = one easily tricked
11. e _ _ _ _ _ _ _ _ _ _ = castrated
12. m _ _ _ _ _ _ _ _ _ _ = a meek or timid person

I've mentioned that I've received a lot of flak for this book being too crusty, and I find this quite funny. In films and in our culture cuss words seem to rule. Every other word seems to be a pejorative. The same folks who are appalled at this college vocabulary will laugh and laugh at a comedian's gutter mouth. And, we give lip service to telling our children, "cussing makes you sound ignorant." What I've done (or tried to do) is give people the option to say something different, to say a pejorative that's actually intelligent. This should help anyone to not rely on obscenities.

Basic Barbs

> ➤ **demirep** = a kept woman; a prostitute
> ➤ **gadfly** = any large fly that bites livestock, or one whose complaining bothers you and/or stirs you into action.
> ➤ **gammer** = an elderly woman
> ➤ **goon** = a weirdo
> ➤ **paparazzi** = freelance photographers
> ➤ **rummy** = a drunkard

Brainy Barbs

1. **fusty old gammer** (fŭs´ tē)   Anyone fusty is stale and/or old-fashioned. From Old French, *fust* = a wine cask > Early Modern English, *fust* = a musty smell.

> *If you want to avoid old age, hang yourself in youth.*
> —*Yiddish proverb*

2. **gabbling goon** (găb´ ling)   Who can make out what this imbecile says? His rapid tongue or meaningless speech frustrates the intelligent listener. The root gab means to chatter. From Medieval English, *gabbe*.

> *Much chatter, little wit.*
> —*Portuguese proverb*

3. **restless gadabout** (găd´ ə bout´)   To gad is to move aimlessly and restlessly about, especially looking for gossip; hence, the noun gadabout came from the verb phrase "gad about". From Late Middle English, *gad* = to hurry.

> *Whomever gossips to you will gossip about you.*
> —*Spanish proverb*

4. galling paparazzi (gôl´ ing) Gall means something is bitter or severe, bitter in spirit, or rudely bold. One could say, "The unmitigated gall of that gasconading goofball." Galling, however, primarily means something is irritating or exasperating. From Old English, *gealle* = a blister.

> I like long walks,
> especially when they are taken by people who annoy me.
> —*Fred Allen*

5. gangly scrounger (gang´ lē) Think of Ichabod Crane: thin, tall and awkward. This word is a possible derivation of gangrel = a lanky beggar

> We tolerate shapes in human beings
> that would horrify us if we saw them on a horse.
> —*W. R. Inge*

6. garbling rummy (gärb´ ling) To garble is to distort, confuse or mix up part of a story. From Italian, *garbellare* = to sift.

> Unintelligible language is a lantern without a light.
> —*Johnson*

7. garish goofball (gâr´ ĭsh) Anyone garish is far too showy and/or wears make-up and clothes that are too bright. From Medieval English, *gauren* = to stare.

> What counts is not how many animals were killed to make the fur
> but how many animals the woman had to sleep with to get a fur.
> —*Angela LaGreca*

8. garrulous gadfly (gâr´ ə ləs) Yap, yap, yap. Anyone who is garrulous is excessively talkative about insignificant matters. From Latin, *garrire* = to chatter.

> When ideas fail, words come in handy.
> —*Goethe*

9. gasconading bag of hot air (găs´ kə nād´ ing) The blokes of Gascony, France, were reputed to be boastful and blustering; hence, to gasconade is to brag in a blustering manner

> Little dogs make the most noise.
> —*Maori proverb*

10. gaudy demirep (gô´ dē) What she wears is showy and lacks good taste. Gaudy comes from an obsolete English word, gaud, which was a cheap, showy trinket.

> You'd be surprised how much it cost to look this cheap.
> —*Dolly Parton*

Quiz 32

Match the definitions with the words on the left.

Brainy Barbs

___ 1. fusty
___ 2. gabbling
___ 3. gadabout
___ 4. gall
___ 5. gangly
___ 6. garble
___ 7. garish
___ 8. garrulous
___ 9. gasconade
___10. gaudy

a. bitter or severe; rude boldness
b. excessively talkative about unimportant matters
c. one looking for gossip
d. stale and/or old-fashioned
e. thin, tall and awkward
f. to brag in a blustering manner
g. to chatter meaninglessly
h. to distort part of a story
i. too showy (fits two words)

Basic Barbs

___11. gammer
___12. paparazzi
___13. gadfly
___14. rummy
___15. demirep

j. a complainer
k. a drunkard
l. a kept woman; a prostitute
m. freelance photographers
n. an elderly woman

Get A Spine, Part 2

(cark, cringe, dastardly, diffident, grovel, inhibited,)
(niddering, quail, recreant, skittish, skulk, lily-livered, wimp)

Match.

1. i _ _ _ _ _ _ _ _ = holding back, repressed
2. d _ _ _ _ _ _ _ _ = shy, lacking self-confidence
3. s _ _ _ _ _ _ _ = playfully coy; easily frightened
4. g _ _ _ _ _ = cower in a prostrate position
5. q _ _ _ _ = draw back in fear
6. n _ _ _ _ _ _ _ _ = mean, cowardly
7. c _ _ _ _ _ = shrink back in fear
8. s _ _ _ _ = to sneak in a cowardly way
9. r _ _ _ _ _ _ _ = one who is cowardly; traitorous
10. d _ _ _ _ _ _ _ _ = cowardly; mean
11. c _ _ _ = worry
12. l _ _ _ - _ _ _ _ _ _ _ = cowardly, timid
13. w _ _ _ = a weak person

Grisly List 33

You won't find the word groak in your dictionary. Nor will you find it in most unabridged dictionaries. In fact, until recently, it was only in an out of print book titled: "The Dictionary for the Vulgar Tongue". So why have I included it? I kept seeing it crop up in various wordbooks, so who knows? It may be coming back into fashion. That's how it is with language. It is constantly evolving. Every year words are added and subtracted from our dictionary. Language is not static. Your use or nonuse of it determines how it changes.

Basic Barbs

➤ **galoot** = an uncouth, clumsy idiot, sloppily dressed
➤ **groak** = an archaic word, a groak is a person who waits by the table begging for morsels with mournful, pleading eyes
➤ **malcontent** = a dissatisfied or rebellious person
➤ **popinjay** = a haughty person
➤ **spieler** = a talker who tries to sell or persuade
➤ **underling** = an inferior, subordinate
➤ **waif** = a homeless, friendless person or child; in the model industry, the waif-look is an excessively thin model
➤ **zombie** = In Haiti, a corpse brought back to robot-like life, the walking dead; one who acts like a zombie

Brainy Barbs

1. **gaunt waif** (gônt) Thin and bony, this grim soul's figure makes the living look like the dead. From Latin, *galbinus* = greenish-yellow.

> *He looked like Death taken seasick.*
> —Swinburne

2. **gawkish groak** (gôk´ ĭsh) To gawk is to stare with your eyes bugged out in an idiotic way. From a dialect of English, *gowk* = an idiot.

> *When a finger points at the moon,*
> *the imbecile looks at the finger.*
> —Chinese proverb

3. **gibbering puddinghead** (jĭb´ ər ing) This is one more idiot chattering, speaking a nonsensical language. The noun derivative is gibberish. The origin is uncertain but the word is imitative of nonsense.

> **TOMBSTONE EPITAPH:**
> *While swimming he yelled, "Help!"*
> *But we thought he said, "kelp!"*

4. glowering malcontent (glou´ ər ing)   To glower is to sullenly stare, scowl, or glare menacingly. From Middle Low German, *gluren* = to leer.

> *His eye, once so kindly, could have been grafted on*
> *to the head of a man-eating shark and no questions asked.*
> —*P. G. Wodehouse*

5. gluttonous blob (glŭt´ ə nəs)   Ooh, this blimp can eat. And eat! And eat!! From Latin, *gluttire* = to devour.

> *The glutton digs his grave with his teeth.*
> —*English proverb*

6. gnathonic underling (nă thän´ ĭk)   A gnathonic person is fawning and flattering. The word is taken from a character named Gnatho in Terrence's play, "Eunuchus", who was notorious for being a sycophant.

> **TOMBSTONE EPITAPH:**
> *An underling all of his life*
> *Croaked when he saw*
> *His boss with his wife*

7. gormless zombie (gôrm´ lĭs)   Slow-witted and senseless, a gormless person fails to pay attention, fails to notice things. From Gothic, *gaumjan* = to heed, to notice + less.

> *Puppets, who, though on idiotism's dark brink,*
> *because they've heads, dare fancy they can think?*
> —*Wolcott*

8. grandiloquent spieler (grăn dĭl´ ə kwənt)   A grandiloquent person is pompous and bombastic. From Latin, *grandis* = great + *loqui* = to speak.

> *He can compress the most words*
> *into the smallest idea of any man I ever met.*
> —*Lincoln*

9. grandiose popinjay (grăn´ dē ōs´)   Anyone or anything grandiose is either impressive or tries to seem impressive. From Latin, *grandis* = great.

> *My right elbow has a fascination that few can resist.*
> —*W. S. Gilbert,*
> *The Mikado*

10. grizzling galoot (grĭz´ ling)   To grizzle is to complain, grumble or mutter. Chiefly British, the word is derived from Middle High German, *grisgramen* = to gnash one's breath.

> *The dogs bark but the caravan moves on.*
> —*Arabic proverb*

Quiz 33

Match the definitions with the words on the left.

Brainy Barbs

__ 1. gaunt	a.	complaining, grumbling
__ 2. gawk	b.	eating excessively
__ 3. gibber	c.	fawning and flattering
__ 4. glower	d.	impressive
__ 5. gluttonous	e.	pompous and bombastic
__ 6. gnathonic	f.	scowl
__ 7. gormless	g.	slow-witted and senseless
__ 8. grandiloquent	h.	speak nonsensically
__ 9. grandiose	i.	stare with mouth open
__10. grizzling	j.	thin and bony

Basic Barbs

__11. waif	k.	a haughty person
__12. malcontent	l.	an unhappy or unruly person
__13. underling	m.	a homeless child
__14. zombie	n.	a talker who tries to persuade
__15. spieler	o.	an inferior, subordinate
__16. popinjay	p.	an uncouth, clumsy idiot
__17. galoot	q.	a corpse brought back to life

Get a Spine, Part 3

(cocker, cosset, enervate, impotent)

Match and unscramble.

1. c _ _ _ _ t = treat like a pet
2. i _ _ _ _ _ _ _ = ineffective, powerless
3. e _ _ _ _ _ _ _ = weaken
4. c _ _ _ _ _ = pamper, coddle

(craven, pusillanimous, quaver, quiver, squeamish, timorous)

5. mortious = fearful   _____
6. sueamqish = easily sickened; easily offended   _____
7. veriuq = tremble   _____
8. uaqver = tremble   _____
9. mnisilulaopus = cowardly   _____
10. ranevc = cowardly   _____

Grisly List 34

Aristotle said that wit is educated insolence. If this is true, then it is important to practice being insolent and to study those who have mastered the art of being witty. It certainly helps to have a masterful command of words, but it is even more important that one knows how to put those words together. Sometimes, just a few words will do. Churchill was known for having that kind of wit. At a dinner party a gossip seated next to him said, "Mr. Churchill, I have placed a bet that I can get more than two words out of you." Mr. Churchill replied, "You lose."

Basic Barbs

➤ **bootlicker** = one who tries to gain favor from others by behaving like a slave, a brownnoser

➤ **gorgon** = from Greek mythology, a woman with snakes for hair, and to behold her would turn you to stone; an ugly, repulsive woman

➤ **greenhorn** = an inexperienced person

➤ **gyp** = (adj.) to cheat another; (noun) or one who gyps, a swindler

➤ **yahoo** = a country imbecile

Brainy Barbs

1. **grotesque gorgon** (grō tĕsk´) This hag is one ugly witch. Grotesque literally means a picture in a cave (grotto) from the designs that were made on Roman cave walls, in which people and animals were painted with plant life in a bizarre way. It now can describe anything bizarre, ludicrously absurd or ugly.

> *Beauty is only skin deep, but ugly goes clear to the bone.*
> —*Murphy's Law*

2. **grousing yahoo** (grous´ ing) One who is grousing is a nagging complainer. From Middle French, *groucier* = to growl.

> *Had we not faults of our own,*
> *we should take less pleasure in complaining of others.*
> —*Fenelon*

3. **groveling bootlicker** (grŏv´ əl ing) To grovel is to cower in a prostrate position. From Middle English, *grufelinge* = on one's face, prone.

> *Those who are surly and imperious to their inferiors*
> *are generally humble, flattering, and cringing to their superiors.*
> —*Fuller*

4. **grubby little stinker** (grŭb´ ē)   Anything (or anyone) grubby is infested with grubs (small larvae of an insect) or dirty or simply inferior. From Medieval English, *grubben* = to dig.

> *You look like the second week of the garbage strike.*
> —Neil Simon

5. **gruff old bag of bones** (grŭf)   This one is rough in the way he/she acts and/or speaks. From German, *grob* = rough, uncouth.

> **TOMBSTONE EPITAPH:**
> *If you can read this, you're too close;*
> *get off my grave, idiot!*
> —Glen Super

6. **guileful gyp** (gīl´ fəl)   Watch out. This gyp is clever at deceit and full of trickery. From Old English, *wigle* = witchcraft.

> *It is morally wrong to allow suckers to keep their money.*
> —"Canada Bill" Jones.

7. **gullible greenhorn** (gŭl´ ə bəl)   A gullible person is easily cheated, too trusting and believes too easily. From Middle English, *golle* = silly fellow, literally, an unfledged bird + able.

> *The more crap you believe, the better off you are.* —Charles Bukowski

8. **gulositous gobbler** (gyū lŏs´ ĭ təs)   A greedy glutton, he/she wants and wants! From Late Latin, *gulosus* = gluttonous > *gula* = throat.

> *For their love lies in their purses,*
> *and whoso empties them by so much*
> *fills their hearts with deadly hate.*
> —William Shakespeare,
> Richard II

9. **hackneyed writer** (hăk´ nēd)   A hackney is horse used for ordinary travel, or the carriage for such travel, or a hackney can be a drudge, from which we get the word hack, a literary drudge. Anything hackneyed is so trite, so ordinary by overuse that it is annoying. From Middle English, *hakene* < Hackney = an English village.

> *When in doubt, have two guys come through the door with guns.*
> —Raymond Chandler

10. **hapless nincompoop** (hăp´ lĭs)   Anyone hapless is without luck. From Old English, *haeppen* = to go by chance + less.

> *My father gave me a bat for Christmas.*
> *The first time I tried to play with it, it flew away.*
> —Rodney Dangerfield

Quiz 34

Match the definitions with the words on the left.

Brainy Barbs

___ 1. grotesque   a. bizarre, ludicrously absurd
___ 2. grouse   b. commonplace by overuse
___ 3. grovel   c. cower in a prostrate position
___ 4. grubby   d. full of trickery
___ 5. gruff   e. greedy, gluttonous
___ 6. guileful   f. infested with grubs or dirty
___ 7. gullible   g. nag, complain
___ 8. gulositous   h. rough in manner and/or speech
___ 9. hackneyed   i. too trusting, believe too easily
___10. hapless   j. without luck

Basic Barbs

___11. gorgon   k. a country imbecile
___12. yahoo   l. a woman with snakes for hair
___13. bootlick   m. an inexperienced person
___15. gyp   n. to cheat another
___16. greenhorn   o. try to gain favor from others by acting slavish

Class And No Class, Part 1

(aristocracy, blue blood, fascist, intelligentsia, masses,)
(meritocracy, mobocracy, plebeian, plutocracy, anarchist)

Match.

1. p _ _ _ _ _ _ _ _ _ = government by the rich
2. f _ _ _ _ _ _ _ = member of a dictatorship typified
             by hostile nationalism
3. a _ _ _ _ _ _ _ _ _ _ _ = elite privileged class
4. m _ _ _ _ _ _ _ _ _ _ _ = the intellectual elite
5. m _ _ _ _ _ _ _ _ _ = rule by the mob
6. m _ _ _ _ _ = the vast numbers of lower, working class people
7. i _ _ _ _ _ _ _ _ _ _ _ _ _ _ = intellectuals, the educated class
8. p _ _ _ _ _ _ _ = one of the lower class; a vulgar person
9. b _ _ _ b _ _ _ _ = from nobility
10. a _ _ _ _ _ _ _ _ = believes in no government

Groucho Marx was another great wit. A guest of his, upon leaving, turned to Groucho and said, "Oh, I'd like to say goodbye to you wife." Not skipping a beat Groucho quipped, "Wouldn't we all." There are plenty of times we wish we'd had said the right remark at the right moment, but that takes practice like anything else. If you take the time to study the great wits like you do the vocabulary, you might be surprised at just how witty you can be.

Basic Barbs

➤ **bemired** = stuck or covered in slime or mud
➤ **egotist** = one who is self-centered and conceited
➤ **gigolo** = a male prostitute
➤ **hydra** = a nine-headed monster from Greek mythology

Brainy Barbs

1. **hebetating hick** (hĕb´ ĭ tāt´ ing) This one is becoming more stupid or dull by the minute. From Latin, *hebeture* = to make dull.

Likely comment:
What Einstein meant to say was, uh, what he meant to, uh, uh, I forgot what I was, uh, me forget, duh, duh, goober, uh, oof. Arf! Arf!

Your response:
Here boy, fetch the stick.

2. **high-falutin garbage** (hī fə lŏŏt´ ĭn) This comes from an altered form of high-floating and it is a humorous way to say something is pompous, bombastic or pretentious.

He can compress the most words
into the smallest ideas of any man I ever met.
—Abraham Lincoln

3. **hircine gigolo** (hûr´ sīn) One who is hircine behaves like a goat; thus, it can be interpreted as lustful and horny. From Latin, *hircus* = goat.

Men are creatures with two legs and eight hands.
—Jayne Mansfield

4. **histrionic ham** (hĭs´ trē ŏn´ ĭk) This ham overacts with buffoonish hilarity using gesticulating gyrations. From Latin, *histro* = actor.

One more drink and I'll be under the host.
—Dorothy Parker

5. the bemired hoi polloi (hoi´ pə loi´)   Hoi polloi in Greek means "the many". It has become a term of contempt synonymous with the masses, the lower class, the common ruck, the great-unwashed etc.

The nose of the mob is its imagination.
By this, at any time, it can be quietly led.
—*Edgar Allan Poe*

6. homicidal maniac (häm´ ə sīd´ əl)   Murder anyone? This one wants to criminally kill. From Latin, *homo* = man + *caedere* = to cut, kill.

If once a man indulges himself in murder,
very soon he comes to think little of robbing;
and from robbing he comes next to drinking and Sabbath-breaking,
and from that to incivility and procrastination.
—*Thomas De Quincy*

7. horripilating hydra (hô rǐp´ ə lāt´ ing)   This monster makes your hairs stand up from fear or disgust. From Latin, *horripilare* = to bristle with hairs.

There is no terror in the bang, only in the anticipation of it.
—*Alfred Hitchcock*

8. hubristic egotist (hyōō brǐs´ tǐk)   The hubris of someone is their excessive pride. The Ancient Greeks felt that this was a great character flaw, which would ultimately lead to one's downfall. The adjective, hubristic, can be used to characterize anyone filled with this excessive pride.

Egotism is the anesthetic that dulls the pain of stupidity.
—*Frank Leahy*

9. iconoclastic radical (ī kǒn´ ə klăst)   In the 8th-century Greek Orthodox Church, an iconoclast was a member of a faction that believed in the elimination of icons. Now anyone iconoclastic attacks traditional beliefs and values. From Late Greek, *eikon* = an image + *klaein* = to break.

Every revolution evaporates
and leaves behind only the slime of a new bureaucracy.
—*Franz Kafka*

10. ignoble ratfink (ǐg nō´ bəl)   The formal definition of ignoble is anything not belonging to nobility, but its standard usage denotes one who has no honor. From Latin, *ignobilis* = not noble.

He has every attribute of a dog except loyalty.
—*Thomas P. Gore*

Quiz 35

Match the definitions with the words on the left.

Brainy Barbs

__ 1. hebetate
__ 2. high-falutin
__ 3. hircine
__ 4. histrionic
__ 5. hoi polloi

__ 6. homicidal
__ 7. horripilating
__ 8. hubristic
__ 9. iconoclastic
__10. ignoble

a. attacking traditional beliefs
b. become more stupid or dull
c. filled with excessive pride
d. like a goat
e. making your hairs stand up from fear or disgust
f. murderous
g. pompous, bombastic
h. the masses, the lower class
i. using gesticulating gyrations
j. without honor

Basic Barbs

__11. hydra
__12. egotist
__13. gigolo
__14. bemired

k. a nine-headed monster
l. a male prostitute
m. is self-centered, conceited
n. covered in slime or mud

Class And No Class, Part 2

(ruck, booboisie, ochlocratic, elitist, dregs, hoi polloi,)
(preppy, upstart, arriviste, reactionary)

Unscramble.

1. loochcratic = government by the mob   _____
2. ttsiile = believes government should be controlled by the best   _____
3. greds = the bottom class in society: _____
4. kcur = a mass of common people   _____
5. bbsoooiie = the social class of stupid and gullible people   _____
6. ohi pooill = in Greek it means "the many"   _____
7. vatrriise = one who has recently acquired wealth by unscrupulous means   _____
8. ppprey = a preparatory school student,   _____
9. starutp = one who's recent wealth has led to pretentious behavior   _____
10. reyacitonar = an extreme conservative   _____

LE MOT QUOTE 20

Match each quote with the appropriate word.

1. Uneasy lies the head that wears the crown.
   —Shakespeare

2. Only the shallow know them selves. —Oscar Wilde

3. Poor fellow, he suffers from files. —Aneurin Bevan

4. They never taste who always drink
   They always talk who never think. —Prior

_ a. functionary

_ b. frothy

_ c. garrulous

_ d. fretful

LE MOT QUOTE 21

Match each quote with the appropriate word.

1. Their kitchen is their shrine, the cook their priest,
   the table their altar, and their belly their God.
   —Buck

2. The surest way of making a dupe is to let your victim
   think you are his. —Bulwer

3. One is easily fooled by that which one loves.
   —Moliere,
   Tartuffe

4. Men are women's playthings. —Victor Hugo

_ a. guileful

_ b. gluttonous

_ c. gullible

_ d. femme fatale

LE MOT QUOTE 22

Match each quote with the appropriate word.

1. If an unlucky man were to sell shrouds,
   people would stop dying. —Arab proverb

2. Papa loved Mamma
   Mamma loved men
   Mamma's in the graveyard
   Papa's in the pen. —Carl Sandburg

3. It is hard to fight against impulsive desire;
   whatever it wants it will buy at the cost
   of the soul. —Heraclitus

4. I've got to take under my wing, tra la
   A most unattractive thing, tra la
   With a caricature of a face. —W. S. Gilbert

___ a. grotesque

___ b. hapless

___ c. homicidal

___ d. gulositous

Chapter 8

Words are like money; there is nothing so useless, unless when in actual use. —Samuel Butler

Grisly List 36

Have you ever thought about *when* you study? Most students see studying as some kind of intellectual marathon, but very little learning takes place when you are pouring hours and hours of time over a book. No. It's much more important to spend fifteen minutes of study and then take a break. Fifteen minutes here, another fifteen there. It all adds up. And in the end, you'll retain more of the information.

Basic Barbs

➤ **impose** = to obtrude oneself on others
➤ **malapert** = an impudent, saucy person, shamelessly disrespectful, rude
➤ **mischievous** = playfully causing trouble or irritation
➤ **scofflaw** = a habitual offender of the law
➤ **whelp** = the young offspring of a dog or wolf; or an impudent youth

Brainy Barbs

1. **ignominious disgrace** (ĭg´ nə mĭn´ ē əs)   Shame! Anything ignominious implies an utter loss of self-respect rendering someone a complete disgrace. From Latin, *ignominia* = without a name.

   Under this flabby exterior is an enormous lack of character.
   —Oscar Levant

2. **slow-witted ignoramus** (ĭg´ nə rā´ məs)   Ignoramus is a fancy w a y to call someone stupid. It was a name given to a lawyer in Ruggle's play, Ignoramus (1615) and literally in Latin means, 'we take no notice'.

   To be ignorant of one's ignorance is the malady of ignorance.
   —A. B. Alcott

3. **imbruted beast** (ĭm brūt´ ĭd)   An imbruted lout is one who has sunk to the level of a brute, a beast. From Latin, *im* = into + *brutus* = stupid.

   I never met a man I didn't want to fight.
   —Lyle Alzado

4. mischievous imp (ĭmp) An imp is a young demon or a mischievous child not unlike a scampish squirt or a puckish pain in the neck. From Greek, *empyta* = offspring, a shoot of a plant.

Favorite motto:
Have joybuzzer—will travel.

5. impecunious beggar (ĭm´ pə kyū´ nē əs) Anyone impecunious is without money. From French, *impecunieux* = without wealth.

If a poor man asks for alms and you have nothing to give,
console him with words, for it is forbidden to chastise a poor man,
or raise your voice against him, since his heart is broken.
—Maimonides

6. impenitent scofflaw (ĭm pĕn´ ə tənt) This one is without shame, regret or remorse. From Latin, *impaenitens* = not repentant.

Since I wronged you, I have never liked you.
—Spanish proverb

7. imposing imperialist (ĭm pēr´ ē əl ĭst) An imperialist is prone to dominate the political, economic affairs of weaker governments. From Latin, *imperare* = to command.

In the eyes of empire-builders men are not men, but instruments.
—Napoleon I.

8. imperious backbreaker (ĭm pēr´ ē əs) One who is imperious is too bossy. From Latin, *imperios* = commanding, tyrannical.

I hold it better for the ruler to be feared than to be loved.
—Machiavelli

9. impertinent malapert (ĭm pûr´ tĭ nənt) Saucy and rude, this wench never shows proper respect. From Late Latin, *impertinens* = not belonging.

Women complain about premenstrual syndrome,
but I think of it as the only time of the month that I can be myself.
—Roseanne Barr

10. impetuous whelp (ĭm pech´ ū əs) Rash, this one always jumps in before thinking of the consequences. From Latin, *impertere* = to rush upon.

Hasty climbers have sudden falls.
—English proverb

Quiz 36

Match the definitions with the words on the left.

Brainy Barbs

___ 1. ignominious   a. a stupid person
___ 2. ignoramus   b. young demon or a mischievous child
___ 3. imbruted   c. completely disgraceful
___ 4. imp   d. like a brute
___ 5. impecunious   e. prone to dominate the affairs of weaker governments
___ 6. impenitent   f. rash
___ 7. imperialistic   g. saucy and rude
___ 8. imperious   h. too bossy, commanding, tyrannical
___ 9. impertinent   i. without money
___10. impetuous   j. lacking shame, regret

Basic Barbs

___11. fraud   k. an impudent, saucy person
___12. mischievous   l. playfully causes trouble
___13. whelp   m. a cheat or an impostor
___14. malapert   n. the young offspring of a dog
___15. impose   o. to obtrude oneself on others
___16. scofflaw   p. a habitual offender of the law

A Real Drag

(obtrusive, interloper, officious, onerous, abrasive, buttinski,)
(insufferable, proleptic, umbrageous, vexatious)

Match.

1. a _ _ _ _ _ _ _ = irritating
2. b _ _ _ _ _ _ _ _ = one who butts in to other people's business
3. i _ _ _ _ _ _ _ _ _ _ _ = intolerable
4. i _ _ _ _ _ _ _ _ _ = one who meddles in others affairs
5. o _ _ _ _ _ _ _ _ _ = offering unwanted advice
6. o _ _ _ _ _ _ = burdensome
7. p _ _ _ _ _ _ _ _ = given to anticipating another's arguments
8. u _ _ _ _ _ _ _ _ _ _ = easily offended
9. v _ _ _ _ _ _ _ _ _ = annoying
10. o _ _ _ _ _ _ _ _ = intruding, interfering, pushy; blatant

Grisly List 37

Where one studies may be just as important as *when* one studies. If you have a book in your hand, why lock yourself up in a library or a closet? You can take a book with you anywhere: a park, the beach, or the mountains. If you're reading this in prison, well, uh, I'm afraid I can't help you there. But as for the rest of you, make your study time part of your recreation and your recreation part of your study time.

Basic Barbs

➤ **fledgling** = a young bird just ready for flight; an inexperienced person
➤ **fury** = extreme anger; an extremely angry person, especially a woman
➤ **lout** = a clumsy idiot
➤ **moocher** = one who begs and lives off others
➤ **pauper** (pô´ pər) = one who lives on charity
➤ **spitfire** = a highly excitable person, especially a woman
➤ **twerp** = a nerd

Brainy Barbs

1. **impolitic fledgling** (ĭm pŏl´ ĭ tĭk) This one's unwise, impractical, careless, lacking shrewdness. Im is a variation of in, a Latin prefix meaning not + from Greek, *politicos* = of a citizen.

> *Before you beat the dog,*
> *learn the name of its master.*
> —Chinese proverb

2. **importuning moocher** (ĭm´ pôr tūn´ ing) To importune is to shamelessly beg, to annoy with insistent requests. From Latin, *importunus* = unsuitable, troublesome.

> *If a beggar be placed*
> *in the midst of a grove of pear trees,*
> *even there he will beg.*
> —Indian proverb

3. **impotent pauper** (ĭm´ pə tənt) Literally impotent means ineffective and powerless, but it also carries the stigma of sexual dysfunction. From Latin, *in* = not + *potis* = able.

> *Powerlessness frustrates;*
> *absolute powerlessness frustrates absolutely.*
> —Russell Baker

4. impoverished wreck (ĭm pŏv´ ər ĭsht)   This poor wreck has been deprived of the ability to make a living and thus, reduced to poverty. From Latin, *pauper* = poor.

> *O God! that bread should be so dear,*
> *and flesh and blood so cheap!*
> —Thomas Hood

5. imprudent spitfire (ĭm prūd´ ənt)   Without any thought of the consequences, this one is rash and indiscreet.   From Latin, *in* = not + *prouidens* = foreseeing.

> *Fools rush in where angels fear to tread.*
> —Pope

6. impudent fury (ĭm´ pyə dənt)   Saucy, impertinent and shameless, this one will spit your face. From Latin, *impudens* = not modest.

> *If you spit in a harlot's face she says it's raining.*
> —Yiddish proverb

7. inane flake (ĭ nān´)   Anyone inane is empty-headed and foolish. From Latin, *inanis* = empty.

> *A fool in a hurry drinks tea with a fork.*
> —Chinese proverb

8. inarticulate twerp (ĭn´ är tĭk´ yə lĭt)   This is another blithering idiot who can't speak coherently, who mumbles, sputters and falters in speech. From Latin, *in* = not + *articulatus* = to separate into joints.

> *Birds are entangled by their feet*
> *and men by their tongues.*
> —Thomas Fuller

9. incendiary lout (ĭn sĕn´ dē er´ ē)   An incendiary person willfully stirs up strife. From Latin, *incendi* = fire.

> *He who incites to strife is worse than he who takes part in it.*
> —Aesop

10. incoherent imbecile (ĭn´ kō hēr ənt)   When something is incoherent it's not sticking together; if a person is incoherent they are rambling and/or unintelligible because the words don't "stick together". From Latin, *in* = not + *co* = together + *haerere* = to stick.

> *Many a man's tongue shakes out his master's undoing.*
> —Shakespeare

Quiz 37

Match the definitions with the words on the left.

Brainy Barbs

__ 1. impolitic
__ 2. importune
__ 3. impotent
__ 4. impoverished
__ 5. imprudent
__ 6. impudent
__ 7. inane
__ 8. inarticulate
__ 9. incendiary
__10. incoherent

a. empty-headed; foolish
b. ineffective and powerless
c. in poverty
d. impertinent and shameless
e. annoy with insistent requests
f. unintelligible (fits two words)
g. unwise (fits two words)
h. willfully stirring up strife

Basic Barbs

__11. fledgling
__12. mooch
__13. spitfire
__14. lout
__15. pauper

i. a clumsy idiot
j. to beg
k. a highly excitable woman
l. one who lives on charity
m. young bird just ready for flight

Hard To Control, Part 1

(foment, fractious, froward, incendiary, instigating, mutinous, factious,)
(militate, saboteur, contumacious, restive, seditious, refractory)

Unscramble.

1. metailit = work against   _____
2. fsuoitca = causing groups to split and fight   _____
3. timunous = revolting against authority   _____
4. stinigagtin = urging on to some evil purpose   _____
5. ceninyarid = fiery; willfully stirring up strife   _____
6. femont = stir up trouble   _____
7. suoitcarf = rebellious   _____
8. warford = not easily controlled   _____
9. yortcfarer = hard to control: stubborn   _____
10. cnuaiusocmto = obstinately resisting authority,   _____
11. siverte = restless, fidgety; unruly   _____
12. suoitides = stirring up discontent   _____
13. rtbsaoeu = one who uses treachery,
              subversion to undermine a nation   _____

They say the average person spends two years of his life waiting at stoplights. I don't know about you but that makes me feel like I'm in prison. But it doesn't have to be that way. Make a list of all the words you miss on each test. Read them and their proper definitions onto a cassette. Pop it into your car cassette player. And, presto! Now you can listen to this anywhere, with any boring occupation: doing the dishes, the laundry, jogging etc. Remember: don't overdo it. Try fifteen-minute study breaks while you are bogged down in heavy traffic. You'll probably find that it even calms you down while on freeway. Why? Because you won't feel like you are wasting your time.

Basic Barbs

➢ **barfly** = one who spends most of his time drinking in taverns
➢ **bluenose** = a puritanical person, a prude
➢ **delinquent** = adj., failing to do what is lawful; noun, one failing to obey the law, especially a juvenile
➢ **ne'er-do-well** = one who never does anything well
➢ **sloth** = a lazy person
➢ **vandal** = Vandals were a Germanic tribe who sacked Rome in 455 AD; one who destroys others' property out of malice

Brainy Barbs

1. **incompetent ne'er-do-well** (ĭn kŏm´ pĭ tənt) Inept, this flop isn't capable of doing a task right. From Latin, *in* = not + *competere* = be qualified.

> *A girl who can't dance says the band can't play.*
> —Yiddish proverb

2. **incorrigible vandal** (ĭn kôr´ ĭ jə bəl) Habitually bad, this one cannot be reformed. From Latin, *in* = not + *corrigere* = to lead straight.

> *Give a woman an inch and she'll park her car on it.*
> —E. P. B. White

3. **inculcating schoolmaster** (ĭn´ kŭl kāt´ ing) To inculcate is to teach with boring and forceful repetition. From Latin, *inculcatus* = to tread down.

> *The average schoolmaster is and always must be essentially an ass,*
> *for how can one imagine an intelligent man*
> *engaging in so puerile an avocation?*
> —H. L. Mencken

4. indecorous comment (ĭn dĕ´ kōr əs)   To be decorous is to conform to what is proper in decent society.   Hence, an indecorous comment is indecent, improper, and tasteless.   From Latin, *in* = not + *decorus* = becoming, in good taste.

A man's venom poisons himself more than his victim.
—Charles Buxton

5. penniless indigent (ĭn´ dĭ jĕnt)   Lacking the basic necessities of life, this poor one needs a handout. From Latin, *indigere* = to be in need.

A fool and his money are soon parted.
—English proverb

6. indignant bluenose (ĭn dĭg´ nənt)   This one is ticked off, angry or scornful. From Latin, *in* = not + *dignari* = to deem worthy.

Moral indignation is jealousy with a halo.
—H. G. Wells

7. indocile delinquent (ĭn dŏs´ ĭl)   One who is indocile is not easy to teach or discipline. From Latin, *in* = not + *docilis* = easily taught.

Never try to teach a pig to sing;
you'll waste your time and you'll annoy the pig.
—Unknown

8. indolent sloth (ĭn´ də lənt)   Anyone indolent is sluggish, lazy, showing a dislike for work, without an interest in anything. In Medicine, indolent characterizes a disease that is slow to heal or doesn't cause any pain. From Latin, *in* = not + *dolere* = to feel pain.

Hard work never killed anybody, but why take a chance?
—Charlie McCarthy
(Edgar Bergen)

9. indurate mule (ĭn´ dŏŏ rĭt)   Indurate can mean hardened, callous or stubborn. From Latin, *indurare* = to make hard.

Worse than a bloody hand is a hard heart.
—Shelley, Percy Bysshe

10. inebriated barfly (ĭn ē´ brē āt´ əd)   This is just a fancy way of saying someone is drunk. From Latin, *inebriare* = to intoxicate.

Someone took the cork out of my lunch.
—W. C. Fields

Quiz 38

Match the definitions with the words on the left.

Brainy Barbs

__ 1. incompetent	a. angry or scornful
__ 2. incorrigible	b. drunk
__ 3. inculcate	c. habitually bad
__ 4. indecorous	d. hardened, callous or stubborn
__ 5. indigent	e. indecent, improper
__ 6. indignant	f. inept
__ 7. indocile	g. not easy to teach or discipline
__ 8. indolent	h. lazy
__ 9. indurate	i. lacking the basic necessities
__10. inebriated	j. to teach by endless repetition

Basic Barbs

__11. vandal	k. a lazy person
__12. bluenose	l. a puritanical person, a prude
__13. powder keg	m. an explosive personality
__14. sloth	n. destroys others' property
__15. barfly	o. spends time drinking in taverns

Hard To Control, Part 2

(intractable, unbridled, feral, incorrigible, indocile, unbitted, iconoclast,)
(insubordinate, insolent, recalcitrant, obstreperous, intransigent)

Match and unscramble.

1. corinelrigib = cannot be reformed,
   habitually bad   _____
2. dinolice = not easy to teach or discipline _____
3. bunridled = unrestrained, wild   _____
4. bunitted = unrestrained, wild   _____
5. rafel = wild   _____

6. r _ _ _ _ _ _ _ _ _ _ = not complying
7. i _ _ _ _ _ _ _ = boldly disrespectful
8. i _ _ _ _ _ _ _ _ _ _ _ _ = disobedient
9. i _ _ _ _ _ _ _ _ _ = one who attacks traditional beliefs
10. o _ _ _ _ _ _ _ _ _ _ _ = noisy, unruly
11. i _ _ _ _ _ _ _ _ _ _ _ = refusing to agree
12. i _ _ _ _ _ _ _ _ _ = hard to manage, unruly

Grisly List 39

If your primary goal is to learn vocabulary and you're not merely reading this for entertainment, then I think it's important that you focus on the words you don't know. Make sure you write down all the words you have difficulty with and scan them every so often. Keep scanning again and again until they are fixed in your long-term memory.

Basic Barbs

➢ **bungler** = an inept or clumsy numskull
➢ **claqueur** (klă kûr´) = a member of a claque, a group hired to applaud and laugh at theaters, performances, nightclubs etc.
➢ **introvert** = one who is interested more in himself than others
➢ **no-account** = a worthless person
➢ **obstructionist** = one who obstructs progress

Brainy Barbs

1. **inefficacious no-account** (ĭn´ ĕ fĕ kā´ shəs) This flake is ineffective. From Latin, *in* = not + *efficax* = effectual.

> We are all of us failures—at least, the best of us are.
> —James M. Barrie

2. **inept bungler** (ĭn ĕpt´) This one is unfit, awkward and inefficient.

> The ass knows seven ways to swim;
> when he falls into the water, he forgets them all.
> —Armenian proverb

3. **inexorable obstructionist** (ĭn ĕk´ sər´ ə bəl) An inexorable person is unyielding and cannot be moved. From Latin, *in* = no, not, without + *exorare* = to move by urgent requests.

> He's a fool that will not yield.
> —Shakespeare

4. **infamous outlaw** (ĭn´ fə məs) Anyone infamous is bad, *real* bad, and famous for being bad. From Latin, *infamis* = disgraced.

> Likely comment:
> This town ain't big enough for the both of us.

> Your response:
> Okay. We'll start expanding. Bring in new businesses, attract the tourists, lay down a ground plan, build more suburbs, parks, restaurants, maybe a movie theme park.

5. infatuated dope (ĭn făch´ ū ā´ tĭd)   To infatuate is to cause someone to lose their sense of common sense, or arouse another to be foolishly in love, a love that is without any depth. To be infatuated is to be stupidly in love. From Latin, infatuare = to be made a fool < fatuus = foolish.

> Love is being stupid together.
> —Paul Valery

6. infernal hellhound (ĭn fûr´ nəl)   This fiend is cooking up some hellish plot. From Latin, infernus = underground, lower.

> **TOMBSTONE EPITAPH:**
> She's gone to meet her maker
> Since heaven wouldn't take her

7. selfish ingrate (ĭn´ grāt n. and adj.)   An ingrate is one who is ungrateful. From Latin, in = not + gratus = grateful.

> I gave him a staff for his support
> and he uses it to break my head.
> —Indian proverb

8. ingratiating claqueur (ĭn grā´ shē ā´ ting)   This one tries to gain another's favor by conscious effort to achieve an advantage. From a Latin phrase, in gratiam = for the favor.

> Charm is a way of getting the answer yes
> without asking a clear question.
> —Albert Camus

9. inhibited introvert (ĭn hĭb´ ĭ təd)   To be inhibited is to hold back. It is synonymous with shy, timid. From Latin, inhibitus = to hold in.

> Of all base passions, fear is the most accursed.
> —Shakespeare,
> Henry VI

10. inimical cutthroat (ĭ nĭm´ ĭ kəl)   Anyone inimical is like an enemy, hostile and unfriendly. From Latin, inimicus = hostile.

> God, save me from my friends,
> I can protect myself from my enemies.
> —Marshal de Villars

Quiz 39

Match the definitions with the words on the left.

Brainy Barbs

___ 1. inefficacious   a. famous for being bad
___ 2. inept   b. fiendish
___ 3. inexorable   c. ineffective
___ 4. infamous   d. like an enemy, hostile
___ 5. infatuated   e. shy
___ 6. infernal   f. stupidly in love
___ 7. ingrate   g. to bring oneself into another's favor by conscious effort
___ 8. ingratiate   h. unfit, awkward and inefficient
___ 9. inhibited   i. an ungrateful person
___10. inimical   j. unyielding

Basic Barbs

___11. bungler   k. absorbed in oneself
___12. obstructionist   l. an inept or clumsy numskull
___13. claqueur   m. one hired to applaud and laugh at performances
___14. introvert   n. one who obstructs progress

Bad To The Bone, Part 1

(ugsome, malicious, invidious, Hydra, ominous, lapidate, culpable,)
(abhorrent, baneful, bête noire, nocent, remorseless, reprehensible)

Match.

1. m _ _ _ _ _ _ _ _ = spiteful
2. l _ _ _ _ _ _ _ = throw stones
3. o _ _ _ _ _ _ = threatening, sinister
4. r _ _ _ _ _ _ _ _ _ _ = cruel, pitiless
5. i _ _ _ _ _ _ _ _ = exciting ill-will or envy
6. h _ _ _ _ = nine-headed monster
7. c _ _ _ _ _ _ _ = deserving blame
8. r _ _ _ _ _ _ _ _ _ _ _ _ = worthy of blame
9. u _ _ _ _ _ = horrid, loathsome
10. n _ _ _ _ _ = harmful; criminal
11. a _ _ _ _ _ _ _ _ = hateful, causing disgust
12. b _ _ _ n _ _ _ _ = a person feared, hated
13. b _ _ _ _ _ _ = deadly

Grisly List 40

Some people have wonderful jobs. They go to work like it's a ballgame. While there, they are filled with rapture. When they go home to their loved ones, they are ecstatic and filled with the glorious energy their job has given them. Then there are the rest of us. We hate our job. We go to work like we'd walk into hell. While there, we live our lives in dread and doom. When we go home, we are so exhausted we have no energy left for our children or ourselves. That's why I believe work is best place for you to study. If you can find pockets of time where you won't get into trouble, go over the book or share it with a friend. Revel in joy that while that while someone else is paying you, you are doing something wonderfully selfish.

Basic Barbs

➢ **git** = British slang word for a foolish idiot
➢ **gourmand** = one who enjoys eating too much
➢ **infidel** = one with no religious beliefs
➢ **serf** = a slave, one bound to his master's land
➢ **skank** = slang, an ugly woman or a woman with a bad reputation
➢ **thrall** = a slave

Brainy Barbs

1. **iniquitous infidel** (ĭ nĭk´ wĭ təs)   From Latin, *iniquus* = not equal, iniquity now signifies a lack of righteousness; wickedness; and injustice.

> *A wicked man is his own hell.*
> —Thomas Fuller

2. **innocuous lamebrain** (ĭ nŏk´ yū əs)   Innocuous either means harmless or so irritatingly dull as to be annoying. From Latin, *in* = not + *nocere* = to hurt.

> *After making love I said to my girl. "Was it good for you, too?"*
> *And she said, "I don't think this was good for anybody."*
> —Garry Shandling

3. **insatiable gourmand** (ĭn sā´ shə bəl)   This porker can't be satisfied. From Latin, *in* = not + *satiare* = to fill full, to provide with enough.

> *To a drunkard, no liquor is bad;*
> *to a merchant, no money is tainted;*
> *to a lecher, no woman is ugly.*
> —Talmud

4. insensate bonehead (ĭn sĕn´ sāt) This one has no sensations, no feelings, no sensitivity, no sense and no intelligence. From Late Latin, *insensatus* = irrational < *in* = without + *sensatus* = gifted with sense.

> When you use your brain it's a violation of the child-labor law.
> —Joe E. Lewis

5. insidious cheat (ĭn sĭd´ ē əs) Anyone insidious is crafty, sly and more dangerous than seems apparent. From *insidiae* = an ambush.

> First secure an independent income, then practice virtue.
> —Greek proverb

6. insipid git (ĭn sĭp´ ĭd) Dull and tasteless, this one is too boring. From Latin, *in* = not + *sapidus* = savory.

> A bore is someone who when you ask him how he is, tells you.
> —Unknown

7. insipient thrall (ĭn sĭp´ ē ənt) This is just another erudite way to call someone stupid. Don't confuse insipient with the homonym, incipient, which means "in the first stage of existence": e.g. as in an incipient illness. If you do you'll end up being called an incipient, insipient thrall. From Latin, *insipiens* = unwise, foolish.

> The Lord made Adam. The Lord made Eve
> He made them both a little naive.
> —E. Y. Harburg

8. insolent skank (ĭn sə lənt) One who is insolent is boldly rude, disrespectful. From Latin, *in* = not + *solere* = to be accustomed.

> I told my girl friend that unless she expressed her feelings
> and told me what she liked I wouldn't be able to please her,
> so she said, "Get off me."
> —Garry Shandling

9. insolvent serf (ĭn sŏl´ vənt) One who insolvent is unable to pay his debts. From Latin, *in* = not + *solvere* = to loosen.

> Owe no man anything.
> —Romans 12: 8

10. instigating irritant (ĭn´ stə gāt ing) This renegade tries to urge you on, often to some evil purpose. From Latin, *instigatus* = goaded on.

> Anarchy is the stepping stone to absolute power.
> —Napoleon

Quiz 40

Match the definitions with the words on the left.

Brainy Barbs

___ 1. iniquitous   a. boldly disrespectful
___ 2. innocuous   b. can't be satisfied
___ 3. insatiable   c. dangerously crafty
___ 4. insensate   d. dull (fits two words)
___ 5. insidious   e. stupid
___ 6. insipid   f. urge on to some evil purpose
___ 7. insipient   g. unable to pay debts
___ 8. insolent   h. unrighteous; wicked
___ 9. insolvent   i. no sensations or intelligence
___10. instigate

Basic Barbs

___11. infidel   j. a slave, (fits two words)
___12. git   k. woman with a bad reputation
___13. thrall   l. British slang for a foolish idiot
___14. skank   m. one with no religious beliefs
___15. serf

Bad To The Bone, Part 2

(culprit, pernicious, insidious, reprobate, unscrupulous)
(baleful, minacious, repugnant, unconscionable)

Unscramble.

1. lufelab = harmful, threatening   _____
2. misinaocu = threatening   _____
3. suncrulupous = without a conscience or morals   _____
4. connusecilonab = without a conscience   _____
5. pugernant = distasteful, offensive   _____
6. pulcrit = one guilty of or charged with a crime   _____
7. nieciporus = harmful by insidiously weakening   _____
8. sindsiiou = more dangerous than seems apparent, crafty   _____
9. ebroprate = a scoundrel, mischievous rogue, lost in sin   _____

LE MOT QUOTE 23

Match each quote with the appropriate word.

1. Marriage is the only war
   in which you sleep with the enemy. —Unknown

2. More are drowned in drink than in water.
   —Scottish proverb

3. Shall we go on conferring our Civilization upon the peoples that sit in darkness, or shall we give those poor things a rest? —Mark Twain

4. Shame is an ornament to the young;
   a disgrace to the old. —Aristotle

5. With endless pain this man pursues
   What, if he gain'd, he could not use;
   And t'other fondly hopes to see
   What never was, no e'er shall be. —Matthew Prior

___ a. imperialist

___ b. ignominious

___ c. impolitic

___ d. inebriated

___ e. inimical

LE MOT QUOTE 24

Match each quote with the appropriate word.

1. A kick in the ass is a step forward. —Unknown

2. Most of the time, he sounds like he has a mouth full of wet toilet paper. —Rex Reed
   (about Marlin Brando)

3. A fool who wants to hang himself, grabs a knife.
   —Jewish proverb

___ a. insipient

___ b. instigate

___ c. incoherent

LE MOT QUOTE 25
Match each quote with the appropriate word.

1. One ungrateful man does an injury to all who stand in need of aid. —Publius Syrus

2. Some act first, think afterward, and then repent forever. —C. Simmons

3. The contagion of crime is like that of the plague. Criminals collected together corrupt each other. They are worse than ever when, at the termination of their punishment, they return to society.
   —Napoleon

4. They can gas me, but I am famous. I have achieved in one day what it took Robert Kennedy all his life to do. —Sirhan Sirhan

___ a. imprudent

___ b. infamous

___ c. incorrigible

___ d. ingrate

Chapter 9

Words, with their weight, fall upon the picture like birds of prey. —Jules Renard

Grisly List 41

If you've followed my advice thus far, you've probably noticed a side benefit to knowing these words: people actually think you're smart. It never fails. All you have to do is drop one measly little word that no one else but you knows into a conversation and everyone thinks you're Einstein. Now you can be ethical and tell them, "No, no, I'm not really smart. I just read this great book "Vicious Vocabulary," but I don't expect that. What I expect is that you'll smile smugly and let them wallow in their ignorance since that's exactly what I would do.

Basic Barbs

➢ **contrarian** = one who always disagrees
➢ **gatecrasher** = one who attends events without an invitation
➢ **helot** = one of the class of serfs in ancient Sparta, a slave
➢ **juicehead** = a drunkard
➢ **runagate** = a traitor, a deserter
➢ **stickler** = an uncompromising person

Brainy Barbs

1. **insubordinate helot** (ĭn´ sə bor´ də nĭt) This one is disobedient and insolent. From Latin, *in* = not + *sub* = under + *ordinaire* = to order.

   Boldness, without rules of property, becomes insubordination.
   —Confucius

2. **insufferable headache** (ĭn sŭf´ ər ə bəl) This one is so bothersome that it is intolerable. From Latin, *ne* = no, not + *sufferre* = endure

   I'm going to memorize your name and throw my head away.
   —Oscar Levant

3. **intemperate juicehead** (ĭn tĕm´ pər ĭt) One that is intemperate lacks restraint, self-control, especially with alcohol. From Latin, *in* = not + *temperare* = to keep correct degree, regulate.

   My uncle was the town drunk and we lived in Chicago.
   —George Gobel

4. **interminable ink-slinger** (ĭn tûr´ mə nə bəl)   Anything interminable is so lengthy, dull or exasperating that it seems without an end. From Latin, *in* = without + *terminare* = to end.

> *Imbeciles are writing the lives of other imbeciles every day.*
> —Agatha Christie

5. **internecine runagate** (ĭn´ tər nĕs´ ēn)   Anyone who is internecine is harmful to both sides involved in a conflict or full of slaughter. From Latin, *inter* = between + *necare* = to kill.

> *For every back there is a knife.*
> —Corporate proverb

6. **intolerable contrarian** (ĭn tŏl´ ər ə bəl)   Anyone intolerable is too painful to be endured! From Latin, *intolerabilis*.

> *I'm going to memorize your name and throw my head away.*
> —Oscar Levant

7. **intractable stickler** (ĭn trăk´ tə bəl)   This unruly stick-in-the-mud is hard to manage, hard to move, and consequently, hard to get along with. From Latin, *in* = not + *tractare* = to haul.

> *An obstinate man does not hold opinions, but they hold him.*
> —Pope

8. **intransigent hardcase** (ĭn trăn´ sĭ jənt)   This one is unbending, stubborn and refuses to agree. From Latin, *in* = not + *transigere* = to come to a settlement.

> *Like all weak men, he laid an exaggerated stress*
> *on not changing one's mind.*
> —W. Somerset Maugham,
> *Of Human Bondage*

9. **intrusive gatecrasher** (ĭn trū´ sĭv)   Anyone intrusive is intruding, pushy, invasive. From Latin, *intrusus* = pushed in.

> **TOMBSTONE EPITAPH:**
> *He asked for directions*
> *At the house of corrections*

10. **inveterate criminal** (ĭn vĕt´ ər ĭt)   Inveterate means anything that has been so firmly established over a long period of time it is now habitual and deep-rooted. From Latin, *inveterare* = to make or become old.

> *Habit, if not resisted, soon becomes necessity.*
> —St. Augustine

Bad To The Bone, Part 3

(infernal, ignoble, homicidal, sanguinary, nonfeasant, imbruted,)
(misfeasor, internecine, undermine, mortiferous, maleficent)

Match.

1. h _ _ _ _ _ _ _ _ = murderous
2. i _ _ _ _ _ _ _ = sunk to the level of a brute
3. m _ _ _ _ _ _ _ _ _ _ = deadly
4. i _ _ _ _ _ _ _ _ _ _ _ = harmful to both sides involved in a conflict; full of slaughter
5. n _ _ _ _ _ _ _ _ _ = failure to do what duty requires
6. m _ _ _ _ _ _ _ _ _ = harmful, evil
7. u _ _ _ _ _ _ _ _ = dig beneath, wear away at the base; weaken by insidious means
8. i _ _ _ _ _ _ = dishonorable
9. m _ _ _ _ _ _ _ _ = one who does a lawful act in an unlawful way so that others are hurt
10. i _ _ _ _ _ _ _ = hellish, fiendish
11. s _ _ _ _ _ _ _ _ _ = attended with blood; bloodthirsty

Grisly List 42

Reading this book doesn't have to be a solo experience. There are others who will share your interest in these acerbic aspersions. Hopefully, they don't own any guns, knives, poison or any of that plastic explosive stuff. And hopefully, they have a sense of humor. So, if you haven't already done this, I suggest you look for some compatriot with whom you can laugh as you peruse these pages. What's that? You can't find anyone? Then it's time you tried the "Vicious Vocabulary Dating Method." Just head down to your local pub, or coffee house or house of ill repute and approach the first hunk or babe or whatever and say, "Wow, you have to read this!" Then read them one of your favorite aspersions. If he/she responds, you've found your date.

Basic Barbs

➢ **controversialist** = one who thrives on controversy
➢ **Don Juan** = from Spanish legends, a male addicted to the perpetual seduction of women
➢ **provocateur** = one who enjoys provoking others, inciting them to anger, strife; an agent provocateur is a secret agent who incites others to break the law in order to arrest them.
➢ **roundheel** = a woman who yields readily to sexual intercourse
➢ **virago** = a shrewish woman; a manlike female

Brainy Barbs

1. **invidious gossip** (ĭn vĭd´ ē əs) This one stirs up envy between friends by inciting animosity. From Latin, *invidios* = envious.

> *He that cannot possibly mend his own case*
> *will do what he can to impair another's.*
> —*Francis Bacon*

2. **irascible controversialist** (ī răs´ ə bəl) Easily angered, this pain looks for things to get in a huff about. From Latin, *irasci* = to be angry.

> *An angry man opens his mouth and shuts his eyes.*
> —*Marcus Parcius Cato*

3. **irate virago** (ī´ rāt, ī rāt´) This virago is furious, incensed, fuming. From Latin, *irasci* = to be angry.

> *Anger would inflict punishment on another;*
> *meanwhile, it tortures itself.*
> —*Publilius Syrus*

4. **irksome provocateur** (ûrk´ səm) An irksome irritant is tiresome, and annoying. From Medieval English, *irken* = to loathe, to be weary of.

> I don't pay any attention to him. I don't even ignore him.
> —Samuel Goldwyn

5. **irrational crackpot** (ĭ răsh´ ə nəl) Not a lick of sense. This one lacks reason and thus isn't playing with a full deck. From Latin, *in* = not, without + *ratio* = a consideration, reason, strategy.

> There is a mutiny in 's mind.
> —William Shakespeare,
> *King Henry*

6. **ithyphallic Don Juan** (ĭth´ ə făl´ ĭk) Originally, ithyphallic referred to the erect phallus carried in the festival of Bacchus. Now it can describe any lustful, obscene person. From Latin, *ithys* = straight + *phallus* = a likeness of the penis venerated as a symbol of procreation.

> When the prick stands, the brains get buried in the ground.
> —Yiddish proverb

7. **jabbering monkey** (jăb´ ər ing) To jabber is to talk fast and nonsensically. From Late Middle English, it is probably imitative of nonsensical speech.

> They talk most that have the least to say.
> —Prior

8. **jackleg fumbler** (jăck´ lĕg) Jackleg is an alteration of the British word blackleg, a name for one who replaces a worker on strike. Hence, a jackleg laborer is unskilled or untrained and possibly unscrupulous.

> What he lacks in intelligence he more than makes up for in stupidity.
> —Anonymous

9. **jaded roundheel** (jā´ dĭd) This one is either worn-out or dulled from overindulgence. A jade is either a worn-out horse or a disreputable woman. From Old Norse, *jalda* = a mare.

> For the lips of the adulteress drip honey….
> but in the end she is bitter gall.
> —Proverbs 3:4

10. **Janus-faced two-timer** (jā´ nəs făst) From Roman mythology, Janus is a Roman god with two faces. Now it refers to anyone being deceitful, two-faced.

> Who dares think one thing and another tell,
> my heart detests him as the gates of hell.
> —Homer

Quiz 42

Match the definitions with the words on the left.

Brainy Barbs

__ 1.	invidious	a.	angry
__ 2.	irascible	b.	deceitful
__ 3.	irate	c.	easily angered
__ 4.	irksome	d.	incompetent; makeshift
__ 5.	irrational	e.	lacking reason
__ 6.	ithyphallic	f.	lustful, obscene
__ 7.	jabbering	g.	stirs up envy, ill will
__ 8.	jackleg	h.	talking fast and nonsensical
__ 9.	jaded	i.	tiresome and annoying
__10.	Janus-faced	j.	worn-out from overindulgence

Basic Barbs

__11.	provocateur	k.	a shrewish woman
__12.	Don Juan	l.	yields easily to sex
__13.	roundheel	m.	addicted to seducing women
__14.	virago	n.	enjoys provoking others

Bad To The Bone, Part 4

(unregenerate, contemptible, villainous, loathsome,)
(nemesis, odious, callous, tactless, sadistic)

Match.

1. s _ _ _ _ _ _ _ = gets sexual kicks by giving pain
2. t _ _ _ _ _ _ _ = without consideration for others
3. c _ _ _ _ _ _ = uncaring, unfeeling
4. l _ _ _ _ _ _ _ _ _ = excites hate and fear
5. o _ _ _ _ _ = hated
6. n _ _ _ _ _ _ = an unbeatable rival
7. c _ _ _ _ _ _ _ _ _ _ _ = worthless, despised
8. u _ _ _ _ _ _ _ _ _ _ _ _ = not born again;
9. v _ _ _ _ _ _ _ _ _ = evil, wicked

Grisly List 43

You shouldn't use these words with every Tom, Dick or Harry that you meet. Nor should you use these words with your spouse, your parents, your children or, (God forbid!) your boss! No. Savor these words and use them at the most opportune moment. That point in time when the world falls away silently waiting with baited breath for that magical utterance out of your silver lips. Then and only then, you can drop the insult with the thud of Thor's hammer as everyone gazes in awe.

Basic Barbs

➢ **crepehanger** = a pessimistic person
➢ **lackey** = a servant or a servile brown-noser
➢ **lollygagging** = wasting time
➢ **lug** = slang for a large numskull
➢ **slouch** = an inept, awkward, lazy person

Brainy Barbs

1. **jaundiced crepehanger** (jŏn´ dĭst) Jaundice is a liver disease that causes the face and eyes to turn yellow, but jaundiced also means when one's view has been "colored" i.e. altered or distorted, especially when one's view is distorted by prejudice. From Latin, *galbinus* = yellowish.

> *Prejudice is the child of ignorance. —Hazlitt*

2. **jeering lackey** (jēr´ ing) To jeer is to make fun or laugh in a rude manner. The origin of jeer is unknown.

> *How are you holding up during the lithium shortage?*
> *—David Letterman*

3. **jejune airhead** (jĭ jūn´) Anything or anyone jejune is barren or dull. From Latin, *jenunus* = empty, dry, barren.

> *She was blond, she was tan, and now she's gone.*
> *—quote from a "friend" of Nicole Simpson*

4. **bloodsucking jingo** (jing´ gō) A jingo is overly patriotic and too eager to go to war. It was derived, in 1878, from an English song, "We don't want to fight but my jingo if we do, we've got the ships we've got the men, we've got the money too." Jingo may have initially been a euphemism for Jesus or Jinko, a Basque word for God. You can use the adjective and call someone a jingoistic bloodsucker.

> *Patriotism is the willingness to kill and be killed for trivial reasons.*
> *—Bertrand Russell*

5. **overpowering juggernaut** (jŭg´ ər nôt´)   Juggernaut comes from Sanskrit meaning "lord of the world". It is the incarnation of Vishnu, the Hindu god, whose idol when carried on a cart during religious rites so excited worshipers that they hurled themselves under the wheels and were crushed. Hence, a juggernaut is anything or anyone that demands blind devotion, terrible sacrifice or any terrible, irresistible force.

> Men are idolaters, and want something to look at and kiss and hug,
> or throw themselves down before; they always did, they always will;
> and if you don't make it of wood, you must make it of words.
> —Oliver Wendell Holmes, Sr.

6. **jugulating killer** (jū´ gyə lāt´ ing)   To jugulate is to cut a throat, probably a jugular vein. From Latin, *jugulare* = to cut the throat of.

> I have the perfect cure for a sore throat: cut it.
> —Alfred Hitchcock

7. **lachrymose loser** (lăk´ rə mōs)   Poor tearful, little thing, this one cries easily. From Latin, *lacrima* = tear.

> Tears are the silent language of grief.
> —Voltaire

8. **lackadaisical slouch** (lăk´ ə dā´ zĭ kəl)   One who is lackadaisical is lethargic, listless or lazy. From an archaic expression, *lackadaisy*, which is a variation of *lackaday*, an alteration of *alack a day* = an expression of dismay.

> Never put off until tomorrow
> what you can do the day after tomorrow.
> —Mark Twain

9. **lollygagging laggard** (lăg´ ərd)   This slowpoke is either always falling behind or just plain late. From Norwegian, *lagga* = to go slowly.

> If a thing's worth doing, it's worth doing late.
> —Frederick Oliver

10. **lambasting lug** (lăm băst´ ing)   Lambasting means to beat or scold severely. From Old Norse, *lam* = to lame + *beysta* = to beat; to attack with words.

> **TOMBSTONE EPITAPH:**
> Our lives were spared of this lambasting lug
> When he tried to lambaste a Mafia thug

Quiz 43

Match the definitions with the words on the left.

Brainy Barbs

__ 1. jaundiced   a. barren, dull
__ 2. jeer   b. demands blind devotion
__ 3. jejune   c. is always falling behind
__ 4. jingoistic   d. too eager to go to war
__ 5. juggernaut   e. prejudiced
__ 6. jugulate   f. showing a lack of interest
__ 7. lachrymose   g. tearful
__ 8. lackadaisical   h. to beat or scold severely
__ 9. laggard   i. to cut a throat
__10. lambaste   j. to make fun in a rude way

Basic Barbs

__11. lackey   k. a pessimistic person
__12. slouch   l. a servant;
                         a servile brown-noser
__13. lollygag   m. slang for an inept, awkward,
                         lazy person
__14. lug   n. slang for a large numskull
__15. crepehanger   o. waste time

Down In The Goondocks

(moron, gormless, gullible, ignoramus,)
(credulous, fatuous, addlebrained, simper, inane, imbecile)

Match.

1. m _ _ _ _ = one with an I.Q. of 50 to 70
2. i _ _ _ _ _ _ _ _ = an idiot
3. g _ _ _ _ _ _ _ = slow-witted
4. g _ _ _ _ _ _ _ = believe too easily
5. f _ _ _ _ _ _ = happy to be stupid
6. c _ _ _ _ _ _ _ _ = believing too easily
7. i _ _ _ _ = empty; foolish
8. i _ _ _ _ _ _ _ = an idiot
9. a _ _ _ _ _ _ _ _ _ _ _ = confused, illogical
10. s _ _ _ _ _ = smile in a silly, stupid way

Most of you will spend about one third of your life sleeping. Others will have trouble with insomnia. And then there are those sluggards who never really wake up. In any case, your sleep time need not be a waste. Without a lot of fanfare, try looking over a chapter right before you hit the sack. Then as you wake, briefly give it another glance. Try the test after breakfast. Some people believe that when you study in this way the material ends up bouncing around in your head while you're sleeping. It seems to work for me. It is just one more way to make the effort of studying effortless.

Basic Barbs

> **freeloader** = one who habitually imposes on others for food, lodging etc.
> **harlot** = a whore
> **lounger** = a lazy person
> **scumbag** = a worthless person who deserves your hate
> **sluggard** = a habitually lazy person
> **swine** = a hog, boar; slang for a disgusting person

Brainy Barbs

1. **languid couch potato** (lang´ gwĭd) To be languid is to be weak, with no interest and little animation. Don't confuse this with langourous which has the connotation of listlessness from laziness or bad weather or daydreaming. From Latin, *languidus* = faint.

> *They laboriously do nothing.*
> *—Seneca*

2. **lapidating witch-hunters** (lăp´ ĭ dāt ing) These dolts like to stone people to death. From Latin, *lapidarius* = of stone.

> *It is often pleasant to stone a martyr,*
> *no matter how much we admire him.*
> *—John Barth*

3. **larcenous swine** (lär´ sə nəs) This one is prone to steal. From Latin, *latrocinari < latro* = mercenary soldier.

> *Thieves for their robbery have authority when judges steal themselves.*
> *—Shakespeare,*
> *Measure for Measure*

4. **lascivious harlot** (lə sĭv´ ē əs)   Lascivious is lustful, with a tasteless interest in sex. From Latin, *lascivas* = wanton, sportive.

> *My sister claimed sexual harassment on the job,*
> *which was a little surprising, since she's a hooker.*
> —George Miller

5. **lassitudinal lounger** (lăs´ ĭ tūd´ ĭ nəl)   This one is weary to the bone, weary from strain and effort. It also has the connotation of lazy indifference. From Latin, *lassus* = faint, weary.

> *Some people have a perfect genius*
> *for doing nothing, and doing it assiduously.*
> —Haliburton

6. **lecherous old goat** (lĕch´ ər əs)   This goat is excessively, offensively lustful. From Old French, *lechier* = to live a debauched life; literally, to lick.

> *At age 82, I sometimes feel like a twenty-year-old,*
> *but there is seldom one around.*
> —Milton Berle

7. **freeloading leech** (lēch)   A leech is a worm that sucks your blood. As slang, a leech is a mooch, sponger, or freeloader. From Old English, *lucan* = to pull out.

> *Beggars should be abolished.*
> *It annoys one to give to them,*
> *and it annoys one not to give to them.*
> —Friedrich Wilhelm Nietzsche

8. **lethargic sluggard** (lə thär´ jĭk)   This one is slow, tired and dull from illness or overeating. From Greek, *lethe* = forgetfulness + *argos* = idle.

TOMBSTONE EPITAPH:
Back in five minutes.

9. **lewd scumbag** (lūd)   Anyone lewd is inordinately lustful, indecent. From Medieval English, *lewede* = vile < ignorant.

> *Flies spread disease—keep yours zipped.*
> —Unknown

10. **libertine primitive** (lĭb´ ər tēn´)   A libertine has no moral or sexual restraint. From Latin, *libertinus* = of a freedman.

TOMBSTONE EPITAPH:
He lusted for sin
But disease did him in

Quiz 44

Match the definitions with the words on the left.

Brainy Barbs

__ 1. languid
__ 2. lapidate
__ 3. larcenous
__ 4. lascivious
__ 5. lassitudinal
__ 6. lecherous
__ 7. leech
__ 8. lethargic
__ 9. lewd
__10. libertine

a. a parasite
b. overly lustful (fits 3 words)
c. one with no moral restraint
d. slow, tired and dull
e. thieving, given to stealing
f. to stone people to death
g. weary from strain and effort
h. lazy or dull from illness

Basic Barbs

__11. swine
__12. harlot
__13. lounger
__14. freeload
__15. sluggard
__16. scumbag
__17. languorous

i. hogs
j. limpness from bad weather
k. a lazy person (fits two words)
l. a whore
m. a worthless person
n. habitually impose on others

Stupid Is As Stupid Does

(nincompoop, asinine, naive, Neanderthal, nescient, obtuse,)
(opaque, stunted, troglodyte, unwitting)

Match.

1. n _ _ _ _ _ _ _ _ _ = an idiot, fool
2. u _ _ _ _ _ _ _ _ = not aware
3. t _ _ _ _ _ _ _ _ _ = a caveman
4. N _ _ _ _ _ _ _ _ _ _ = a prehistoric subspecies of man
5. s _ _ _ _ _ _ = hindered in growth or development
6. o _ _ _ _ _ = impervious to light; unintelligent
7. a _ _ _ _ _ _ = like an ass, silly, stupid
8. o _ _ _ _ _ = blunt; intellectually slow
9. n _ _ _ _ _ _ _ = ignorant
10. n _ _ _ _ = foolishly simple; childlike

Grisly List 45

In the last chapter I suggested you study right before you sleep. What about studying when you can't sleep? You're lying there, tossing and turning, looking at the clock as it ticks on and on, dreading the next day. Here's what you do: climb out of bed and into a warm bath, peruse these pages playfully, and drink some hot milk or tea. When you go back to bed you'll sleep like a baby. Furthermore, you'll feel like your time has been well spent. By the way, don't drop the book in the bath.

Basic Barbs

➤ **bureaucrat** = an official who's petty and follows a routine in a pedantic way
➤ **egghead** = one who studies too much, i.e. his large brain makes his head look like an egg
➤ **gabbler** = one who rapidly talks without making much sense
➤ **lecher** = a lustful old man
➤ **Peeping Tom** = one who, for sexual kicks, secretly spies on others disrobing, a voyeur
➤ **shyster** = an unethical lawyer
➤ **slugabed** = one who stays in bed because of laziness
➤ **floozy** = a girl with loose morals

Brainy Barbs

1. **libidinous floozy** (lĭ bĭd´ ə nəs)   This floozy's hot to trot, lustful, lewd etc. The word is based on libido, one's sexual desire. From Latin, *libet* = it pleases.

> *In breeding cattle you need one bull for every twenty-five cows, unless the cows are known sluts.*
> —Johnny Carson

2. **licentious lecher** (lī sĕn´ shəs)   To be licentious is to be sexually and/or morally unrestrained. From Latin, *licere* = to be allowed.

> *You're only as old as the woman you feel.*
> —Groucho Marx

3. **Lilliputian bureaucrat** (lĭl´ ĭ pyū´ shən)   In Jonathan Swift's "Gulliver's Travels", the inhabitants of Lilliput were pint-sized people whose small-minded attitudes matched their height. Use this aspersion when confronting dolts who bicker over petty details.

> *Small and creeping things are the products of petty souls.*
> —Thomas Browne

4. **limacine slimeball** (līm´ ə sīn)   Anyone limacine resembles a slug. From Latin, *limax* = a slug.

> I got some new underwear the other day.
> Well, new to me.
> —Emo Philips

5. **listless slugabed** (lĭst´ lĭs)   This one shows a lack of interest and spirit. From Old English, *lust* = desire, pleasure + *les* = without.

> To try may be to die, but not to care is never to be born.
> —William Redfield

6. **litigious shyster** (lĭ tĭj´ əs)   The plague of modern man: ready to sue at the drop of a hat, this shyster licks his chops at every accident. From Latin, *litigium* = strife < *litigare* = to discuss; hence, to argue.

> For certain people, after fifty,
> litigation takes the place of sex.
> —Gore Vidal

7. **loquacious gabbler** (lō kwā´ shəs)   This one likes to talk, perhaps too much. From Latin, *loqui* = to speak.

> Where there is a surfeit of words,
> there is a famine of intelligence.
> —Indian proverb

8. **loose lothario** (lō thâr´ ē ō´)   A lothario is a seducer of women. Lothario was a character in Nicholas Rave's play, The Fair Penitent.

> A lewd bachelor makes a jealous husband.
> —English proverb

9. **lubricious Peeping Tom** (lū brĭsh´ əs)   Lubricious can mean slippery or shifty or lewd. From Latin, *lubricus* = slippery.

> Women should be obscene and not heard.
> —Groucho Marx

10. **lucubrating egghead** (lū´ kyū brā´ ting)   Some of us who burned the midnight oil to get through college can identify with this definition: working, studying, writing with difficulty late at night. From Latin, *lucubrare* = to work by artificial light.

> Much learning doth make thee mad.
> —Acts 26:24

Quiz 45

Match the definitions with the words on the left.

Brainy Barbs

___ 1. libidinous
___ 2. licentious
___ 3. Lilliputian
___ 4. limacine
___ 5. listless
___ 6. litigious
___ 7. loquacious
___ 8. lothario
___ 9. lubricious
___10. lucubrate

a. a seducer of women
b. lacking interest and spirit
c. like a slug
d. lustful, lewd (fits two words)
e. ready to sue
f. slippery or shifty or lewd
g. small-minded, petty
h. study late at night
i. talking too much

Basic Barbs

___11. floozy
___12. lecher
___13. bureaucrat
___14. slugabed
___15. shyster
___16. gabble
___17. Peeping Tom

j. a foolish or thoughtless girl
k. spies on others disrobing
l. this one lazily stays in bed
m. a pedantic, petty official
n. talk without making sense
o. an unethical lawyer
p. a lustful old man

An Idiot By Any Other Name Would Be As Dumb

(insensate, cretin, stultified, vacuous, infatuated, vapid,)
(myopic, insipient, distrait, impolitic, sciolistic)

Match.

1. v _ _ _ _ _ _ = empty; lacking intelligence
2. s _ _ _ _ _ _ _ _ = made foolish
3. v _ _ _ _ = having lost sparkle; flat, insipid
4. i _ _ _ _ _ _ _ _ _ = stupidly in love
5. c _ _ _ _ _ = an idiot, mentally stunted
6. i _ _ _ _ _ _ _ _ = unfeeling, stupid
7. d _ _ _ _ _ _ _ = absent-minded
8. i _ _ _ _ _ _ _ _ _ = unwise
9. i _ _ _ _ _ _ _ _ = stupid
10. m _ _ _ _ _ = near-sighted
11. s _ _ _ _ _ _ _ _ _ = superficially knowledgeable

LE MOT QUOTE 26

Match each quote with the appropriate word.

1. When the rich wage war, it is the poor who die.
   —Jean-Paul Sartre

2. Men often make up in wrath
   what they want in reason. —Alger

3. Most men are within a finger's breadth of being mad.
   —Diogenes

4. He who sets one foot in the bawdy-house,
   claps t'other in a hospital. —Thomas Fuller

__ a. libertine

__ b. irrational

__ c. irate

__ d. internecine

LE MOT QUOTE 27

Match each quote with the appropriate word.

1. I started out on burgundy
   but soon hit the harder stuff. —Bob Dylan

2. Love grows, lust wastes. —Penn

3. Patriotism is a pernicious,
   psychopathic form of idiocy. —George Bernard Shaw

4. The fire you kindle for your enemy often burns yourself
   more than him. —Chinese proverb

5. The first external revelations of the dry rot in men
   is a tendency to lurk and lounge. —Dickens

__ a. irascible

__ b. jingo

__ c. lascivious

__ d. lassitude

__ e. intemperate

LE MOT QUOTE 28

Match each quote with the appropriate word.

1. Give a man a free hand and he'll run it all over you.
   —Mae West

2. God hath given you one face and you make
   yourselves another. —Shakespeare, <u>Hamlet</u>

3. Our wrangling lawyers are so litigious and busy here
   on earth, that I think they will plead their clients'
   causes hereafter, some of them in hell. —Burton

4. Some men study so much,
   they don't have time to know. —Talmud

5. The followers of a great man often put their eyes out,
   so that they may be the better able to sing his praise.
   —Nietzsche

__ a. lucubrate

__ b. juggernaut

__ c. libidinous

__ d. litigious

__ e. Janus-faced

Chapter 10

Words have users, but as well, users have words.
And it is the users that establish the world's realities.
—Le Roi Jones

Grisly List 46

In the last chapter I suggested you study in the bathtub when you're having trouble with insomnia. But there's another great time to study in the bathtub—on hot days! Imagine this: it's scorching, blistering hot; the damp air weighs on you like a wet wool blanket; you are uncomfortable beyond belief. Go to the bathtub; turn on the cold water; dump some ice into it; pour yourself an ice tea; climb in with your book. Now read.

Basic Barbs

➢ **buffoon** = a fool, a clown
➢ **henchman** = a underling of a crime boss; a criminal
➢ **klutz** = any clumsy stupid person, from German, *klotz*, literally, block of wood
➢ **lounge lizard** = a male who hunts for women at nightclubs
➢ **magpie** = one who talks too much
➢ **schemer** = one who plots schemes
➢ **warlord** = an aggressive tyrant

Brainy Barbs

1. **ludicrous buffoon** (lū´ də krəs) Anything ludicrous is laughable because it's so obviously absurd. From Latin, *ludus* = a play, game.

> *It is only one step from the sublime to the ridiculous.*
> —Napoleon

2. **lugubrious sadsack** (lŏŏ gōō´ brē əs) Anyone lugubrious is sad or so unbelievably sad that it's laughable and ludicrous. From Latin, *lugere* = to mourn.

> *My mother didn't breast-feed me. She said she liked me as a friend.*
> —Rodney Dangerfield

3. **lupine lounge lizard** (lū pīn) Lupine means wolf-like. From Latin, *lupus* = wolf.

> *A gentleman is a patient wolf.*
> —Henrietta Tiarks

4. machiavellian schemer (măk´ ē ə věl´ ē ən)   In Machiavelli's "The Prince" political necessity is placed above morality and deceit as the means used to maintain power by the ruler; hence, anyone machiavellian is characterized by unscrupulous cunning, full of plots and intrigue.

The greatest cunning is to have none at all.
—Carl Sandburg

5. magniloquent magpie (măg nĭl´ ə kwənt)   This pompous, boastful one talks big, but it's only so much hot air. From Latin, *magniloquus* = speaking in a lofty style.

He that speaks lavishly shall hear as knavishly.
—English proverb

6. maladroit klutz (măl´ ə droit´)   This one is clumsy. From French, *mal* = bad + *droit* = right.

Men lose more conquests by their own awkwardness
than by any virtue in the woman.
—Ninon De Enclos

7. evil malefactor (măl´ ə făk´ tər)   This villain is a doer of evil, of crime. From Latin, *malefacere* = to do wrong.

He who greatly excels in beauty, strength, birth, or wealth,
and he, on the other hand, who is very weak, or very disgraced,
find it difficult to follow rational principles.
The one sort grows into violent and great criminals,
the other into rogues and petty rascals.
—Aristotle

8. maleficent terror (mə lĕf´ ĭ sənt)   Likely to cast an evil spell, this terror is harmful and evil. From Latin, *male* = evil + *facere* = to do.

Political power grows out of the barrel of a gun.
—Mao Tse-tung

9. malevolent henchman (mə lĕv´ ə lənt)   To be malevolent is to be malicious, to wish evil on others. From Latin, *male* = ill + *volens* = wishing.

The tyranny of the multitude is a multiplied tyranny.
—Edmund Burke

10. malicious warlord (mə lĭsh əs)   Anyone malicious has an active desire to do harm to others, or to see them suffer. From Latin, *malus* = bad.

A tyrant's breath is another's death.
—English proverb

Quiz 46

Match the definitions with the words on the left.

Brainy Barbs

___ 1. ludicrous
___ 2. lugubrious
___ 3. lupine
___ 4. machiavellian
___ 5. magniloquent

___ 6. maladroit

___ 7. malefactor

___ 8. maleficent
___ 9. malevolent
___10. malicious

a. a doer of evil
b. clumsy
c. laughable, obviously absurd
d. pompous, boastful
e. so unbelievably sad it's
   laughable and ludicrous
f. unscrupulously cunning,
   filled with plots and intrigue
g. with evil intent
   (fits three words)
h. wolf-like

Basic Barbs

___11. warlord
___12. henchman
___13. klutz
___14. magpie
___15. schemer

i. a clumsy stupid person
j. an aggressive tyrant
k. one who plots schemes
l. one who talks too much
m. a criminal

Of All the Idiots I've Loved Before

(acephales, dummkopf, grobian, solecistic, gawk,)
(dunce, numskull, witling, hebetate, insensate)

Unscramble.

1. kawg = stare like an idiot   _____
2. cepahasel = without a head; without a leader   _____
3. lesocitsic = characterized by making errors
   in grammar   _____
4. fmmkodup = idiot in German   _____
5. robigan = the patron saint of idiots   _____
6. beheatte = become stupid   _____
7. cedun = an idiot   _____
8. sunkumll = an idiot   _____
9. tiwling = one who has little wit or intelligence   _____

There's a circle of theorists who believe that if you study while listening to classical music you retain more information. The concept is that the music allows the information to stimulate both sides of the brain. I can't vouch for this, but it seems like a fairly fun and harmless idea. I guess if you followed that logic then studying while listening to rock n roll would stimulate the more primitive parts of the brain. But give it a shot. Put on Hayden or Bach. Sit by a fire and read the book. Give it some time. If you find your testing improves, it worked.

Basic Barbs

> ➤ **flagellant** = one who whips himself to mortify the flesh, usually out of excessive religious devotion
> ➤ **loafer** = one who dawdles about wasting time
> ➤ **minions** = followers, used derisively
> ➤ **moron** = one with an I.Q. of 50 to 70, an idiot
> ➤ **mutant** = one who deviates from parents

Brainy Barbs

1. **malignant mutant** (mə lĭg´ nənt) Like cancer, this mutant has an evil or harmful influence. From Latin, *malignare* = to act maliciously.

> *The entire economy of the Western world*
> *is built on things that cause cancer.*
> —line from the movie <u>Bliss</u>

2. **maligning opponent** (mə līn´ ing) To malign is to slander, to say something destructive. From Latin, *malignus* = wicked, malicious.

> *Even doubtful accusations leave a stain behind them.*
> —Thomas Fuller

3. **malingering loafer** (mə ling´ ər ing) This loafer will fake being ill to get out of work. From French, *malingre* = sickly, infirm.

> *It is better to have loafed and lost than never to have loafed at all.*
> —James Thurber

4. **malleable minions** (măl´ ē ə bəl) To be malleable is to be easily shaped or molded. From Latin, *malleare* = to beat with a hammer.

> *As long as men worship the Caesars and Napoleons,*
> *the Caesars and Napoleons will duly rise and make them miserable.*
> —Aldous Huxley

5. malodorous stinkpot (măl ō´ dər əs)   This one stinks, reeks, smells offensively bad. From Latin, *malus* = bad + *odor* = a smell.

Every stink that fights the ventilator thinks its Don Quixote.
—Stanislaw J. Lec

6. martial barbarian (mär´ shəl)   Anyone martial is eager to fight. From Latin, *Martialis* = of Mars (the god of War).

When you're wounded and left on Afghanistan's plains
And the women come out to cut up what remains
Just roll to your rifle and blow out your brains
An' go to your Gawd like a soldier.
—Kipling

7. over-bearing martinet (mär´ tĭ nĕt´)   Who put this bossy nerd in charge? He thinks he needs to be everybody's disciplinarian. The word comes from General Jean Martinet, a 17th century drillmaster.

Each man is a tyrant in tendency,
because he would impose his idea on others.
—Emerson

8. masochistic flagellant (flăj´ ə lənt)   A flagellant is one who whips himself to mortify the flesh, usually out of excessive religious devotion. From Latin, *flagellans* = whipping.

Masochist: Someone who is only happy when miserable.
—Anonymous

9. maudlin weeper (môd´ lĭn)   Anyone maudlin is idiotically sentimental, usually from too much liquor. From Old French, Madeleine is the French spelling of Magdalene, of the Bible, who was often represented with red eyes from weeping.

Women's weapons, water-drops.
—Shakespeare

10. maundering moron (môn´ dər ing)   To maunder is to move or act in a dreamy, vague way or to speak meaninglessly or incoherently, to ramble carelessly. From Latin, *mendicare* = to beg.

He that knows little often repeats it.
—Thomas Fuller

Quiz 47

Match the definitions with the words on the left.

Brainy Barbs

__ 1. malignant
__ 2. malign
__ 3. malinger
__ 4. malleable
__ 5. malodorous
__ 6. martial
__ 7. martinet
__ 8. masochistic
__ 9. maudlin
__10. maundering

a. one who is bossy
b. derives pleasure from pain
c. eager to fight
d. fake being ill to avoid work
e. foolishly sentimental
f. slander
g. stinks
h. to be easily shaped or molded
i. to move in a dreamy way or to speak meaninglessly
j. with an evil influence

Basic Barbs

__11. flagellant
__12. moron
__13. loafer
__14. minion
__15. mutant

k. one who wastes time
l. follower, used derisively
m. whips himself
n. deviates from parents
o. one with an I.Q. of 50 to 70

Lust In The Dust, Part 1

(amoral, lascivious, lewd, libertine, libidinous, brazen, meretricious,)
(salacious, vulgarian, Sybaritic, unsavory, precocious, slatternly)

Unscramble.

1. lasaciosu = lustful _____
2. bilidinosu = lustful _____
3. weld = lustful; indecent _____
4. morala = not caring about right or wrong _____
5. salucivio = lustful _____
6. bileretin = acts without moral restraints _____
7. yuvnsaor = offensive, immoral _____
8. Sycitbari = loves luxury and self-indulgence _____
9. vulanigar = given to coarse tastes _____
10. coprecious = shows premature behavior _____
11. nezarb = showing no shame _____
12. ylnrettals = untidy, sluttish _____
13. suoicirterem = falsely attractive _____

If you really want to know a subject—teach it. When you take the time to teach a subject to someone else you are more likely to have a sense of mastery over the subject. In part, when you see the difficulty others have in grasping or retaining the material you end up searching for other ways to express it. This cements it into that gray goop between your ears. Am I saying go teach a vocabulary class? No. But if you keep dropping these words into your banter people will ask you what they mean. The more you do this, the more you'll teach yourself.

Basic Barbs

> **crue** = an archaic spelling of crew
> **delude** = mislead or deceive
> **minx** = an impudent, flirtatious, or promiscuous girl
> **mongrel** = a crossbreed dog or a contemptible person
> **motley** = composed of clashing colors
> **motley crue** = a band of misfits
> **tart** = a small pie; a loose woman

Brainy Barbs

1. **mawkish softy** (mô´ kĭsh)   One who is mawkish shows sentiment, tenderness or understanding in false, feeble or repulsive ways.   From Medieval English, *mawke* = maggot. Originally, mawkish meant repulsive but over time came to mean revoltingly sentimental.

The sentimental people fiddle harmonics on the string of sensualism.
—George Meredith

2. **deluded megalomaniac** (mĕg´ ə lō mā´ nē ăk´)   A megalomaniac is one deluded with grandeur and power. From Greek, *megalo* = large + *mania* = madness.

Likely comment:
I am the reincarnation of Napoleon, Julius Caesar and Cleopatra.

Your response:
Well, then you get the check.

3. **melancholy baby** (mĕl´ ən kŏl´ ē)   From Greek, *melancholia* = black bile. In Medieval times it was believed black bile (one of the four humors of the body) caused gloominess and depression; hence, one melancholy (or melancholic) is depressed.

Melancholy is the pleasure of being sad.
—Victor Hugo

4. mendacious mongrel (mĕn dā´ shəs)   Anyone mendacious lies and has told lies in the past. From Late Latin, *mendaci* = given to lying.

> *Satisfy a dog with a bone and a woman with a lie.*
> —*Basque proverb*

5. homeless mendicant (mĕn´ də kənt)   A mendicant is a beggar (sometimes of a religious order) who depends on charity.   From Latin, *mendicus* = having physical defects; hence, poor, a beggar.

> *It's not hard to tell we were poor*
> *when you saw the toilet paper dryin' on the clothesline.*
> —*George "Goober" Lindsey*

6. mephitic motley crue (mə fĭt´ ĭk)   Mephitis is a bad or poisonous odor coming out of the ground from decomposing matter.   So think of a mephitic motley crue as living in the sewer. They stink.

> *A corpse and an uninvited guest stink after a couple of days.*
> —*Mexican proverb*

7. bloodthirsty mercenary (mûr´ sə nĕr´ ē)   A mercenary is influenced by a desire for gain. It can be used as an adjective as in, "His interest in church is completely mercenary." or as a noun, especially when referring to one who has been hired to fight for money, as in, "The mercenaries sacked the defenseless town." From Latin, *merces* = pay, wages.

> *I would wish you good luck, but for all I know you're trying to kill me.*
> —*Jackie Mason*

8. mercurial minx (mər kyŏŏr´ ē əl)   This one is apt to change moods with little cause. From Latin, *mercurialis* = of the God or planet Mercury.

> *I am a feather for each wind that blows.*
> —*Shakespeare*

9. meretricious tart (mer´ ĭ trĭsh´ əs)   This one is seemingly attractive in a shallow or vulgar way but without truly having any real beauty.   From Latin, *meretrix* = a prostitute.

> *Many a man has fallen in love with a girl in a light so dim*
> *he would not have chosen a suit by it.*
> —*Maurice Chevalier*

10. fancy schmancy meritocracy (mer´ ĭ tŏk´ rə sē)   A meritocracy is a system where the intellectual elite attain a special status over others. From Latin, *merere* = to deserve, earn + ocracy.

> *The classes that wash the most are those that work the least.*
> —*G. K. Chesterton*

Match the definitions with the words on the left.

Brainy Barbs

___ 1. mawkish
___ 2. megalomaniac
___ 3. melancholy
___ 4. mendacious
___ 5. mendicant
___ 6. mephitic
___ 7. mercenary
___ 8. mercurial
___ 9. meretricious
___10. meritocracy

a. beggar dependent on charity
b. apt to change moods
c. depressed
d. falsely attractive
e. given to lying
f. influenced by a desire for gain
g. one deluded with power
h. showing feeling in false ways
i. where the educated elite rule
j. with a bad or poisonous odor

Basic Barbs

___11. tart
___12. minx
___13. motley
___14. mongrel
___15. deluded
___16. crue

k. a crossbreed dog
l. a small pie
m. an archaic spelling of crew
n. an impudent girl
o. composed of clashing colors
p. mislead or deceived

Lust In The Dust, Part 2

(bawdy, deviate, unseemly, carnal, perverse, prurient, vitiated,)
(concupiscent, wanton, pander, naughty, lubricious, licentious)

Match.

1. p _ _ _ _ _ _ _ = lustful
2. p _ _ _ _ _ _ _ = deviating from what is considered right or good
3. v _ _ _ _ _ _ _ _ = spoiled; weakened morally
4. w _ _ _ _ _ = sexually loose
5. p _ _ _ _ _ = cater to vile desires
6. n _ _ _ _ _ _ = indecent, mischievous
7. l _ _ _ _ _ _ _ _ _ = slippery; shifty; lewd
8. l _ _ _ _ _ _ _ _ _ _ = lustful, without morals
9. b _ _ _ _ = humorously coarse; lewd
10. d _ _ _ _ _ _ = turn away from what is normal, especially sexually
11. u _ _ _ _ _ _ _ _ = not decent
12. c _ _ _ _ _ = fleshly; sexual
13. c _ _ _ _ _ _ _ _ _ _ _ = with abnormal sexual desire

Grisly List 49

One of the best ways to grasp a subject is to take time to review what you have learned. Don't forget to go back over the quizzes and draw lines from the definitions to the words. You're probably saying, "But that's too easy." That's okay. Learning doesn't have to be difficult. By doing this you are reviewing the information.

Basic Barbs

➤ **Bluebeard** = murderer of women
➤ **crank** = a quarrelsome person
➤ **grunt** = a Vietnam infantryman
➤ **interloper** = a meddlesome person
➤ **leery** = wary, suspicious
➤ **mogul** = a powerful person in an autocratic position
➤ **underhanded** = sly, deceitful

Brainy Barbs

1. **militant grunt** (mĭl´ ĭ tənt) We need someone willing to fight, to lay down his life so that we can kick back to blow bubbles in the park. And we need this grunt stationed far, far away. From Latin, *miles* = soldier.

   Governments need to have both shepherds and butchers.
   —Voltaire

2. **militating interloper** (mĭl´ ĭ tāt´ ing) To militate is to work against something. From Latin, *militat* = to serve as a soldier.

   An open foe may prove a curse
   but a pretended friend is worse.
   —John Gay

3. **minacious vulture** (mĭ nā´ shəs) This vulture is threatening, hostile. From Latin, *minari* = to threaten < *minae* = projecting points of walls.

   It only takes my little fingers to blow you away.
   —Elvis Costello

4. **minatory mogul** (mĭn´ ə tôr ē) Anyone minatory is threatening or menacing. From Latin, *minari* = to threaten.

   You can get more with a kind word and a gun
   than you can with a kind word alone.
   —Al Capone

5. misanthropic crank (mĭs´ ən thrōp)   A misanthrope hates mankind; hence, anyone misanthropic despises mankind. Don't confuse this with misandrist, one who hates men. From Greek, *misein* = to hate + *anthropos* = a man.

> Hell is other people.
> —Jean Paul Sartre

6. rotten miscreant (mĭs´ krē ənt)   A miscreant is one who believes a religious faith which is regarded as false or one who is evil and criminal. From Medieval French, *miscreant* = unbelieving.

> All spirits are enslaved that serve things evil.
> —Percy Bysshe Shelley

7. underhanded misfeasor (mĭs fē´ zər)   A misfeasor does a lawful act in an unlawful way that ends up hurting others. From Medieval English, *mis* = ill, wrong + Latin, *facere* = to do.

> I have never seen a situation so dismal
> that a policeman couldn't make it worse.
> —Brendan Behan

8. misogynous Bluebeard (mĭ sŏ´ jĕ nĭst)   This one hates women. This is the adjective form of misogyny. You can also call someone a misogynist. From Greek, *misos* = hatred + *gyno* = female.

> If you catch a man, throw him back.
> —Women's Lib slogan

9. leery misologist (mĭ sŏl´ ə jĭst)   Don't try to reason with a misologist. This one hates or distrusts reason or enlightenment. The noun is misology. From Greek, *miso* = to hate + *logos* = a word, thought.

> He who refuses to learn deserves extinction.
> —Hillel

10. bullheaded misoneist (mĭs´ ō nē ĭst)   A misoneist hates innovation, change or anything new. From Greek, *miso* = to hate + *neos* = new.

> He has a first-rate mind until he makes it up.
> —Violet Bonham-Carter

Quiz 49

Match the definitions with the words on the left.

Brainy Barbs

___ 1. militant
___ 2. militate
___ 3. minacious
___ 4. minatory
___ 5. misanthropic
___ 6. miscreant
___ 7. misfeasor
___ 8. misogynous
___ 9. misologist
___10. misoneist

a. does a lawful act in an illegal way which hurts others
b. hateful of women
c. hating mankind
d. one that hates innovation
e. one that distrusts reason
f. one who is evil and criminal
g. threatening (fits two words)
h. to work against something
i. willing to fight

Basic Barbs

___11. leery
___12. Bluebeard
___13. mogul
___14. interloper
___15. grunt
___16. underhanded

j. a meddlesome person
k. a powerful person in an autocratic position
l. a Vietnam infantryman
m. murderer of women
n. wary, suspicious
o. sly, deceitful

Lust In The Dust, Part 3

(jaded, profligate, raffish, scatological, ruttish,)
(venerious, voyeur, rakish, hedonist, Epicurean)

Match.

1. r _ _ _ _ _ _ = rakish, vulgar
2. r _ k _ _ _ = lacking moral restraint, raffish
3. v _ _ _ _ _ _ _ _ = hunting, sexual desire
4. s _ _ _ _ _ _ _ _ _ _ _ = fixated with excrement or obscenity
5. v _ _ _ _ _ = one who derives sexual pleasure from peeping at others disrobed
6. r _ _ _ _ _ _ = in sexual heat
7. h _ _ _ _ _ _ _ = one devoted to pleasure as the chief aim in life
8. e _ _ _ _ _ _ _ _ = seeker of sensuous pleasure
9. p _ _ _ _ _ _ _ _ _ = an immoral person
10. j _ _ _ _ = worn out from over use

I knew someone that wanted to go to Japan and be fluent in the language before he left. What he did is spend the next year—morning, noon and night—studying and practicing Japanese. By the time he left he could speak Japanese with ease. Prior to this chapter, I've suggested that you not spend more than fifteen minutes in any given study period as you go through this book. But there is another approach that, depending on your goals, you may want to try—the immersion method. Immerse yourself in this subject, morning, noon and night. The positive feedback that you'll get is your progress will be so obvious to you and others that the effort will have felt worthwhile.

Basic Barbs

➤ **double-dealing** = deceiving, treacherous
➤ **drag** = one who is a pain to be around
➤ **has-been** = one who is no longer famous
➤ **scapegoat** = one who takes the blame for others
➤ **stick-in-the-mud** = one refusing to budge
➤ **wisecracker** = a smart aleck

Brainy Barbs

1. **mad monomaniac** (mŏn´ ə mā´ nē ăk) Monomania is a partial insanity over one idea; hence, a monomaniac is obsessed with one thing and one thing only, forever fixated on that illusive thing, person, or idea. From Greek, *monos* = alone, combined with *mania* = madness.

Adhesion to one idea is slavery.
—*Bovee*

2. **monotonous lowbrow** (mə nŏt´ ə nəs) Anyone monotonous is tiresome because his/her voice doesn't vary and drones on interminably. From Greek, *mono* = one + *tonos* = strain, tone, mode.

He is not only dull himself, he is the cause of dullness in others.
—*Samuel Johnson*

3. **mordacious joker** (môr dā´ shəs) This joker has a keen or biting w i t, or maybe he just likes to bite. From Latin, *mordacitas* = given to biting.

True wit is nature to advantage dressed,
What oft was thought but ne'er so well expressed.
—*Alexander Pope*

4. mordant wisecracker (môr´ dənt)   Anything mordant is either biting and sarcastic or corrosive. From Latin, *mordere* = to bite.

Sharp wits, like sharp knives, do often cut their owner's fingers.
—*Arrowsmith*

5. moribund has-been (môr´ ə bŭnd´)   Going once, twice, gone! This person is dying, checking out, kicking the bucket, pushing up daisies, fading fast, petering out, biting the dust. From Latin, *moribundus* = dying.

Either this man is dead or my watch has stopped.
—*Groucho Marx*

6. morose drag (mə rōs´)   This drag is so sullen and gloomy. From Latin, *morosus* = peevish, fretful.

The only cure for grief is action. —*G. H. Lewes*

7. mortiferous butcher (môr tĭf´ ər əs)   Beware! This one is deadly. From Latin, *mortiferus* = death-bearing.

We kill everybody, my dear.
Some with bullets, some with words
and everybody with our deeds.
We drive people into their graves
and neither see it nor feel it.
—*Maxim Gorky*

8. mortified scapegoat (môr´ tə fīd´)   To mortify is to punish oneself by self-denial or to humiliate. Anyone mortified has been humiliated. From Latin, *mortificare* = to kill, destroy.

My one regret in life is that I'm not someone else.
—*Woody Allen*

9. double-dealing mountebank (moun´ tə bangk´)   This one is a charlatan, a fake. From Italian, *montimbanco* = one who climbs on a bench.

Quacks pretend to cure other men's disorders,
but fail to find a cure for their own.
—*Cicero*

10. mulish stick-in-the-mud (myū´ lĭsh)   Anyone mulish is like a mule; hence, stubborn. Mule comes from Latin, *mulus*.

There are two kinds of fools:
those who can't change their opinions
and those who won't.
—*Josh Billings*

Quiz 50

Match the definitions with the words on the left.

Brainy Barbs

___ 1. monomaniac   a. charlatan, a fake
___ 2. monotonous   b. deadly
___ 3. mordacious   c. dying
___ 4. mordant   d. humiliated
___ 5. moribund   e. obsesses with one thing
___ 6. morose   f. stubborn
___ 7. mortiferous   g. sullen and gloomy
___ 8. mortified   h. voice doesn't vary
___ 9. mountebank   i. with biting wit
                                (fits two words)
___10. mulish

Basic Barbs

___11. has-been   j. takes the blame for others
___12. wisecracker   k. deceiving, treacherous
___13. stick-in-the-mud   l. one refusing to budge
___14. double-dealing   m. one who is a pain to be around
___15. scapegoat   n. a smart aleck
___16. drag   o. one who is no longer famous

Woke Up On The Wrong Side Of The Bed, Part 1

(choleric, crabbed, crotchety, crusty, curmudgeon, disgruntled,)
(indignant, inimical, irascible, irate, splenetic, testy)

Match.

1. i _ _ _ _ _ _ _ = like an enemy, hostile
2. i _ _ _ _ _ _ _ _ = easily angered
3. i _ _ _ _ = angry
4. i _ _ _ _ _ _ _ _ = expressing anger or scorn
5. s _ _ _ _ _ _ _ _ = bad-tempered, of the spleen
6. t _ _ _ _ = irritable
7. c _ _ _ _ _ _ _ = bad-tempered
8. c _ _ _ _ _ = bad-tempered
9. c _ _ _ _ _ _ = bad tempered
10. c _ _ _ _ _ _ _ _ = full of stubborn notions, twisted, eccentric
11. d _ _ _ _ _ _ _ _ _ _ = peevishly unhappy
12. c _ _ _ _ _ _ _ _ _ = a surly, bad-tempered person

LE MOT QUOTE 29

Match each quote with the appropriate word.

1. Every murderer is probably somebody's old friend.
   —Agatha Christie

2. The artistic temperament is a disease
   that afflicts amateurs. —G. K. Chesterton

3. A man's worst enemy can't wish him
   what he thinks up for himself. —Yiddish proverb

4. Men's vows are women's traitors. —Shakespeare

5. A man may build himself a throne of bayonets
   but he can't sit on it. —Inge

_ a. mercurial

_ b. mortiferous

_ c. masochistic

_ d. mendacious

_ e. martial

LE MOT QUOTE 30

Match each quote with the appropriate word.

1. Join the army, see the world,
   meet interesting people, and kill them.
   —Anti-war slogan

2. Always tell the truth in the form of a joke.
   —Armenian proverb

3. One dies only once, and it's for such a long time!
   —Moliere

4. From powerful causes spring the empiric's gains.
   Man's love for life, his weakness and his pains
   these first induce him the vile trash to try
   then lend his name that others too may buy.
   —Crabbe

_ a. mercenary

_ b. mordacious

_ c. moribund

_ d. mountebank

LE MOT QUOTE 31
Match each quote with the appropriate word.

1. Any girl can be glamorous; all you have to do
   is stand still and look stupid. —Hedy Lamarr

2. He that flings dirt at another dirties himself most.
   —English proverb

3. When a man is intoxicated by alcohol,
   he can recover, but when intoxicated by power,
   he seldom recovers. —James F. Byrnes

4. For it's "Tommy this an' Tommy that,
   and "Chuck 'im out, the brute."
   But it's "Savior of 'is country," when
   the guns begin to shoot.
   —Kipling

__ a. militant

__ b. meretricious

__ c. malign

__ d. megalomaniac

Chapter 11

Those things for which we find words
are things we have already overcome.
—Nietzsche

In Chapter 50 I suggested you try the immersion method of studying the text, but I've also suggested you browse through at your leisure. Then again you can always do both. Read through the book in a cavalier way. Once through, go back and plow through it again with more passion.

Basic Barbs

➤ **cipher** = zero; a person of no importance
➤ **idealogue** = slang for one who adheres to particular idea or philosophy
➤ **mimbo** = slang for a male bimbo
➤ **mobocracy** = government ruled by the mob
➤ **plebeian** = a lower class or vulgar person
➤ **schnook** = one easily cheated
➤ **scoundrel** = a villain
➤ **urchin** = an unkempt, mischievous child; a sea urchin is a small soft-bodied sea animal encased in a shell

Brainy Barbs

1. **mundane plebeian** (mŭn dān´) Literally, it means "of the world", but it also refers to anything as ordinary. From Latin, *mundus* = world.

> *An ox remains an ox, even if driven to Vienna.*
> —Hungarian proverb

2. **mussitating mob** (mŭs´ ĭ tā´ ting) They mumble and grumble almost silently. You see their mouths move but you can't quite make out what they are saying. From Latin, *mussitare* = to mutter.

> *When people cease to complain, they cease to think.*
> —Napoleon

3. **mutinous mobocracy** (myūt´ ĭnəs) Anyone mutinous is revolting against authority. From Old French, *meute* = a riot.

> *No one can go on being a rebel too long
> without turning into an autocrat.*
> —Lawrence Durrell

4. **myopic idealogue** (mī ŏp´ ĭk)   Literally, myopic means near-sighted, but it also denotes a lack of foresight or a preoccupation with the minor details. From Greek, *myops* = shortsighted, blinking.

> *Looking at small advantages*
> *prevents great affairs from being accomplished.*
> —*Confucius*

5. **naive schnook** (nä ēv´)   Anyone naive is childlike and foolishly simple; hence, gullible. From Latin, *nativas* = natural.

> *One woman I was dating said,*
> *"Come on over, there's nobody home."*
> *I went over—nobody was home.*
> —*Rodney Dangerfield*

6. **narcissistic mimbo** (när´ sĭ sĭs´ tĭk)   In Greek mythology, Narcissus fell in love with his own reflection. A narcissistic person is excessively self-centered, self-absorbed, self-infatuated.

> *There but for the grace of God, goes God.*
> —*Winston Churchill*

7. **lowbred Neanderthal** (nē ăn´ dər thôl)   This one is a prehistoric subspecies of man or any brutish person. From German, it literally means, Neander valley, where the Neanderthal man was first discovered.

> *While Darwinian Man, though well behaved,*
> *at best is only a monkey shaved.*
> —*Gilbert*

8. **nebulous cipher** (nĕb´ yə ləs)   A nebula is a vast, indistinct cloud of stars seen too far away to be seen clearly. So, nebulous is anything that is unclear, vague or indefinite. I've combined it with the word cipher to describe one of the indistinct pawns in life, taking up space, but not discernable from the masses. From Latin, *nebula* = vapor, mist, cloud.

> *I'm trying to arrange my life so that I don't even have to be present.*
> —*Unknown*

9. **necessitous street urchin** (nə sĕs´ ĭ təs)   Anyone necessitous is needy. From Latin, *necessarius* = needful.

> *It is no disgrace to be poor, but it might as well be.*
> —*Jim Grue*

10. **nefarious scoundrel** (nĭ fâr´ ē əs)   This scoundrel is wicked and immoral. From Latin, *nefarius* = impious, abominable.

> *Evil enters like a needle and spreads like an oak tree.*
> —*Ethiopian proverb*

Quiz 51

Match the definitions with the words on the left.

Brainy Barbs

__ 1. mundane   a. a prehistoric subspecies of man
__ 2. mussitate   b. childlike and foolishly simple
__ 3. mutinous   c. terribly in love with oneself
__ 4. myopic   d. mumble almost silently
__ 5. naive   e. near-sighted
__ 6. narcissistic   f. needful
__ 7. Neanderthal   g. ordinary
__ 8. nebulous   h. revolting against authority
__ 9. necessitous   i. unclear, vague or indefinite
__10. nefarious   j. wicked

Basic Barbs

__11. scoundrel   k. a lower class or vulgar person
__12. cipher   l. a male bimbo
__13. mimbo   m. government ruled by the mob
__14. schnook   n. one stuck to one idea
__15. mobocracy   o. one easily cheated
__16. idealogue   p. villain
__17. plebeian   q. zero; one of no importance

Woke Up On The Wrong Side Of The Bed, Part 2

(cantankerous, churlish, contentious, disputatious, dissident,)
(divisive, dyspeptic, glower, malcontent, surly)

Match.

1. d _ _ _ _ _ _ _ _ = having impaired digestion; grouchy
2. d _ _ _ _ _ _ _ = causing factions or disagreements
3. d _ _ _ _ _ _ _ _ = not agreeing
4. c _ _ _ _ _ _ _ _ _ _ _ = bad-tempered
5. c _ _ _ _ _ _ _ _ _ _ _ = always ready to argue
6. c _ _ _ _ _ _ _ _ = surly; stingy; hard to manage
7. s _ _ _ _ = bad-tempered
8. m _ _ _ _ _ _ _ _ _ _ = dissatisfied or rebellious
9. g _ _ _ _ _ = scowl, an angry glare
10. d _ _ _ _ _ _ _ _ _ _ _ = ready to argue

Grisly List 52

Take a look at this next list. What may surprise you is this: if you've lived long enough you probably know people that fit these descriptions. Scary, isn't it? At first, these slurs seem unreal, but over time, they wind up naming someone you know.. Carl Jung, the noted psychologist, felt that if one can put a name on something, it then takes power out of that image. That is my hope: not that you wallow down the alley puling, "Oh, my God, I'm surrounded by incompetents;" but having named your nightmare he/she has become your nightmare no more.

Basic Barbs

➤ **anarchist** = one who believes the best government is no government or one who advocates social disorder
➤ **hellion** = one fond of devilry or mischief
➤ **ninny** = a fool
➤ **nag** = to annoy by constant complaining; one who nags, especially a woman; a female horse
➤ **cannon fodder** = a derogatory term for military men who are expendable

Brainy Barbs

1. **negligible cannon fodder** (nĕg´ lĭ jə bəl)   Anyone negligible is disregarded because he's unimportant. Don't confuse this with negligent. When one is negligent one has failed in some task due to carelessness or inattention. From Latin, *neg* = not + *legere* = to pick up + IBLE.

> *He had the sort of face that, once seen, is never remembered.*
> —Oscar Wilde

2. **deadly nemesis** (nĕm´ ĭ sĭs)   That life-long enemy whom you've never been able to beat is back and snapping at your heels. In Greek mythology, Nemesis is the god of retribution.

> *He hasn't an enemy in the world—but all his friends hate him.*
> —Eddie Cantor

3. **nepotistic politician** (nĕ´ po tĭs´ tĭc)   This one shows favoritism, especially to relatives. From Latin, *nepos* + *potis* = grandson + nephew

> *If the camel once gets his nose in the tent,*
> *his body will soon follow.*
> —Arabic proverb

4. nescient nitwit (nĕsh´ ənt, nĕsh´ ē ənt) Lacking any clue, this nitwit is ignorant and lacks experience. From Latin, *nesciens* = to be ignorant.

> Only two things are infinite:
> the universe and human stupidity,
> and I'm not sure about the former.
> —Albert Einstein

5. nettling nag (nĕt´ ling) Nettle is a plant that stings; hence, to nettle is to irritate. A nettling person is irritating and annoying. From Medieval English, *netlen*.

> Better to live on a corner of the roof
> than to share a house with a quarrelsome wife.
> —Proverbs 21:9

6. niddering ninny (adj. or n. nĭd´ ər ing) A mean or cowardly person, this ninny would abandon his kids for fear of getting his toe stubbed. From Icelandic, *nithingr* = to act basely.

> Cowards never use their might
> But against such as will not fight.
> —Samuel Butler

7. niggardly spender (nĭg´ ərd lē) This one is stingy. From Norwegian, *gnigga* = to be stingy.

> He read in the paper that it takes ten dollars a year
> to support a kid in India. So he sent his kid there.
> —Red Buttons

8. nihilistic anarchist (nī ə lĭs´ tĭk) Nihilism is the denial of any basis for truth; the rejection of morality, religion. In politics, a nihilist believes only violent overthrow can change the existing social structure. From Latin, *nihilum* = nothing.

> There is no gravity. The earth sucks.
> —Graffito

9. Noachian hermit (nō ā´ kē ən) Noachian means of the time of Noah or it can also mean ancient.

> I prefer old age to the alternative.
> —Maurice Chevalier

10. nocent hellion (nō´ sənt) Nocent means harmful, injurious or criminal. From Latin, *nocens* = doing harm.

> A thief believes everybody else steals.
> —Ed Howe

Quiz 52

Match the definitions with the words on the left.

Brainy Barbs

___ 1. negligible   a. ancient
___ 2. nemesis   b. denying any basis for truth;
                        rejecting morality, religion
___ 3. nepotistic   c. disregarded as unimportant
___ 4. nescient   d. harmful, injurious or criminal
___ 5. nettling   e. ignorant
___ 6. niddering   f. irritating and annoying
___ 7. niggardly   g. life-long enemy
___ 8. nihilistic   h. mean or cowardly
___ 9. Noachian   i. showing favoritism to relatives
___10. nocent   j. stingy

Basic Barbs

___11. cannon fodder   k. believes in no government
___12. hellion   l. fool
___13. anarchist   m. one fond of devilry or mischief
___14. ninny   n. expendable military men
___15. nag   o. to annoy by complaining;
                      a female horse

Ninety-Nine Bottles Of Beer On The Wall

(bacchanalian, bibulous, debauched, decadent, degenerate,)
(depraved, deviant, dissipated, dissolute)

Unscramble.

1. isedusolt = immoral, dissipated   _____
2. disedsitap = wasted away having indulged
                  in booze, gambling etc.   _____
3. pedradev = morally corrupt   _____
4. egedenerat = morally corrupt   _____
5. cadeentd = declining, morally depraved   _____
6. evidant = turning from what is normal   _____
7. ebaueddch = given to immoral living   _____
8. biulobus = addicted to booze   _____
9. cabanachlian = like a drunken orgy   _____

Grisly List 53

There are visual learners, those who learn primarily by seeing; aural learners, those who learn primarily by hearing; and kinesthetic learners, those who learn primarily by doing. However, all learners benefit in some way by all three approaches. When you read the words on the page you are visually learning. When you sound them out you are aurally learning. If you write them down, or draw a picture you are kinesthetically learning. The process is now in your muscle memory. Take time to write these words down to fix them in your muscle memory.

Basic Barbs

➤ **blight** = a pestilence; any person or thing that withers one's hopes or ambitions
➤ **chump** = one who is easily cheated, a fool, an idiot
➤ **Circe** = an enchantress who turned men into pigs; see Circean
➤ **drone** = a stingless male bee who doesn't gather honey; any loafer who lives off the work of others
➤ **hatchet man** = a professional killer
➤ **naughty** = wicked; disobedient; obscene
➤ **nudnik** = Yiddish, a stupid, annoying pest
➤ **wannabe** = one who tries to be something but lacks the skill or talent to do so

Brainy Barbs

1. **nocuous hatchet man** (nŏk´ yū əs) This one's poisonous, harmful to health, noxious. From Latin, *nocere* = to hurt, injure.

2. **noisome nudnik** (noi´ səm) A noisome person is harmful, and/or smells bad. From a Latin phrase, *in odio* = in ill will > annoy > noy + some.

The drug he gave me, which he said was precious and cordial to me,
have I not found it murd'rous to th' senses?
—Shakespeare

3. **nondescript drone** (nŏn´ dĭ skrĭpt´) Anyone nondescript has no definite class or type. There is nothing that distinguishes this drone out of the crowd. From Latin, *non* = not + *descriptus* = described.

One could not even dignify him with the name of stuffed shirt.
He was simply a hole in the air.
—George Orwell

4. forgettable nonentity (nŏn ĕn´ tĭ tē)   Nonentity means something is not existing, but it can also describe a person of little or no importance. From Latin, *non* = not + *entitas* = being.

> Glory is fleeting, but obscurity is forever.
> —Napoleon Bonaparte

5. nonfeasant official (nŏn fē´ zənt)   One who is guilty of nonfeasance has failed to do what duty requires. This reminds me of the Los Angeles Meter Officer who placed a parking ticket on a vehicle where the driver sat hunched over with a bullet in his head. From Latin, *non* = not + *facere* = to do.

> He who holds the ladder is as bad as the thief.
> —German proverb

6. nonplused chump (nŏn plŭsd´)   To be nonplused is to be so utterly perplexed that one is unable to speak or act further. From Latin, *non* = not + *plus* = further.

> At six I was left an orphan.
> What on earth is a six-year-old supposed to do with an orphan?
> —Anonymous

7. notorious Circe (nō tôr´ ē əs)   Not only is she bad to the bone, she's famous for it. From Late Latin, *notoria* = news, information.

> The popularity of the bad man is as treacherous as he is himself.
> —Pliny the Younger

8. noxious blight (nŏk´ shəs)   Anyone noxious causes injury to health and/or morals. From Latin, *nocere* = to hurt, injure.

> If it tastes good, it's trying to kill you.
> —Roy Qualley

9. nugatory wannabe (nū´ gə tôr´ ē)   Anyone or anything that is nugatory is worthless. From Latin, *nugae* = trifles.

> You may marry the man of your dreams,
> but 15 years later you're married to a reclining chair that burps.
> —Roseanne Barr

10. naughty nymphomaniac (nĭm´ fō mā´ nē ăk)   This woman has an uncontrollable desire for sex. Once upon a time, that was a plus; now it can be a death sentence. The word derived from Greek, *nymph* = a nature goddess + *mania* = madness.

> You can lead a horticulture, but you can't make her think.
> —Dorothy Parker

Quiz 53

Match the definitions with the words on the left.

Brainy Barbs

___ 1. nocuous
___ 2. noisome
___ 3. nondescript
___ 4. nonentity

___ 5. nonfeasant
___ 6. nonplused
___ 7. notorious
___ 8. noxious

___ 9. nugatory
___10. nymphomaniac

a. completely perplexed
b. failing to do duty
c. famous and bad
d. harmful to health
   (fits three words)
e. having no definite class
f. worthless
g. not existing
h. a woman who has an
   uncontrollable desire for sex

Basic Barbs

___11. naughty
___12. wanna be
___13. blight
___14. Circe
___15. drone

___16. nudnik

i. loafer who lives off of others
j. a pestilence
k. a stupid, annoying pest
l. turned men into pigs
m. tries to be something
   but lacks the skill
n. wicked; disobedient

Put A Cork In It

(barfly, crapulous, dipsomaniac, inebriated, intemperate,)
(lush, potvaliant, sodden, souse)

Match.

1. l _ _ _ = a drunk
2. p _ _ _ _ _ _ _ _ _ = brave because of alcohol
3. b _ _ _ _ _ = one who frequents bars
4. c _ _ _ _ _ _ _ _ = drunk
5. d _ _ _ _ _ _ _ _ _ _ = an alcoholic
6. s _ _ _ _ _ = drunk
7. s _ _ _ _ = a drunkard
8. i _ _ _ _ _ _ _ _ _ = drunk
9. i _ _ _ _ _ _ _ _ _ _ = lacking restraint

Grisly List 54

If you take the time to write the words down you will also be improving your spelling, and a misspelled word is a big faux pas. One spelling blunder can make you look like a complete nincompoop. And don't think your spellchecker is going to help. Many of these words have nuances that won't be picked up. Spellchecker can't tell the difference between insipient and incipient. One exercise you might want to try is to give yourself a spelling test. Find the words that you misspell and then write them three times.

Basic Barbs

> **busybody** = one who intrudes and meddles in other people's affairs
> **pawn** = the lowest piece in a chess game; one who is manipulated by another
> **numskull** = an idiot
> **obsolescent** = something is in the state of becoming obsolete
> **ogress** = the female of ogre, a fabled man-eating giant
> **stiff** = Stiff is a slang word for corpse, specifically one in rigor mortis, but it also has the additional meaning of anyone who is useless or ineffective.

Brainy Barbs

1. **obese tub of lard** (ō bēs´) Being fat was once considered a sign of wealth. Times have changed. From Latin, *obedere* = to devour.

He must have had a magnificent build
before his stomach went in for a career of its own.
—*Margaret Halsey*

2. **obdurate numskull** (ŏb´ dŏŏ rĭt) This hardhearted, stubborn one has a mulish attitude. From Latin, *obdurare* = to harden.

I refuse to admit I'm more than fifty-two,
even if that does make my sons illegitimate.
—*Nancy Astor*

3. **obfuscating oddball** (ŏb´ fŭs kāt ing) When you need clarity, when you need things to be perfectly clear, avoid this oddball. This oddball clouds over and muddles what needs to be said. From Late Latin, *obfuscatus* = darkened.

I wish people who have trouble communicating would just shut up.
—*Tom Lehrer*

4. **objurgating ogress** (ŏbʹ jər gāʹ ting)   To objurgate is to criticize severely. From Latin, *objugare* = chastise, to rebuke.

> The blow of a whip raises a welt,
> but a blow of the tongue crushes bones.
> —Ecclesiasticus 28:27

5. **close-minded obscurant** (əb skyŏŏrʹ ənt)   This person tries to stop the spread of knowledge. From Latin, *obscurus* = dark.

> Pedantry crams our heads with learned lumber,
> and takes out our brains to make room for it.
> —Colton

6. **obsequious wart** (əb sēʹkwē əs)   This overly submissive one is much too willing to serve. From Latin, *obsequi* = to comply with.

> Coercion created slavery, the cowardice of slaves perpetuated it.
> —Rousseau

7. **obsolete pawn** (ŏbʹ sə lēt)   Anything obsolete is no longer needed. Of course, you can always use the word obsolescent, which means something is in the state of becoming obsolete. From Latin, *obsolescere* = to go out of use.

> It is better to be looked over than be overlooked.
> —Mae West

8. **obstipated stiff** (ŏbʹ stə pāʹ təd)   This stiff is obstinately constipated. Give him some prunes. From Late Latin, *obstipatio* = close pressure.

> People who never get carried away should be.
> —Malcolm Forbes

9. **obstreperous stinkard** (əb strĕpʹ ər əs)   Anyone obstreperous is noisy and unruly. From Latin, *obtrepere* = to roar at.

> If a child shows himself to be obstreperous,
> he should be quietly beheaded at the age of twelve,
> lest he grow to maturity, marry, and perpetuate his kind.
> —Don Marquis

10. **obtrusive busybody** (əb trū sĭv)   This one intrudes, interferes without invitation. It can also mean something is conspicuous, blatant. From Latin, *ob* = toward + *trudere* = to thrust.

> I can't remember your name, but don't tell me.
> —Alexander Woollcott

Quiz 54

Match the definitions with the words on the left.

Brainy Barbs

___ 1. obese
___ 2. obdurate
___ 3. obfuscate
___ 4. objurgate

___ 5. obscurant
___ 6. obsequious
___ 7. obsolete
___ 8. obstreperous

___ 9. obtrusive
___10. obstipated

a. cloud over and muddle
b. fat
c. hardhearted, stubborn
d. intrude without invitation and
   get in the way
e. noisy and unruly
f. no longer needed, out of use
g. overly submissive
h. one who tries to stop
   the spread of knowledge
i. obstinately constipated
j. to criticize severely

Basic Barbs

___11. pawn
___12. ogress
___13. numskull
___14. obsolescent
___15. busybody

k. one controlled by another
l. becoming obsolete
m. meddles in other's affairs
n. an idiot
o. the female of ogre

Party Hard

(Rabelaisian, rambunctious, raucous, roguish,)
(roisterous, rumbustious, waggish)

Match.

1. r _ _ _ _ _ _ = playfully mischievous
2. R _ _ _ _ _ _ _ _ _ _ = lustfully humorous
3. r _ _ _ _ _ _ = loud and rowdy
4. r _ _ _ _ _ _ _ _ _ _ _ = wild, unruly
5. r _ _ _ _ _ _ _ _ _ = rowdy
6. w _ _ _ _ _ _ = playfully humorous
7. ro _ _ _ _ _ _ _ = rough merrymaking; blustery

It is one thing to recognize a word on a test. It is another thing to use it correctly in your speech. But it is another jump to use it in your writing. And if you want to improve your writing, then you have to write. So take the time to write sentences using the words below. Make the sentences as ridiculous or as serious as you want. This will help your memory of the words, your spelling, and your craft as a writer.

Basic Barbs

- ➢ **albatross** = a web-footed bird; one considered a burden or jinx
- ➢ **ogre** = a man-eating monster
- ➢ **rabble** = a wild mob; the lower class
- ➢ **sellout** = one who has compromised morals for cash; anything, e.g. a concert, that has sold out
- ➢ **snitch** = to steal or be an informer
- ➢ **snoop** = to pry or one who pries into others' business

Brainy Barbs

1. **obtuse ogre** (əb tūs´) To be obtuse is to be blunt or intellectually slow. From Latin, *obtusus* = to be blunted, dull.

> *It is the dull man who is always sure,*
> *and the sure man who is always dull.*
> —H. L. Mencken

2. **ochlocratic rabble** (ŏk´ lə kră´ tĭk) An ochlocratic government is run by a riotous mob. From Greek, *ochlos* = mob.

> *The tyranny of the multitude is multiplied tyranny.*
> —Edmund Burke

3. **odious stalkarazzi** (ō´ dē əs) This one is hated and fills others with disgust. From Latin, *odium* = hatred.

> *One should hate nobody whom one cannot destroy.*
> —Goethe

4. **officious snoop** (ə fĭsh´ əs) An officious person is always offering unwanted and unasked for advice. From Latin, *officiosus* = conformable to duty.

> *You will always find some Eskimos*
> *ready to instruct the Congolese*
> *on how to cope with heat waves.*
> —Stanislaw Lec

5. **oleaginous sneak** (ō´ lē ăj´ ə nəs) Yuck! Oleaginous means to have the nature of oil or to be unctuous, objectionably debonair and charming, smooth. From Latin, *oleaginus* = of the olive.

> You're where you should be all the time
> and when you're not
> you're with a wife of a close friend.
>
> —Carly Simon

6. **ominous shadow** (ŏm´ ə nəs) Anything ominous is threatening and sinister, foreshadowing the evil, dread, or death that lurks just ahead. From Latin, *ominosus* = portentous.

> <u>Likely comment:</u>
> Your days are numbered.
>
> <u>Your response:</u>
> Well, it's a good thing I can't count.

7. **onerous albatross** (ŏn´ ər əs, ōn´ ər əs) This one is an incredible burden. From Latin, *onus* = a load.

> It is not the load but the overload that kills.
>
> —Spanish proverb

8. **opaque flunky** (ō pāk´) Anything opaque is impervious to light, loosely transparent, or stupid. From Latin, *opacus* = shady.

> When you go to a mind reader, do you get half price?
>
> —Ben Creed

9. **ophidian snitch** (ō fĭd´ ē ən) This snitch is like a snake. From Greek, *ophis* = snake, serpent.

> You snakes! You brood of vipers!
>
> —Jesus of Nazareth,
> Luke 23:33

10. **opprobrious sellout** (ə prō brē əs) Anything opprobrious is shameful, disgraceful or conveys ridicule, contempt, or severe condemnation. From Latin, *opprobrius* = reproach.

> One of the misfortunes of our time
> is that in getting rid of false shame
> we killed off so much real shame as well.
>
> —Louis Kronenberger

Quiz 55

Match the definitions with the words on the left.

Brainy Barbs

__ 1. obtuse
__ 2. ochlocratic
__ 3. odious
__ 4. officious
__ 5. oleaginous
__ 6. ominous
__ 7. onerous
__ 8. opaque
__ 9. ophidian
__10. opprobrious

a. burdensome
b. government run by riotous mob
c. hated
d. impervious to light
e. blunt or dull
f. offering unwanted advice
g. of or like snakes
h. oily, greasy
i. shameful, disgraceful
j. threatening and sinister

Basic Barbs

__11. rabble
__12. snitch
__13. albatross
__14. ogre
__15. snoop

k. web-foot bird; a burden or jinx
l. a man-eating monster
m. a wild mob; the lower class
n. to steal or be an informer
o. pries into others' business

Followers And Brownnosers, Part 1

(beadle, brownnoser, complaisant, compliant, docile, ductile,)
(underling, ingratiate, malleable, minions, slavish, truckle, belaud)

Match.

1. b _ _ _ _ _ _ _ _ _ = one who flatters just to get something
2. b _ _ _ _ _ = a minor official
3. u _ _ _ _ _ _ _ _ _ = an inferior, a subordinate
4. s _ _ _ _ _ _ = like a slave
5. m _ _ _ _ _ _ _ _ = able to be shaped; trainable
6. m _ _ _ _ _ _ = followers, used disdainfully
7. i _ _ _ _ _ _ _ _ _ _ = bring oneself into another's favor
by conscious effort
8. d _ _ _ _ _ _ = easily molded or led
9. d _ _ _ _ _ = easily led
10. c _ _ _ _ _ _ _ _ = yielding
11. c _ _ _ _ _ _ _ _ _ _ _ = willing to please
12. b _ _ _ _ _ = to praise excessively, especially sarcastically
13. t _ _ _ _ _ _ = to submit obsequiously

LE MOT QUOTE 32

Match each quote with the appropriate word.

1. Rebellion to tyrants is obedience to God.
   —Thomas Jefferson

2. Whenever nature leaves a hole in a person's mind,
   she generally plasters it over with a thick coat
   of self-conceit. —Longfellow

3. By the pricking of my thumbs,
   something wicked this way comes. —Shakespeare

4. It is the enemy whom we do not suspect
   who is the most dangerous. —Rojas

__ a. nemesis

__ b. narcissistic

__ c. nefarious

__ d. mutinous

LE MOT QUOTE 33

Match each quote with the appropriate word.

1. The most infamous are fond of fame;
   and those who fear not guilt, yet start at shame.
   —Churchill

2. That woman speaks eighteen languages,
   and can't say no in any of them. —Dorothy Parker

3. No one is as deaf as the man who won't listen.
   —Jewish proverb

4. Warm up a frozen snake and she will bite you.
   —Armenian proverb

__ a. nymphomaniac

__ b. notorious

__ c. obdurate

__ d. ophidian

LE MOT QUOTE 34

Match each quote with the appropriate word.

1. If I die, I forgive you; if I live, we'll see.
   —Spanish proverb

2. A mob is the scum that rises
   upmost when the nation boils. —Dryden

3. I count him lost, who is lost to shame. —Plautus

4. Awkward, embarrassed, stiff, without the skill
   Of moving gracefully or standing still,
   One leg, as if suspicious of his brother,
   Desirous seems to run away from t'other.
   —Charles Churchill

__ a. opprobrious

__ b. ominous

__ c. ochlocratic

__ d. maladroit

Chapter 12

All words are pegs to hang ideas on.
—Henry Ward Beecher

Grisly List 56

Let me suggest again that you practice the pronunciation of each word. This is important for two reasons: One, as I've mentioned before, pronouncing the word will help you better remember the word; And two, if you mispronounce the word in a social setting it can be as egregious as misspelling a word in a business letter. Either way you look like an idiot. So, take the time to practice enunciating each word. It will give you the confidence you need to use it when you need it.

Basic Barbs

➤ **lummox** = a clumsy, ungainly person
➤ **oaf** = Originally, oaf was an elf but it now denotes a clumsy idiot.
➤ **penny pincher** = one who is excessively frugal, a miser
➤ **thug** = a member of a former religious organization of India that murdered and robbed in the service of Kali, a goddess of destruction; a rough, brutal hoodlum

Brainy Barbs

1. **oppugnant thug** (ə pŭg´ nənt) Anyone oppugnant is hostile and antagonistic. It comes from the same Latin word from which we get pugnacious, *pugna* = a fight.

> *The world is a madhouse,*
> *so it's only right that it is patrolled by armed idiots.*
> —Brandan Behan

2. **oscitant lummox** (ŏs´ ĭ tənt) Oscitancy is the action of yawning or the condition of being drowsy or dull. This one is drowsy and dull. From Latin, *oscitant* = yawning.

> *Life is one long process of getting tired.*
> —Samuel Butler

3. **ostentatious yuppie** (ŏs´ tĕn tā´ shəs) Anyone ostentatious shows a pretentious display of wealth. From Latin, *ostendere* = to show.

> *If you stay in Beverly Hills too long you become a Mercedes.*
> —Robert Redford

4. **otiose baggage** (ō´ shē ōs´, ō´ tē ōs´)   This one is useless, worthless or lazy. From Latin, *otium* = leisure.

> Many are idly busy. Domitian was busy,
> but then it was at catching flies.
> —Jeremy Taylor

5. **ovine oaf** (ō´ vīn)   Anyone ovine is like a sheep. From Latin, *ovis* = sheep.

> Make thyself a sheep and the wolf is ready. —Russian proverb

6. **palavering putz** (pə lăv´ ər ing)   To palaver either means to chat in an idle way or to try to charm or cheat someone by one's talk. From Portuguese, *palavra* = a word , speech.

> **TOMBSTONE EPITAPH:**
> Though his words were quite sweet
> The cannibals need meat
> So they munched on his hide
> From his head to his feet

7. **pandering pimp** (păn´ dər ing)   This pimp tries to cater to your vile, evil, incestuous desires. The word, pander, comes from the Greek name, Panderos, a character in the Iliad who acted as a romantic go-between for Troilus and Cressida.

> I see the devil's hook, and yet cannot help nibbling at his bait.
> —M. Adams

8. **paranoid loonytoon** (pâr´ ə noid)   Overly suspicious, this one has delusions of persecution. From Greek, *para* = beside + *nous* = the mind.

> When dealing with the insane, the best method is to pretend to be sane.
> —Hermann Hesse

9. **exiled pariah** (pə rī ə)   This poor sot, this outcast is despised and rejected by the community. Originally, a pariah was the lowest class in India, an untouchable. From Tamil, *parai* = a drum: the pariah was the hereditary drumbeater.

> Loneliness is the ultimate poverty. —Abigail Van Buren

10. **parsimonious penny pincher** (pär´ sə mō´ nē əs)   Excessively frugal, this penny pincher is fearful of being wasteful. From Latin, *parcere* = to spare.

> Save a little money each month and at the end of the year
> you'll be surprised at how little you have.
> —Ernest Haskins

Quiz 56

Match the definitions with the words on the left.

Brainy Barbs

___ 1. oppugnant
___ 2. oscitant
___ 3. ostentatious
___ 4. otiose
___ 5. ovine
___ 6. palaver
___ 7. pander
___ 8. paranoid
___ 9. pariah
___10. parsimonious

a. an outcast
b. cater to vile, evil desires
c. drowsy and dull
d. excessively frugal
e. hostile and antagonistic
f. lazy
g. like sheep
h. having delusions of persecution
i. a affected show of wealth
j. to cheat another by one's talk

Basic Barbs

___11. oaf
___12. lummox
___13. thug
___14. penny pincher

k. a clumsy, ungainly person
l. a miser
m. a rough, brutal hoodlum
n. an elf; a clumsy idiot

Followers And Brownnosers, Part 2

(subservient, gnathonic, uxorious, servile, doting, biddable, castrated,)
(thrall, smarmy, claqueur, fawn, helot, obsequious, sequacious, stooge)

Match.

1. d _ _ _ _ _ = weak-minded; foolishly fond
2. g _ _ _ _ _ _ _ _ = fawning
3. b _ _ _ _ _ _ _ = obedient
4. s _ _ _ _ _ _ _ _ _ _ = submissive
5. u _ _ _ _ _ _ _ _ = excessively devoted to one's wife
6. s _ _ _ _ _ _ = like a slave
7. s _ _ _ _ _ _ _ _ = tending to follow a leader, lacking self-will
8. c _ _ _ _ _ _ _ _ = one who is hired to clap and laugh at theaters
9. o _ _ _ _ _ _ _ _ _ = overly submissive
10. f _ _ _ = flatter slavishly
11. c _ _ _ _ _ _ _ _ = with the testicles removed
12. s _ _ _ _ _ = an actor who serves as the butt of the jokes
13. h _ _ _ _ = a class of serfs in ancient Sparta
14. t _ _ _ _ _ = a slave
15. s _ _ _ _ _ = characterized by oily, insincere flattering

Grisly List 57

Are you the type that gets behind on writing letters? Then why not use this book as a way to catch up? Just grab a bunch of postcards, some stamps, this book, and then sit down to write. Don't be too verbose. Keep it simple like: "Hi mom. Everything's great here except for the pathological killer that crept into the apartment last night. Kisses, your loving son." Or how about, "Dear Dad, I ran into some pedestrian clone. Send money." You get the idea. Have fun with it.

Basic Barbs

> ➤ **booboisie** = the social class of the stupid and gullible
> ➤ **clone** = a duplicate produced by genetic engineering
> ➤ **prig** = an annoying, pedantic person or anyone who is overly precise, proper and haughty in following rules
> ➤ **priggish** = one who is pointlessly precise about conformity, fussy about unimportant details, and self-righteous in an irritating way
> ➤ **puppet** = as slang a puppet is anyone controlled by another
> ➤ **sot** = a drunkard
> ➤ **wiseacre** = a fool who thinks he's wise, from Middle Dutch, *wijsseggher*, truthsayer; a smart aleck, wise guy

Brainy Barbs

1. **pathetic puppet** (pə thět´ ĭk) One that is pathetic is either pitiful or miserably inadequate. From Greek, *pathos* = suffering.

Women live like bats or owls, labor like beasts, and die like worms.
—Margaret Cavendish

2. **pathological liar** (păth´ ə lŏj´ ĭ kəl) Pathological is anything related to disease, or it can also describe anyone governed by an excessive compulsion because of a mental disease. From Greek, *pathos* = suffering, disease.

I don't buy temporary insanity as a murder defense.
Cause people kill people. That's an animal instinct.
I think breaking into someone's home and ironing
all their clothes is temporary insanity.
—Sue Kolinsky

3. **patronizing wiseacre** (pā´ trə nī´ zing) To patronize is to treat another in a condescending way. From Latin, *patronus* = a protector.

TOMBSTONE EPITAPH:
He talked down to others like he was the rave
Now dogs look down as they piss on his grave

4. **Pavlovian dog** (păv lô´ vē ən)   Ivan Pavlov was a Russian physiologist who studied behavior by training dogs to salivate. So, a Pavlovian dog is trained to salivate but it can be a wonderful slur for anyone who behaves in such a slobbering fashion.

He's the kind of a man a woman would have to marry to get rid of.
—Mae West

5. **peccable sot** (pĕk´ ə bəl)   A peccable person is liable to sin or error. Don't confuse this with peccant which means one is already sinning. From Latin, *peccare* = to sin.

Oh Lord, help me to be pure, but not yet.
—St. Augustine

6. **peculating trustee** (pĕk´ yə lā´ ting)   To peculate is to steal money entrusted to one's care. From Latin, *peculari* = to embezzle < *peculium* = private property < *pecus* = cattle.

Is it a bigger crime to rob a bank or to open one?
—Ted Allan

7. **priggish pedagogue** (pĕd´ ə gŏg´)   A pedagogue is a teacher, but it usually denotes one who is pedantic and/or dogmatic. From Greek, *paidagogos* = a boy's tutor.

Deep versed in books, and shallow in himself.
—Milton

8. **pedantic prig** (pə dăn´ tĭk)   A pedantic person stresses the trivial points of learning. From French, *pedant* = schoolmaster.

Academic tenure encourages pedants to become fossils.
—Leo Rosten

9. **pedestrian clone** (pə dĕs´ trē ən)   A pedestrian is one who travels on foot but it can also describe something or someone who is ordinary, run-of-the-mill. From Latin, *pedester* = on foot.

The trouble with some women
is that they get all excitedabout nothing
—and then marry him.
—Cher

10. **pedicular booboisie** (pə dĭk´ yə lər)   Literally, it means filled with lice, but it also describes one considered lousy. From Latin, *pedis* = a louse.

The lean lice bite most.
—Polish proverb

Followers And Brownnosers, Part 3

(unctuous, wheedle, Barmecidal, sycophant, bathetic,)
(drudge, lackey, oleaginous, parasite, toad, bootlicker)

Unscramble and match.

1. merbadical = pretended hospitality   _____
2. edehwle = influences by flattery   _____
3. cuntusou = oily, smooth and deceitful   _____
4. coyspanth = one who flatters in order
    to get something   _____

5. o _ _ _ _ _ _ _ _ _ = oily, greasy
6. b _ _ _ _ _ _ _ = insincerely sentimental
7. t _ _ _ = a sycophant, brownnoser
8. l _ _ _ _ _ = a servant or a brownnoser
9. d _ _ _ _ _ = one who does menial work
10. p _ _ _ _ _ _ _ = lives at other's expense
11. b _ _ _ _ _ _ _ _ _ = a brownnoser

One of the words from the basic list, parasite, has a rather curious and interesting past. It comes from the Greek word, *parasitos*, which means one who sits at the table of another; thus a parasite is a person in ancient Greece, who flattered and amused his host in return for free meals. Now it depicts one who lives at the expense of another without offering anything in return, similar to a sponge, a hanger-on or a leech. In biology, a parasite not only lives off another organism, but it also harms it.

Basic Barbs

- ➤ **cheap-skate** = a miser
- ➤ **fiend** = an evil spirit; a wicked, cruel person
- ➤ **fusspot** = one who fusses over nothing
- ➤ **grubber** = one who toils for his daily bread
- ➤ **nitpicker** = one who finds faults over insignificant things
- ➤ **parasite** = one who lives at the expense of another without offering anything in return
- ➤ **plutocracy** = government by the wealthy
- ➤ **prima donna** = the principal female singer in an Opera, or any arrogant, vain or temperamental person, especially a woman

Brainy Barbs

1. **peevish prune** (pē´ vĭsh) A peevish person is impatient and hard to please. From Medieval English, *pevish* = spiteful.

   My license plate says PMS. Nobody cuts me off. —Wendy Liebman

2. **pejorative nitpicker** (pĭ jôr´ ə tĭv) Pejorative is usually applied to words whose meaning has changed for the worse, but it can also be used to describe someone who is disparaging, derisive or the like. From Latin, *pejore* = to make worse.

   When one is not good oneself,
   one likes to talk of what is wrong with others.
   —Yugoslavian proverb

3. **pelting plutocracy** (pĕl´ ting) Don't confuse pelting with the verb pelt, which means to attack with repeated blows or missiles; its origin is obscure but it connotes anyone who is mean and/or miserly. From Danish, *pjalt* = rags.

   TOMBSTONE EPITAPH:
   They rode in style in long limousines
   But the ride was cut short by the guillotine.

4. penurious cheapskate (pə nŏŏr´ ē əs)   Penurious can mean stingy, or poor or both stingy and poor. From Latin, *penuria* = want.

> *Man hoards himself when he has nothing to give away.*
> *—Edward Dahlherg*

5. perfidious fiend (pər fĭd´ ē əs)   Perfidy is the premeditated breaking of faith. A perfidious fiend is treacherous. From Latin, *perfidios* = faithless, dishonest.

> *Alas, they had been friends in youth;*
> *but whispering tongues can poison truth.*
> *—Samuel Taylor Coleridge*

6. perfunctory grubber (pər fŭngk´ tə rē)   Anything perfunctory is done in a routine fashion, without care. From Latin, *perfungi* = to get rid of.

> *Most men in a brazen prison live,*
> *Where, in the sun's hot eye,*
> *With heads bent o'er their toil, they languidly*
> *Their lives to some unmeaning taskwork give,*
> *Dreaming of naught beyond their prison wall.*
> *—Matthew Arnold, <u>A summer night</u>*

7. perjuring jackal (pûr´ jûr ing)   On the witness stand, this one lies under oath. From Latin, *perjurus* = breaking oath.

> *His face was filled with broken commandments.*
> *—John Masefield*

8. pernicious parasite (pər nĭsh´ əs)   Anyone pernicious is harmful by insidiously weakening you. From Latin, *perniciosus* = destructive.

> *Destroy the seed of evil, or it will grow up to your ruin.*
> *—Aesop*

9. persnickety fusspot (pər snĭk´ ĭ tē)   This fusspot is too precise and fussy. From Scottish, perhaps derived from a child's word for particular, *pertickie*.

> *Nancy Reagan fell down and broke her hair. —Johnny Carson*

10. pert prima donna (pûrt)   This one is bold, saucy and forward. From Old French, *apert* = open, free; hence, impudent < Latin, *apertus* = open. Check Chapter 17 and compare this to malapert, From Latin, *mal apert* = badly opened, ill taught.

> **TOMBSTONE EPITAPH:**
> She wanted a world on her own terms
> Now she's food for maggots and worms.

Quiz 58

Match the definitions with the words on the left.

Brainy Barbs

___ 1. peevish
___ 2. pejorative
___ 3. pelting
___ 4. penurious
___ 5. perfidious
___ 6. perfunctory
___ 7. perjure
___ 8. pernicious
___ 9. persnickety
___ 10. pert

a. bold, saucy and forward
b. disparaging, derisive
c. hard to please, impatient
d. insidiously weakening
e. in a routine way, without care
f. lie under oath
g. mean, miserly
h. stingy and/or poor
i. too precise and fussy
j. treacherous

Basic Barbs

___ 11. prima donna
___ 12. pelt
___ 13. fiend
___ 14. plutocracy

k. government by the wealthy
l. an evil spirit
m. vain or temperamental person
n. attack with repeated blows

A Little Pessimistic

(dour, funereal, fatalist, misanthrope, misandrist)
(obscurant, dystopia, misoneist, misologist)

Match.

1. m _ _ _ _ _ _ _ _ _ _ = one who hates people
2. f _ _ _ _ _ _ _ = one who believes life is controlled
by inevitable fate
3. d _ _ _ _ _ _ _ = a dreadful place
4. m _ _ _ _ _ _ _ _ = one who hates innovation or change
5. m _ _ _ _ _ _ _ _ _ = hatred of reason or enlightenment
6. d _ _ _ = severe; gloomy
7. f _ _ _ _ _ _ _ _ = gloomy
8. m _ _ _ _ _ _ _ _ _ _ = one who hates men
9. o _ _ _ _ _ _ _ _ _ = one who tries to stop the spread of learning

I've suggested in previous chapters that you focus on the words that you miss on the tests. That is still a good idea, but I have another one. Try keeping a list of your favorite words, words that you are most likely to use because they appeal to you in some way. These words will be easier for you to memorize and add to your speech. You don't need to spend more than few minutes each day looking them over. In no time at all you will find them deeply imbedded in your long-term memory.

Basic Barbs

➢ **hen** = a chicken; a slang term for a female nag
➢ **mouthpiece** = slang term for a lawyer
➢ **rogue** (rōg) = A rogue is a rascal and a rascal could be a thief, a con, a philanderer or simply a mischievous boy
➢ **snot** = slang, a disrespectful, haughty person
➢ **tightwad** = a stingy person
➢ **zealot** = member of a radical Jewish sect that resisted Roman rule in the first century AD; a zealous or fanatically committed person

Brainy Barbs

1. **pertinacious zealot** (pûr´ tə nā´ shəs)   Stubborn to the end, this pain never says die. From Latin, *pertinacia* = stubbornness.

> *In the friendship of an ass expect nothing but kicks.*
> —Indian proverb

2. **perverse stalker** (pər vûrs´)   To be perverse is to deviate from what is considered right or good, or to be stubborn in what is wrong. From Latin, *pervertare* = to pervert.

> *She sleeps alone at last.*
> —Robert Benchley
> (on the death of a promiscuous actress)

3. **pesky critters** (pĕs´ kē)   Any critters that are pesky are annoying and troublesome. The word is a blend of pest + (ri)sky.

> *Never lend your car to anyone to whom you have given birth.*
> —Erma Bombeck

4. **pestiferous rogue** (pĕ stĭf´ ər əs)   Anything pestiferous is diseased, evil or simply mischievous. From Latin, *pestes* = a plague + *ferre* = to bear.

> *Disease is the retribution of outraged nature.*
> —Hosea Ballou

5. pettifogging mouthpiece (pĕt´ ē fŏg ing)　A pettifogger is a lawyer who handles petty cases using unethical methods; a cheater; a quibbler. From Middle Dutch, *voeger* = one who arranges things.

> *Two farmers each claimed to own a certain cow.*
> *While one pulled on its head and other pulled on its tail,*
> *the cow was milked by a lawyer.*
> —*Jewish parable*

6. pettish hen (pĕt´ ĭsh)　Originally pettish meant one was like a pet, that is, like a spoiled child. Now it means one cross and peevish. From French, *petit* = little, used as an endearment, *mon petit* = "my little one".

> **FAMOUS LAST LINES:**
> *Either they go, or I do.*
> —*Oscar Wilde,*
> *of his new bedroom curtains*

7. petulant snot (pĕch´ ə lənt)　One that is petulant is peevish, froward, and impatient. From Latin, *petulant* = impudent.

> *Keep your paws off. He's mine.*
> —*Amanda,*
> <u>*Melrose Place*</u>

8. two-timing <u>philanderer</u> (fĭ lăn´ dər ər)　To philander is to love insincerely, to flit from affair to affair especially when married. From Greek, *philos* = loving + *andros* = a man.

> *Never make the big pitch until the second date.*
> *If her eyes don't quite track, it's a sign of a sure kill.*
> —*international swordsman*

9. phlegmatic slug (flĕg măt´ ĭk)　Think of phlegm, snot! In medieval times it was believed that phlegm was one of the four humors that controlled the human personality. This one is sluggish and stolid.

> *When I feel like exercising I just lie down until the feeling goes away.*
> —*Robert M. Hutchins*

10. picayunish tightwad (pĭk´ ē yŭn´ ĭsh)　One who is picayunish is either worthless, or concerned with unimportant details. From French, *picaillan* = small change.

> <u>*Likely comment:*</u>
> *Gee. When our dinner bill is $1.29,*
> *how do we split the check evenly?*
>
> <u>*Your response:*</u>
> *Right between your eyes.*

Quiz 59

Match the definitions with the words on the left.

Brainy Barbs

__ 1. pertinacious
__ 2. perverse
__ 3. pesky
__ 4. pestiferous
__ 5. pettifogger
__ 6. pettish
__ 7. petulant
__ 8. philander
__ 9. phlegmatic
__10. picayune

a. annoying and troublesome
b. an unethical lawyer
c. peevish (fits two words)
d. diseased, evil or mischievous
e. like snot: sluggish and stolid
f. make love insincerely
g. of little value
h. stubborn to the end
i. deviate from what is right

Basic Barbs

__11. snot
__12. zealot
__13. mouthpiece
__14. rogue
__15. tightwad

j. fanatically committed person
k disrespectful, haughty person
l. a stingy person
m. rascal
n. slang term for a lawyer

Cry Me A River

(dejected, despondent, disconsolate, distraught,)
(dolorous, sullen, lachrymose, lugubrious, maudlin,)
(mawkish, melancholy, morose, saturnine)

Match.

1. d _ _ _ _ _ _ _ _ _ = upset
2. d _ _ _ _ _ _ _ _ _ _ _ = beyond any comfort
3. d _ _ _ _ _ _ _ _ _ _ = loss of courage or hope
4. d _ _ _ _ _ _ _ = in low spirits
5. s _ _ _ _ _ = morose; depressed
6. d _ _ _ _ _ _ _ = sad
7. s _ _ _ _ _ _ _ _ _ = sluggish, gloomy
8. m _ _ _ _ _ = sullen; gloomy
9. m _ _ _ _ _ _ _ _ _ = sad
10. m _ _ _ _ _ _ = foolishly sentimental
11. m _ _ _ _ _ h = false or feeble sentimentality; sickening
12. l _ _ _ _ _ _ _ _ _ _ = sad, especially in a ludicrous way
13. l _ _ _ _ _ _ _ _ _ = tearful

I've struggled whether or not to use any words that were synonymous with fat. Fat is a feminist issue. Women grow up inundated with images of emaciated models and it's no wonder that they end up hating their own bodies. Men as well (especially boys) are picked on for their size. On the other hand, this *is* vicious vocabulary. I've expurgated this book so as to offend the least amount of people possible. Hence, what I've done is include words that make fun of the shrimps as well. I simply offer up this paragraph to you as food for thought. Perhaps someday people will stop and think of how they treat the weight-challenged crowd.

Basic Barbs

➢ **autocrat** = one with unlimited power
➢ **beadle** = a minor official. From Old English, *bydel* = herald.
➢ **beadledom** = an officious, and stupid display of authority
➢ **partisan** = one devoted to one party
➢ **palooka** = a big clumsy dope, especially, an inept athlete
➢ **sponge** = slang, one who lives off others or soaks up the booze

Brainy Barbs

1. **pillaging pirate** (pĭl´ ĭj ing)   To pillage is to violently strip property or money from a victim. From Middle French, *pillar* = to rob.

> *Hitler is a monster of wickedness,*
> *insatiable in his lust for blood and plunder...*
> *So now this bloodthirsty guttersnipe*
> *must launch his mechanized armies*
> *upon new fields of slaughter, pillage and devastation.*
> —Winston Churchill

2. **pilfering pickpocket** (pĭl´ fər ing)   A pilfering person steals small items and usually steals habitually. From Middle French, *pelfre* = stolen goods.

> *He without benefit of scruples*
> *His fun and money soon quadruples*
> —Ogden Nash

3. **pinguid beadle** (pĭn´ gwĭd)   This is a fancy way to call someone fat. From Latin, *pinguis* = fat.

> *If you want to look young and thin, hang around old fat people.*
> —Jim Eason

4. piscine sponge (pĭsˊ īn) Literally, piscine means like or resembling a fish, but it has the connotation of someone who drinks booze like a fish drinks water. From Latin, *piscis* = fish.

I can't die until the government finds a safe place for my liver.
—Phil Harris

5. plagiarizing copycat (plāˊ jə rīˊ zing) To plagiarize is to take other's ideas and pass them off as one's own. From Latin, *plagiarius* = kidnaper.

A plagiarist should be made to copy the author a hundred times.
—Karl Kraus

6. pockmarked palooka (pŏkˊ märktˊ) To be pockmarked is to be scarred and pitted from pimples or small pox, etc. From Old English, *poc* = a pustule.

Now there's a face for radio.
—Paul Attanasio,
Quiz Show

7. useless pococurante (pō kō kū rănˊ tē) In Italian, a pococurante is indifferent, careless and can be used as an adjective or a noun. From Latin, *paucus* = few + *cura* = care.

He did nothing in particular, and did it very well.
—W. S. Gilbert

8. polemic partisan (pə lĕmˊ ĭk) Anyone polemic (or polemical) is either controversial or argumentative. From Greek, *polemos* = a war.

People generally quarrel because they cannot argue.
—G. K. Chesterton

9. gutless poltroon (pŏl trūnˊ) A poltroon is a contemptible coward! Chicken, that is. The word is a derivative of poultry. From Old Italian, *poltrone* = idler, coward, literally, one who lies in bed.

Among ten men nine are sure to be women.
—Turkish proverb

10. pompous autocrat (pŏmˊ pəs) A pompous person is full of self-importance, often expressing this by being overly serious or eloquent. From Greek, *pompe* = solemn procession.

Don't remind a vain man of his pimples.
—Russian proverb

Quiz 60

Match the definitions with the words on the left.

Brainy Barbs

__ 1. pillage
__ 2. pilfer
__ 3. pinguid
__ 4. piscine
__ 5. plagiarize
__ 6. pockmarked
__ 7. pococurante
__ 8. polemic
__ 9. poltroon
__10. pompous

a. a chicken or coward
b. controversial; argumentative
c. fat
d. full of self-importance
e. like or resembling a fish; drunk
f. steal
g. tardy, late
h. to be scarred from pimples
i. take another's ideas and pass them off as one's own
j. to violently strip property or money from a victim

Basic Barbs

__11. palooka
__12. sponge
__13. beadle
__14. beadledom
__15. partisan
__16. autocrat

k. one devoted to one party
l. a minor official
m. a stupid display of authority
n. slang, one who lives off others
o. an inept athlete
p. one with unlimited power

Lazy Good-For-Nothings, Part 1

(bootless, dawdle, dilatory, fainéant, indolent, lackadaisical,)
(laggard, languid, lassitude, procrastinate)

Match.

1. d _ _ _ _ _ = waste time
2. d _ _ _ _ _ _ _ = late, tardy
3. p _ _ _ _ _ _ _ _ _ _ _ = put off tasks until a later time
4. b _ _ _ _ _ _ _ = useless
5. f _ _ _ _ _ _ _ = lazy
6. i _ _ _ _ _ _ _ = disliking work, lazy
7. l _ _ _ _ _ _ = slowpoke, one falling behind
8. l _ _ _ _ _ _ _ _ _ _ _ = showing a lack of interest
9. l _ _ _ _ _ _ = weak; wanting in interest
10. l _ _ _ _ _ _ _ _ = weary in body and mind; lazy indifference

LE MOT QUOTE 35

Match each quote with the appropriate word.

1. Behind every argument is someone's ignorance.
   —Louis D. Brandeis

2. Borrowed thoughts, like borrowed money,
   only show the poverty of the borrower.
   —Lady Blessington

3. He that falls into sin is a man; that grieves at it,
   is a saint; that boasteth of it, is a devil. —Thomas Fuller

4. Violence is the last refuge of the incompetent.
   —Isaac Asimov

5. Women still remember the first kiss
   after men have forgotten the last.
   —Remy de Gourmont

__ a. oppugnant

__ b. peccable

__ c. philanderer

__ d. plagiarize

__ e. polemic

LE MOT QUOTE 36

Circle the word that best fits the quote.

Brimful of learning, see the pedant stride,
bristling with horrid Greek, and puffed with pride!
A thousand authors he in vain has read,
and with their maxims stuffed his empty head;
and thinks that without Aristotle's rules,
reason is blind, and common sense a fool!
—Boileau

a. uncouth   b. pedagogue   c. archaic

LE MOT QUOTE 37

Match each quote with the appropriate word.

1. Bureaucracy is a giant mechanism
   operated by pigmies. —Hoore De Balzac

2. Education: the inculcation of the incomprehensible
   into the indifferent by the incompetent.
   —John Maynard Keynes

3. Men are not punished for their sins, but by them.
   —Frank McKinney Hubbard

4. The best way to put an end to the bugs
   is to set fire to the bed. —Mexican proverb

5. Treachery, though at first very cautious,
   in the end betrays itself. —Livy

6. Woe unto them that call evil good, and good evil.
   —Isaiah 5:20

___ a. peccant
___ b. pedantic
___ c. perfidious
___ d. perverse
___ e. pestiferous
___ f. beadle

Chapter 13

When ideas fail, words come in very handy.

—Goethe

The "Review Peu" tests following the chapters help you test your retention of the material. Hopefully, the review has made you think on a deeper level. Some of the quotes are obvious and some are more oblique. Some are silly and some are scary. When you have to think about which quote matches which word, you are more likely to remember the word.

Basic Barbs

➤ **grouch** = one who is bad-tempered, in a foul mood
➤ **gump** = a foolish or dull person
➤ **jailbait** = a teen-aged girl under the age of consent with whom sexual intercourse is classified as statutory rape
➤ **peacock** = a bird: slang for a vain, strutting person
➤ **plodder** = one who moves or works laboriously
➤ **whippersnapper** = a young insignificant, pretentious person

Brainy Barbs

1. **ponderous plodder** (pŏn´ dər əs) Anything ponderous is heavy and bulky, or labored and dull. From Latin, *pondus* = a weight.

> *If the human being is condemned and restricted*
> *to perform the same functions over and over again,*
> *he will not even be a good ant,*
> *not to mention a good human being.*
> —Norbert Wiener

2. **pontificating bother** (pŏn tĭf´ ə kāt ing) To pontificate is to speak in a pompous and dogmatic style. From Latin, *pontifex* = pontiff (a pope or bishop) implying a pontiff is likely to be pompous and dogmatic.

> *A closed mouth gathers no feet.*
> —Unknown

3. **porcine fatso** (pôr´ sīn) Anything porcine is involving or resembling a pig. From Latin, *porcus* = a hog.

> *Outside every fat man there is an even fatter man trying to close in.*
> —Kingsley Amis

4. potvaliant gump (pŏt´ văl yənt)   A potvaliant dolt is brave because he/she is drunk. From English Slang, *potted* = drunk + *valiant* = brave.

> *They were red-hot with drinking,*
> *so full of valor that they smote the air.*
> —Shakespeare

5. preadamic caveman (prē´ ə dăm´ ĭk)   To be preadamic is to have existed before Adam. It also refers to those who believe man existed before Adam. It is formed from the prefix pre + Adam + ic.

> *A man is as old as the woman he feels.*
> —Groucho Marx

6. precipitous grouch (prĭ sĭp´ ĭ təs)   Precipitous indicates something that is steep, but it can also insinuate someone is headlong in disposition, ala Yosemite Sam. From Latin, *praeceps* = headlong.

> *I'm not crazy. I've just been in a very bad mood for forty years.*
> —Robert Harling,
> Steel Magnolias

7. precocious jailbait (prĭ kō shəs)   A precocious person is more developed, the behavior more mature than is anticipated at a particular age. From Latin, *praecoci* = early ripe.

> *Men aren't attracted to me by my mind, but what I don't mind.*
> —Gypsy Rose Lee

8. predatory savage (prĕd´ ə tôr´ ē)   This savage lives by exploiting, plundering, or robbing others. From Latin, *praedari* = to plunder.

> *Don't jump on a man unless he's down.*
> —Finley Peter Dunne

9. preening peacock (prēn´ ing)   To preen is to trim one's feathers, adorn oneself; or to vainly adorn oneself. From Medieval English, *preonen* = prick with a pin.

> *The smaller the mind, the greater the conceit.*
> —Aesop

10. presumptuous whippersnappers (prĭ zŭmp´ chū əs)   Anyone presumptuous takes too much for granted. From Latin, *praesumere* = to undertake beforehand.

> *No young man believes he will ever die.*
> —Hazlitt

Quiz 61

Match the definitions with the words on the left.

Brainy Barbs

__ 1. ponderous   a. brave because one is drunk
__ 2. pontificate   b. exploiting, plundering
__ 3. porcine   c. bulky, or labored and dull
__ 4. potvaliant   d. of or like a pig
__ 5. preadamic   e. old; existed before Adam.
__ 6. precipitous   f. pompous and dogmatic
__ 7. precocious   g. premature
__ 8. predatory   h. steep; headlong in disposition
__ 9. preen   i. takes too much for granted
__10. presumptuous   j. to trim one's feathers,
                                   ;or to vainly adorn oneself

Basic Barbs

__11. whipper snapper   k. a foolish or dull person
__12. peacock   l. an underaged teen-aged girl
__13. jailbait   m. a vain, strutting person, slang
__14. grouch   n. a young pretentious person
__15. gump   o. move or work laboriously
__16. plod   p. a bad-tempered person

Lazy Good-For-Nothings, Part 2

(boondoggle, lethargic, slothful, listless, torpid, malinger,)
(phlegmatic, sedentary, stagnant, otiose)

Unscramble.

1. gicalther = slow, tired, dull   _____
2. lessilt = spiritless, lack of interest   _____
3. limanger = fake illness to get out of work   _____
4. plemathigc = sluggish, stolid   _____
5. desenarty = not moving, always sitting   _____
6. tpdori = sluggish and apathetic   _____
7. hfulstol = lazy, slow   _____
8. stanngat = not moving; foul from not moving;
              sluggish   _____
9. gooneldbog = do inane work to look busy   _____
10. seoito = lazy, useless   _____

Grisly List 62

I've given a great deal of emphasis to the Brainy Barbs in this book without really saying much about the words listed in the Basic Barb list. However, that doesn't mean that they are without merit. Sure, they may not be on your SAT or GRE list, but sprinkling them into your speech can salt up your lexicon. There may be a word in the basic list that you knew but prior to this book you never would have used. After you finish this book, take some time to review the basic lists in the book.

Basic Barbs

➣ **diva** = the lead singer in an opera; a self-inflated, egotistical person who is difficult and peevish

➣ **Gestapo** = the secret police force of Nazi Germany, infamous for its ruthlessness

➣ **grifter** = one who operates a sideshow at a fair or a circus; in slang, a conman, swindler

➣ **idler** = one who is inactive or lazy

➣ **wisenheimer** = a smart aleck, the word is a combination of wise and enheimer which is often the ending to many German family names, e.g. *Oppenheimer, Altenheimer.*

Brainy Barbs

1. **pretentious diva** (prĭ těn´ shəs) This stuck-up snob thinks and acts affectedly superior. From Middle Latin, *praetensus* = alleged.

> *An ounce of pretension is worth a pound of manure.*
> —Steven E. Clark

2. **prevaricating grifter** (prĭ văr´ ĭ kāt ing) A prevaricator is a liar, one who evades the truth. Don't believe a word this creep says. Liar, liar, pants on fire. From Latin, *praevaricatus* = to walk crooked.

> *The masses will more easily fall victim to a big lie than to a small one.*
> —Adolf Hitler

3. **priapic yutz** (prī ăp´ ĭk) Anyone priapic is overly concerned with virility, manliness. From Greek, *priapizein* = to be lewd < *Priapus*, the god of male reproduction.

> *In the past, it was easy to be a Real Man,*
> *All you had to do was abuse women,*
> *steal land from Indians,*
> *and find some place to dump the toxic waste.*
> —Bruce Fierstein

4. primordial slime (prī môr dē əl) A primordial person, out of the depths of time, existed from the very beginning; this one is primitive and original. From Latin, *primus* = first + *ordiri* = to begin.

You remind me of my brother Bosco—only he had a human head.
—Judy Tenuta

5. procrastinating idler (prō krǎs′ tə nāt′ ing) This one puts off doing something. From Latin, *pro* = ahead + *crastinus* = belonging to tomorrow.

If it weren't for the last minute, nothing would get done.
—Unknown

6. Procrustean Gestapo (prō krŭs′ tē ən) In Greek mythology, the giant, Procrustes, would stretch or amputate limbs of his victims so that they would fit his bed. Now it depicts one who ruthlessly forces control.

And if the population should treat us with indignation,
we chop 'em to bits because we like our hamburgers raw.
—Bertolt Brecht

7. prodigal squanderer (prŏd′ ə gəl) The adjective refers to one who is wasteful or extravagantly wild. The noun denotes one who squanders his or her parent's money. From Latin, *prodigere* = to drive away, waste.

He's got a wonderful head for money. There's a long slit on the top.
—David Frost

8. profane menace (prō fān′) Anyone profane shows disrespect for sacred things. From Latin, *profanare* = to desecrate.

With devotion visage, and pious action
we do sugar o'er the devil himself.
—Shakespeare

9. reckless profligate (prŏf′ lə gĭt, gāt) A profligate is given to drink, sex, gambling etc. with such abandon career and marriage suffer. From Latin, *profligare* = to strike to the ground.

A woman drove me to drink
and I never had the courtesy to thank her.
—W.C. Fields.

10. proleptic wisenheimer (prō lĕp′ tĭk) This one anticipates your argument so as to answer back before you've had a chance to respond. From Greek, *prolepsis* = anticipation < *pro* = forward + *lepsis* = to take.

The opposite of talking isn't listening.
The opposite of talking is waiting.
—Fran Lebowitz

Quiz 62

Match the definitions with the words on the left.

Brainy Barbs

___ 1. pretentious   a. act affectedly superior
___ 2. prevaricate   b. anticipate another's argument
___ 3. priapic   c. existing from the beginning
___ 4. primordial   d. given to drink, sex, gambling
                                            with abandon
___ 5. procrastinate   e. overly concerned with virility
___ 6. Procrustean   f. ruthlessly forcing control
___ 7. prodigal   g. disrespectful for sacred things
___ 8. profane   h. to lie, to evade the truth
___ 9. profligate   i. to put off till tomorrow
___10. proleptic   j. wasteful

Basic Barbs

___11. idler   k. a smart aleck
___12. Gestapo   l. one who is inactive or lazy
___13. wisenheimer   m. ruthless secret police force
___14. grifter   n. in slang, a conman, swindler

Lazy Good-For-Nothings, Part 3

(cunctative, drone, goldbricker, idler, loafer, lollygag,)
(oscitant, sloth, slouch, slugabed, sluggard, soporific)

Match.

1. s _ _ _ _ _ _ _ _ = inducing sleep
2. o _ _ _ _ _ _ _ = drowsy, dull
3. g _ _ _ _ _ _ _ _ _ _ = tries to avoid work
4. c _ _ _ _ _ _ _ _ _ = procrastinating
5. i _ _ _ _ = one who is inactive or lazy
6. s _ _ _ _ = a lazy person
7. d _ _ _ _ = a male bee without a sting; any loafer
8. s _ _ _ _ _ _ _ = one who lazily stays in bed
9. s _ _ _ _ _ _ _ = a habitually lazy person
10. s _ _ _ _ _ = an inept, awkward, lazy person
11. l _ _ _ _ _ _ _ = to waste time
12. l _ _ _ _ _ = one who dawdles, wasting time

Grisly List 63

I've encouraged some of you to casually browse through this book, and I've encouraged others to precipitously fling themselves on the material like a rapacious wolf on some hapless sheep. Both are fine. However, what if you don't fit in either camp? You started out dogged and determined but have fizzled out erratic and aimless. That's fine as well. I won't be grading your tests when you finish this book. You will benefit from this verbiage nonetheless. If you are the erratic type, don't feel guilty. Simply use it to your best advantage. When the inspiration comes to go through the text, go through the text. When you feel like setting it down, set it down.

Basic Barbs

> **guttersnipe** = one belonging to the lowest social group in a city, sometimes used for homeless kids, sometimes for filth peddlers
> **Philistine** = a narrow-minded person, devoid of culture, indifferent to art
> **prattler** = one who talks in a childish way

Brainy Barbs

1. **prolix prattler** (prō lĭks´)   This prattler is just exasperatingly wordy. From Latin, *prolixus* = extended.

> *A chattering fool comes to ruin.*
> —Proverbs 10: 8

2. **prosaic scribbler** (prō zā´ ĭk)   Dull! Dull! Dull! This one's writing is like prose and hence, lacking the imagination of poetry. From Latin, *prosa* = straightforward (speech).

> *The Home Beautiful... is a play lousy.*
> —Dorothy Parker

3. **prosy piece of twaddle** (prō´ zē)   Anything prosy is so dull, so tedious because it resembles prose—not poetry. From Latin, *prosa* = straightforward (speech).

> *Some people stay longer in an hour than others do in a month.*
> —William Dean Howells

4. **provincial Philistine** (prə vĭn´ shəl)   This one is rustic, narrow-minded, unsophisticated and uninformed. From Latin, *provincia* = province.

> *Some fellers get credit for being conservative when they're only stupid.*
> —Kin Hubbard

5. **prurient rodent** (prŏŏr´ ē ənt) A prurient person is excessively lustful, lascivious, constantly yearning for sex. From Latin, *prurire* = to itch.

> There is nothing a young man can get by wenching
> but duels, the clap and bastards.
> —Kathleen Winsor

6. **two-faced pseudologist** (sū dŏ´ lō jĭst) A pseudologist is the ultimate craftsman of the big lie. From Greek, *pseudes* = false = *logos* = word, speech.

> There's one way to find out if a man is honest:
> ask him; if he says yes, you know he is crooked.
> —Mark Twain

7. **puckish pain in the neck** (pŭk´ ish) Watch out! This pain is mischievous, likely to set your alarm for three in the morning and hide it under your bed. Puck is a mischievous spirit. From Old Norse, *puki* = a devil or a mischievous demon.

> He that mischief hatcheth,
> mischief catcheth.
> —William Camden

8. **puerile guttersnipe** (pyū´ ər ĭl) This juvenile acts silly, immature and childish. In psychology, puerile is used as a noun to describe people who are self-absorbed. From Latin, *puerilis* = boyish.

> Boys will be boys, and so will a lot middle-aged men.
> —Kin Hubbard

9. **pugilistic blockhead** (pyū´ jə lĭs´ tĭk) A pugilist is a professional boxer, or anyone who likes to fistfight; hence, anyone pugilistic likes to box or fight. From Latin, *pugil* = boxer.

> Make yourself at home, Frank. Hit somebody.
> —Don Rickles,
> to Frank Sinatra

10. **pugnacious scrapper** (pŭg nā´ shəs) Anyone pugnacious is belligerent, prone to fight or quarrel. From Latin, *pugnacitas* = combativeness.

> My kid beat up your honor student.
> —bumper sticker

Quiz 63

Match the definitions with the words on the left.

Brainy Barbs

___ 1. prolix
___ 2. prosaic
___ 3. prosy
___ 4. provincial
___ 5. prurient
___ 6. pseudologist
___ 7. puckish
___ 8. puerile
___ 9. pugilist
___10. pugnacious

a. a professional boxer
b. dull (fits two words)
c. like to fight or quarrel
d. lustful
e. mischievous
f. one who lies
g. rustic, narrow-minded
h. silly, immature and childish
i. too wordy

Basic Barbs

___11. guttersnipe
___12. Philistine

___13. prattle

j. a narrow-minded person
k. one belonging to the lowest social group in a city
l. to talk in a childish way

A Little Too Tight, Part 1

(pedagogue, pedantic, picayunish, priggish, bureaucrat, Lilliputian,)
(pedant, ethnocentric, prig, schoolmarm, tendentious)

Match.

1. l _ _ _ _ _ _ _ _ _ _ = small-minded
2. p _ _ _ _ _ = a teacher who stresses the trivial points in learning
3. p _ _ _ _ _ _ _ = stressing the trivial points of learning
4. p _ _ _ _ _ _ _ _ = a pedantic teacher
5. p _ _ _ _ _ _ _ _ _ = worthless; concerned with trivial matters
6. p _ _ _ _ _ _ _ = annoyingly pedantic, overly prim and proper
7. b _ _ _ _ _ _ _ _ _ = an official who follows a routine pedantically

8. dententious = overly opinionated _____
9. thenorcentic = stuck in one's own cultural prejudices _____
10. shorcolmam = a female schoolteacher, or anyone old-fashioned _____
11. girp = a person who is overly precise and haughty in following rules _____

Grisly List 64

The beauty of words like pulchritudinous and doughty is that even when others know what those words mean, they still don't know what you mean. One word means beautiful and the other means brave. But when used they both come off so overblown that it could be an insult or a compliment. No one will know for sure. Now why is that important? Well, the gift of gab is not only to make things clear but it is also to make things obscure—when one wants to be obscure.

Basic Barbs

➢ **automaton** = a lifeless machine, like a robot. From Greek, *automatos* = self-moving
➢ **intelligentsia** = intellectuals, the educated class
➢ **misandrist** = one who hates men
➢ **pedant** = a teacher who stresses the trivial points in learning
➢ **tripe** = part of the stomach; anything worthless or offensive

Brainy Barbs

1. **pulchritudinous babe** (pŭl´ krĭ tūd´ ĭ nəs) In the strict sense of the word, the definition of pulchritudinous is beautiful, but it is now often used in jest, meaning just the opposite. From Latin, *pulcher* = beautiful.

Beauty is only sin deep.
—Saki

2. **punctilious pedant** (pŭngk tĭl´ ē əs) A punctilious person is overly exacting in observing rules; you get the feeling this pedant has his clock wound a little too tight. From Latin, *punctillum* = a little point.

TOMBSTONE EPITAPH:
Tried to control things a little too tightly
When renal failure caused a death unsightly

3. **purblind automaton** (pûr´ blīnd) This one lacks vision, insight, and/or intelligence. From Medieval English, *pur blind* = completely blind.

Where all think alike, no one thinks very much.
—Walter Lippman

4. **purloining shoplifter** (pər loin´ ing) To purloin is to steal but it can have the added connotation of breaking faith in the act of stealing. From Old French, *purloigner* = remove < from Latin, *longus* = to put far off; hence, purloin developed the sense to make off with.

Opportunity makes the thief.
—English proverb

5. **pusillanimous cream puff** (pyŏŏ´ sə lăn' ə məs)   A pusillanimous person is a coward. From Latin, *pusillus* = tiny, + *animus* = the mind, courage.

> *It is better to die on your feet than live on your knees.*
> —Talmud

6. **putrid pile of tripe** (pyū´ trĭd)   Anyone putrid is rotten and reeking an odor of decay or it can signify something is corrupt and disgustingly bad. From Latin, *putris* = rotten.

> *She's like a rose to me. It smells and so does she.*
> —Homer Haynes

7. **quailing coward** (kwāl´ ing)   To quail is to draw back in fear. From Medieval English, *quail* = to fail, the modern sense of shrink or cower is probably because of the bird by the same name.

> *It is easy to frighten a bull from the window.*
> —Italian proverb

8. **quasi-intelligentsia** (kwā´ zī, or kwŏ´ zī)   Anything quasi isn't real or true. It is often combined with a noun using a hyphen; for example, a quasi-academic, a quasi-hero. From Latin, *quasi* = as if.

> *Everyone agreed that Clevinger was certain*
> *to go far in the academic world.*
> *In short, Clevinger was one of those people*
> *with lots of intelligence and no brains,*
> *and everyone knew it except*
> *those who soon found it out.*
> *In short, he was a dope.*
> —Joseph Heller,
> Catch 22

9. **quavering crybaby** (kwā´ vər ing)   To quaver is to tremble from fear or anxiety or it can describe one who speaks in a trembling voice. From Medieval English, *cwafien* = to tremble. It may also be a blend of quake and waver.

> *Cowards die many times before their deaths;*
> *the valiant never taste death but once.*
> —Shakespeare,
> Julius Caesar

10. **querulous misandrist** (kwer´ ə ləs)   To be querulous is to be complaining and faultfinding. From Latin, *queri* = to complain.

> *Clean your finger before you point your finger at my spots.*
> —Benjamin Franklin

Quiz 64

Match the definitions with the words on the left.

Brainy Barbs

___ 1. pulchritudinous   a. beautiful, often used in jest
___ 2. punctilious   b. complaining and faultfinding
___ 3. purblind   c. cowardly
___ 4. purloin   d. lacking vision, intelligence
___ 5. pusillanimous   e. overly tough in keeping rules
___ 6. putrid   f. not real or true
___ 7. quail   g. rotten, or disgustingly bad
___ 8. quasi   h. steal
___ 9. quaver   i. to draw back in fear
___10. querulous   j. tremble

Basic Barbs

___11. intelligentsia   k. a lifeless machine
___12. tripe   l. stresses minor points in learning
___13. misandrist   m. one who hates men
___14. pedant   n. intellectuals, the learned class
___15. automaton   o. part of the stomach

A Little Too Tight, Part 2

(constrict, fastidious, obstipated, didactic, prude, sectarian, inculcate,)
(bluenose, functionary, dogmatic, punctilious, persnickety, doctrinaire)

Match.

1. p _ _ _ _ _ _ _ _ _ _ = very exacting in observing rules
2. f _ _ _ _ _ _ _ _ _ = not easy to please; too refined, too neat
3. p _ _ _ _ = one overly modest or proper
4. s _ _ _ _ _ _ _ _ = narrow-minded
5. o _ _ _ _ _ _ _ _ _ = obstinately constipated
6. c _ _ _ _ _ _ _ _ = make smaller by squeezing
7. b _ _ _ _ _ _ _ = a puritanical person, a prude
8. d _ _ _ _ _ _ _ = inclined to state their opinion in an arrogant way
9. d _ _ _ _ _ _ _ _ _ _ = holding to a belief system in an
                           unyielding, dogmatic way
10. p _ _ _ _ _ _ _ _ _ _ = too precise, fussy
11. d _ _ _ _ _ _ _ = intended to teach morals; too inclined to teach
12. i _ _ _ _ _ _ _ _ = teach by frequent repetition
13. f _ _ _ _ _ _ _ _ _ _ = an official; bureaucrat

If you're a writer then you might want to look at this book in another light. Why not write a character that uses a certain arcane verbiage? Often in plays, novels or films a character is differentiated by his/her speech. It fits then that one might want to write a character that pontificates using just this kind of vitriolic vocabulary. If you are not a writer then try playing with it. Write a short dialogue between two characters: one an idiot, and another whose vocabulary is difficult to understand.

Basic Barbs

➢ **blubbermouth** = a crybaby
➢ **cagey** = sly, careful not to get caught
➢ **eavesdrop** = to stand on the eavesdrop (just outside the house) and listen to gossip; anytime one listens to gossip
➢ **heel** = a jerk
➢ **luddite** = Ned Ludd, an 18th-century worker, argued machines were taking away jobs from workers. Luddites were workers who destroyed machines that were taking away their jobs.
➢ **riffraff** = worthless, disreputable persons

Brainy Barbs

1. **cagey quibbler** (kwĭb´ lər) This sneak always evades the main point by emphasizing some petty detail. From Latin, *quibus* = to whom, as in, to whom it may concern; this word was common in legal documents.

> *Be these juggling fiends no more believed,*
> *that palter with us in a double sense,*
> *that keep the word of promise to our ear,*
> *and break it to our hope.*
> *—Shakespeare*

2. **eavesdropping quidnunc** (kwĭd´ nŭngk) This one is a gossip or nosy. From Latin, *quid nunc* = what now?

> *Gossip is vice enjoyed vicariously.*
> *—Elbert Hubbard*

3. **deceitful quisling** (kwĭz´ ling) Vidkun Quisling was a Norwegian politician who betrayed his country to the Nazis, and in exchange became a puppet dictator. To call someone a quisling is to call him a traitor of the most despicable sort.

> *Treachery lurks in honeyed words.*
> *—Danish proverb*

4. **quivering blubbermouth** (kwĭv´ ər ing) This trembling geek needs a backbone. From Medieval Danish, *quiveren* = to tremble.

Coward: One who in a perilous emergency thinks with his legs.
—*Ambrose Bierce*

5. **quixotic knight** (kwĭk sŏt´ ĭk) This one is extravagantly chivalrous, impractical. From the fictitious character, Don Quixote, who fought imaginary dragons for damsels of questionable virtue.

He would have killed the deadly dragon
If it hadn't been a Chevy wagon

6. **Rabelaisian rascal** (răb´ ə lā zē ən) Rabelais (1490?-1553) was French satirist and humorist who favored coarse, vulgar humor. Anyone Rabelaisian is given to vulgar tastes.

I drink no more than a sponge. —*Rabelais*

7. **rabid luddite** (răb´ ĭd) Anyone rabid has rabies or is acting as if they are affected by rabies, a disease which causes madness. Foaming at the mouth, this mongrel rampages about out of control. From Latin, *rabidus* = raving, furious < *rabere* = to be madness.

Whom the gods wish to destroy they first make mad.
—*Sophocles*

8. **raffish heel** (răf´ ĭsh) This heel is rakish and vulgar. From Old French, *rif et raf* = every scrape.

Ooooh. Ahhhh. Get out.
—*Andrew Dice Clay's impression of a one-night stand*

9. **rakish wolf** (rā´ kĭsh) A rake is a Lothario, a Romeo, a Don Juan, a womanizer. Lacking moral restraint, anyone rakish preys upon gullible, weak-minded women. From Middle English, *rakel* = rash, wild.

My mother-in-law broke up my marriage.
One day my wife came home early from work
and found us in bed together.
—*Lenny Bruce*

10. **rambunctious riffraff** (răm bŭnk´ shəs) This wild bunch is wildly rough, difficult to control and noisy. The word is a blend of ram + bumptious. Check Chapter 12 for a description of bumptious.

We had to play taps
When the frat floor collapsed

Quiz 65

Match the definitions with the words on the left.

Brainy Barbs

__ 1. quibble   a. affected by rabies, raving
__ 2. quidnunc   b. a gossip
__ 3. quisling   c. a traitor
__ 4. quiver   d. evade the main point
                               by stressing some petty detail
__ 5. quixotic   e. extravagantly chivalrous
__ 6. Rabelaisian   f. given to vulgar tastes
__ 7. rabid   g. lacking moral restraint
__ 8. raffish   h. rakish and vulgar
__ 9. rakish   i. tremble
__10. rambunctious   j. wildly rough, hard to control

Basic Barbs

__11. cagey   k. a cry baby
__12. eavesdrop   l. a jerk, slang
__13. blubbermouth   m. sly, careful not to get caught
__14. heel   n. to listen to gossip
__15. riffraff   o. irrelevant, scandalous people
__16. luddite   p. thinks that machines
                               take away jobs from workers

Countrified

(agrestic, Boeotian, boor, bumpkin, churl,)
(galoot, hick, Philistine, rube, yahoo, provincial)

Match.

1. P _ _ _ _ _ _ _ _ _ = a narrow-minded person devoid of culture
2. a _ _ _ _ _ _ _ = rustic, crude
3. b _ _ _ _ _ _ = a country idiot
4. h _ _ _ = a country idiot
5. y _ _ _ _ = a country idiot
6. g _ _ _ _ _ = an uncouth, clumsy idiot
7. B _ _ _ _ _ _ _ _ = one without cultural refinement
8. r _ _ _ = a country idiot
9. b _ _ _ = a rude, clownish peasant
10. c _ _ _ _ = a peasant, an ill-bred person
11. p _ _ _ _ _ _ _ _ _ = like a province, rustic

LE MOT QUOTE 38

Match each quote with the appropriate word.

1. Fear has the largest eyes of all. —Boris Pasternak

2. The soul of this man is in his clothes. —Shakespeare

3. What he says he doesn't mean,
   and what he means he doesn't say.
   —Jewish proverb

4. Macho doesn't necessarily mean mucho.
   —Zsa Zsa Gabor

   __ a. preen
   __ b. prevaricate
   __ c. quaver
   __ d. priapic

LE MOT QUOTE 39

Match each quote with the appropriate word.

1. To a toad, what is beauty?
   A female with two pop eyes, a wide mouth,
   yellow belly, and spotted back. —Voltaire

2. For virtue's self may too much zeal be had;
   the worst of madness is a saint run mad. —Pope

3. What lies lurk in kisses. —Heinrich Heine

4. A faultfinder complains even
   that the bride is too pretty.
   —Yiddish proverb

   __ a. pseudologist
   __ b. pulchritudinous
   __ c. querulous
   __ d. Quixotic

LE MOT QUOTE 40

Circle the word that best matches the quote.

Punctuality is the virtue of the bored. —Evelyn Waugh

a. quaver   b. priapic   c. punctilious

LE MOT QUOTE 41

Match each quote with the appropriate word.

1. Every murderer is probably somebody's old friend.
   —Agatha Christie

2. The way to be nothing is to do nothing. —Howe

3. While pondering when to begin
   it becomes too late to do. —Quintillian

_ a. nonentity
_ b. mortiferous
_ c. procrastinate

Chapter 14

Ill deeds are doubled with an evil word.
—Shakespeare

Grisly List 66

Scattered throughout this book is an occasional foreign word or two. You'll find them in unabridged dictionaries, but they still are really just a borrowed word. If you really want to sound erudite and elite try saying them with the proper accent and people will think you're some grand pedant. With the French word "arriviste" ask the next Frenchman you meet how to pronounce it and practice until it comes effortlessly out your tongue.

Basic Barbs

➤ **arriviste** (ar´ rē vēst´) = one who has recently acquired wealth by unscrupulous means; from French, "one who has just arrived"
➤ **addlebrained** = confused, illogical
➤ **doggery** = rabble, riffraff
➤ **delinquent** = failing to do one's duty; a young troublemaker
➤ **reactionary** = reacts to political change by going in the opposite direction, an extreme conservative
➤ **scalawag** = a rascal or scoundrel

Brainy Barbs

1. **rampageous doggery** (răm pā´ jəs) A rampageous person is on a rampage; this one is characterized by raging behavior, violently rushing about. From Frank, *rampon* = to creep or crawl < Germanic, *rampa* = a claw.

> The public is a ferocious beast:
> one must either chain it up or flee from it.
> —Voltaire

2. **rank beginner** (rangk) Don't confuse this with the noun rank, as in "He moved up in rank". It's far more interesting when you use it as an adjective, as in "He's a rank beginner." It can mean stinking, flagrant, absolute or growing excessively. From Icelandic, *rakkr* = straight, bold.

> Nobody will use other people's experience,
> nor has any of his own till it is too late to use it.
> —Hawthorne

3. **ranting reactionary** (rănt´ ing) One can only take so much screaming. This one screams and raves. From Dutch, *ranten* = to rave.

A cowardly cur barks more fiercely than it bites.
—*Quintus Curtius Rufus*

4. **rapacious arriviste** (rə pā´ shəs) This is one more plundering, greedy bloodsucker. From Latin, *rapere* = to seize.

Avarice is the sphincter of the heart. —*Matthew Green*

5. **raucous meatball** (rô´ kəs) This one is either loud and rowdy, or harsh and strident. From Indo-European, *reu-* = to give hoarse cries.

*You know your party is out of control
when people you don't even know ask you how the shower works.*
—*Buddy Baron*

6. **rebarbative tough** (rē bär´ bə tĭv) One who is rebarbative is repellent, irritating and/or unattractive. From Middle French, *rebarber* = "to face beard to beard" implying resisting the enemy.

Better an ugly face than an ugly mind. —*James Ellis*

7. **recalcitrant brat** (rĭ kăl´ sĭ trənt) This one obstinately resists authority and will not comply. From Latin, *recalcitrare* = to kick back.

*Students today are tyrants. They contradict their parents,
gobble their food, and tyrannize their teachers.*
—*Socrates*

8. **recidivistic delinquent** (rĭ sĭd´ ə vĭs´ tĭk) This one habitually relapses into former criminal or antisocial behavior. From Latin, *recidiv* = relapse.

As the dog returns to his vomit so a fool repeats his own folly.
—*Proverbs 26: 11*

9. **addlebrained recluse** (rĕk´ lūs) A recluse prefers to be alone, shut away from the rest of the world. From Latin, *recludere* = to shut up.

*Happiness is having a large, loving, caring,
close-knit family in another city.*
—*George Burns*

10. **recreant scalawag** (rĕk´ rē ənt) This one is a coward and/or a traitor. From Old French, *recreare* = to give in in a competition.

*Thou kill'd him sleeping. O brave touch!
Could not a worm, an adder, do so much?*
—*Shakespeare,
A Midsummer Night's Dream*

Quiz 66

Match the definitions with the words on the left.

Brainy Barbs

__ 1. rampage
__ 2. rank
__ 3. rant
__ 4. rapacious
__ 5. raucous
__ 6. rebarbative
__ 7. recalcitrant
__ 8. recidivistic
__ 9. recluse
__10. recreant

a. cowardly and disloyal
b. habitually relapse into former criminal behavior
c. loud and rowdy; or harsh
d. one who prefers to be alone
e. not complying
f. plundering, greedy
g. repellent, irritating and/or unattractive
h. stinking, flagrant, absolute
i. to scream, to rave
j. to violently rush about

Basic Barbs

__11. addlebrained
__12. delinquent
__13. arriviste
__14. reactionary

__15. doggery

k. a young troublemaker
l. an extreme conservative
m. confused, illogical
n. one who has newly acquired wealth by unscrupulous means
o. rabble, riffraff

Out There

(abominable, abysmal, blatant, categorical, flagrant,)
(unmitigated, arrant, rank, infamous, notorious)

Match.

1. b _ _ _ _ _ _ = offensively noisy; conspicuous
2. c _ _ _ _ _ _ _ _ _ _ = without qualifications, absolute
3. a _ _ _ _ _ = absolute, out and out
4. a _ _ _ _ _ _ = bottomless; wretched
5. f _ _ _ _ _ _ _ = glaringly bad
6. r _ _ _ = (one of many definitions) stinking, flagrant
7. a _ _ _ _ _ _ _ _ _ _ = nasty and disgusting
8. u _ _ _ _ _ _ _ _ _ _ = absolute, not lessened
9. n _ _ _ _ _ _ _ _ = famous for being bad
10. i _ _ _ _ _ _ _ = famous for being bad

In Chapter 65 I suggested you write a character whose speech is filled with the kind of vocabulary you can find in this book, but I have a further and maybe better suggestion. Try writing a character that personifies a particular word. Many great writers fill their novels with this kind of subtext. Obsequious, drudge, remorseless, vindictive: when you think of the famous characters in many classic books, don't these words come to mind?

Basic Barbs

➤ **disputant** = one who disputes, debater
➤ **hack** = one hired to do routine, dull writing
➤ **misfit** = one maladjusted and/or disturbingly different
➤ **tyke** = a small child
➤ **valetudinarian** = one who is excessively concerned about health
➤ **racketeer** = one who obtains money illegally, chiefly by bootlegging or extortion.
➤ **renegade** = one who abandons his religion for another, or abandons his party, movement and joins the other side; a traitor

Brainy Barbs

1. **recriminating disputant** (rĭ krĭm´ ə nāt´ ing)   To criminate is to accuse another of a crime. To recriminate is to make counter accusations when confronted with someone accusing you. From Latin, *re* = again, anew + *crimen* = offense.

> *One false knave accuses another.*
> > —*English proverb*

2. **redundant hack** (rĭ dŭn´ dənt)   To be redundant is to use more words than are needed, or to needlessly repeat something. From Latin, *redundare* = to overflow; hence, to be in excess.

> *That which is repeated too often becomes insipid and tedious.*
> > —*Boileau-Despreaux*

3. **refractory misfit** (rĭ frăk´ tə rē)   This misfit is hard to control and stubborn as a mule. From Latin, *refringere* = to turn aside.

> *Obstinacy and vehemency in opinion*
> *are the surest signs of stupidity.*
> > —*Bernard Burton*

4. remorseless racketeer (rǐ môrs´ lǐs)   This one has no conscience, no mercy, no pity. From Latin, *remordere* = to bite again, the connotation being that a conscience bites afterwards + less.

If your beard were on fire, he'd light his cigarette on it.
—Armenian proverb

5. reneging scam-artist (rǐ nǐg´ ing)   To renege is to make a promises, but then back out. From Latin, *re* = again + *negare* = to deny.

Break the deal; face the wheel.
—Tina Turner
from the movie, <u>Thunderdome</u>

6. repining valetudinarian (rǐ pīn´ ing)   To repine is to fret, complain, or be fretfully discontented. From Old English, re + *pinian* = to torment.

I broke-up with my psychiatrist. I told him I had suicidal tendencies.
He told me from now on I had to pay in advance.
—Rodney Dangerfield

7. reprehensible renegade (rĕp´ rǐ hĕn´ sə bəl)   A reprehensible person is worthy of blame. From Latin, *reprehendere* = to hold back, restrain.

The more I see of my representatives the more I admire my dogs.
—Alphonse de Lamartine

8. lowdown <u>reprobate</u> (rĕp´ rə bāt´)   A reprobate person is one who is rejected by God, a scoundrel. From Latin, *reprobatus* = disapproved, rejected.

God bears with the wicked, but not forever.
—Cervantes,
<u>Don Quixote</u>

9. repugnant pimpleface (rǐ pŭg´ nənt)   Repugnant can mean inconsistent or to offer up resistance; but now it seems far more common for it to refer to something as distasteful and offensive. From Latin, *re* = back + *pugnare* = to fight.

I never forget a face but in your case I'll be glad to make an exception.
—Groucho Marx

10. restive tyke (rĕs´ tǐv)   Restive has several meanings: to refuse to go forward; to be unruly; or to be restless, fidgeting. From Latin, *restive* = to stop, stand, rest.

Never raise your hands to your kids. It leaves your groin unprotected.
—Red Buttons

Quiz 67

Match the definitions with the words on the left.

Brainy Barbs

__ 1. recriminate   a. back out of a promise
__ 2. redundant   b. distasteful and offensive
__ 3. refractory   c. hard to control and stubborn
__ 4. remorseless   d. repeating the same thought
__ 5. renege   e. rejected by God, a scoundrel
__ 6. repine   f. to be unruly; or to be restless
__ 7. reprehensible   g. to fret, be fretfully unhappy
__ 8. reprobate   h. to make counter accusations
__ 9. repugnant   i. without mercy or pity
__10. restive   j. worthy of blame

Basic Barbs

__11. tyke   k. a small child
__12. valetudinarian   l. one who disputes, argues
__13. disputant   m. obtains money illegally,
                       esp. by bootlegging, extortion
__14. racketeer   n. hired to do routine, dull writing
__15. renegade   o. a traitor
__16. hack   p. overly fretful about health

They're Coming To Take Me Away, Ha Ha

(irrational, confabulate, deranged, pathological, demented, daft,)
(bedlamite, lunatic, psychopath, maniac, paranoid)

Unscramble.

1. fanocbutale = chat; replace fact with fantasy   _____
2. medented = insane   _____
3. radenged = insane   _____
4. ratrilaion = lacking reason   _____
5. thopalogalic = compulsive   _____
6. rapanodi = overly suspicious
             or has delusions of persecution   _____
7. ladebmite = a lunatic   _____
8. htapohcysp = one who is mentally ill   _____
9. ticanul = insane or utterly foolish   _____
10. cainam = insane   _____
11. fatd = silly, foolish, crazy   _____

Grisly List 68

I've mentioned before that it would be helpful to look at the etymology of a particular word to help you remember the word, but it is also helpful to go over the linguistic derivation of a word so you can use the word more precisely. Sometimes the etymon of a word isn't helpful, i.e. roguish < *rogare* = to beg; other times it's curious, i.e. salacious < *salaci* = to leap. However, at times the original word can help you see the proper twist of how best to use it, as in roister < *ruistre* = ruffian. Review this book, this time looking at all the etymons for each word. Focus on words that you find interesting and unique.

Basic Barbs

> **fanfaron** = one who brags too much,
> from Spanish, *fanfarron* = a braggart
> **jailbird** = one who is or has been in jail
> **grimalkin** = an old female cat; a shrewish old woman
> **saboteur** = one who engages in treacherous and subversive
> action against a nation. From French, *sabater* = to create a loud
> noise with wooden shoes.

Brainy Barbs

1. **reticent doormat** (rĕt´ ĭ sənt)   This one is either habitually silent or unwilling to talk. From Latin, *reticere* = to be silent.

   He knew the precise psychological moment when to say nothing.
   —Oscar Wilde

2. **retrogressive jailbird** (rĕ´ trə grĕs´ ĭv)   To retrogress is to move back to a worse condition. From Latin, *retro* = backward + *gradus* = a step.

   TOMBSTONE EPITAPH:
   Though he tried to jump bail
   He took a bullet in the tail

3. **revanchist saboteur** (rə văn´ shēst)   This one's vengeful spirit is motivated by the need to restore his/her country's territories, power, etc. lost earlier from an enemy. From French, *revanche* = revenge.

   Revenge is a dish that should be eaten cold.
   —English proverb

4. **rhetorical expounder** (rĭ tôr´ ĭ kəl)   Rhetorical is an effective use of words or a stagy display of language. From Greek, *rhetor* = to speak.

   Whoever can speak well can also lie well. —Japanese proverb

5. **ribald chap** (rĭb´ əld) If you like a dirty joke, this chap's the one to ask. This one is given to coarse and vulgar joking. From Old French, *ribaud* = debauchee.

> *Of all the griefs that harass the distressed,*
> *Sure the most bitter is a scornful jest.*
> —Samuel Johnson

6. **rodomontading fanfaron** (rŏd´ ə mŏn tād´ ing) This stormy one arrogantly brags to those unlucky enough to be nearby. Rodomontade was an Italian fictional character from Ariosto's <u>Orlando Rurioso</u> noted for his boasting.

> *The noisiest drum has nothing in it but air.*
> —English proverb

7. **roguish rat** (rō´ gĭsh) Anyone roguish is like a rogue: dishonest or playfully mischievous. Rogue was a 16th century slang term possibly derived from the Latin word, *rogare* = to ask, beg.

> *I prefer rogues rather than fools; for rogues occasionally take a break.*
> —Alexandre Dumas

8. **roisterous brat pack** (roi´ stər əs) This pack parties hard. They laugh. They fight. They swagger. They drink. Swaggering, they laugh while they fight over a drink. They party noisily without restraint. From Medieval French, *ru(i)stre* = ruffian, boor < *ru(i)ste* = rustic.

> *I hate to advocate drugs, alcohol, violence, or insanity to anyone,*
> *but they've always worked for me.*
> —Hunter S. Thompson

9. **rotund grimalkin** (rō tŭnd´) If you like them plump and rounded, then this one's for you. From Latin, *rota* = a wheel.

> *She was so fat, he danced with her for half an hour*
> *before he realized she was still sitting down.*
> —Ed Wynn

10. **rugose fossil** (rū´ gōs, rū gōs´) Anyone rugose is wrinkled, creased. It is usually used to describe leaves but that doesn't mean you can't refer to someone's face as being rugose. From Latin, *ruga* = wrinkle.

> *What is the worst of woes that wait on age?*
> *What stamps the wrinkle deeper on the brow?*
> *To view each loved one blotted from life's page,*
> *And be alone on earth, as I am now.*
> —Lord Byron

Quiz 68

Match the definitions with the words on the left.

Brainy Barbs

___ 1. reticent
___ 2. retrogressive
___ 3. revanchist
___ 4. rhetorical
___ 5. ribald
___ 6. rodomontade

a. proudly brag in a stormy way
b. a stagy display of language
c. dishonest, playfully ill-behaved
d. given to coarse, vulgar joking
e. habitually silent
f. moving backwards to a worse condition

___ 7. roguish
___ 8. roisterous
___ 9. rotund
___10. rugose

g. noisy, without restraint
h. plump and rounded
i. vengeful to another country
j. wrinkled

Basic Barbs

___11. grimalkin

k. an old female cat; a shrewish old woman

___12. boob

l. engages in subversive action

___13. fanfaron

m. one who brags too much

___14. saboteur

n. one who is or has been in jail

___15. jailbird

o. slang term for an idiot

Greed Is Good

(avaricious, edacious, esurient, gluttonous, gulositous,)
(insatiable, voracious, rapacious, glutton)

Match.

1. g _ _ _ _ _ _ _ _ _ = greedy, eat too much
2. e _ _ _ _ _ _ _ = hungry, greedy
3. v _ _ _ _ _ _ _ _ = eating with greediness; immoderate
4. r _ _ _ _ _ _ _ _ = plundering; greedy
5. ed _ _ _ _ _ _ = consuming, devouring
6. a _ _ _ _ _ _ _ _ _ = greedy
7. gu _ _ _ _ _ _ _ _ _ = gluttonous
8. i _ _ _ _ _ _ _ _ _ _ = cannot be satisfied
9. g _ _ _ _ _ _ = one who greedily eats too much

I've thought of another grand place to study—on long flights. If you've ever been stuck on one of those long dreary flights from God-knows-where to Timbuktu, then you know how wasted you feel on the flight and how wasted you feel you've spent your time: you're so cramped, you can't see the movie, the earphones they give you sound like mosquitoes in your ears. It is the perfect place to go over these words. The next time you fly, see how much of this book you can finish. By the time you reach your destination, you will feel the satisfaction of having accomplished an important goal.

Basic Barbs

➤ **shrew** = a scolding woman
➤ **hypocrite** = one who pretends or claims to be virtuous but lacks those qualities
➤ **blasphemer** = one who speaks of God irreverently
➤ **patsy** = one easily swindled; a scapegoat or fall guy; one who is the object of a joke
➤ **clodhopper** = a clumsy idiot
➤ **cut-up** = one who is clownish to get attention

Brainy Barbs

1. **rumbustious clodhopper** (rŭm bŭs shəs)   Wild, unruly, and boisterous, this riotous clodhopper is quick to get out of hand. This possibly comes from a blend of rum, the liquor, and rambunctious.

> *You gotta fight for your right to party.*
> —Beastie Boys

2. **saccharine goody two-shoes** (săk´ ə rĭn)   This one's sweet, maybe too sweet. From Latin, *saccharum* = sugar.

> *Where does the ant die except in sugar?*
> —Malay proverb

3. **sackless patsy** (săk´ lĭs)   Feeble-minded, this patsy lacks energy. From Latin, *saccus* = bag + less.

> *Why don't you bore a hole in your head and let the sap run out?*
> —Groucho Marx

4. sacrilegious blasphemer (săk´ rə lĭj´ əs) This one's disrespectful to anything sacred. From Latin, *sacrilegus* = temple robber.

> *So if you worship me, it will all be yours.*
> —Satan, Luke 4:8

5. sadistic slave driver (sə dĭs´ tĭk) The word sadism came from Marquis de Sade, a nutcase who derived pleasure from giving others pain.

> *Every normal man must be tempted at times*
> *to spit on his hands, hoist the black flag,*
> *and begin slitting throats.*
> —H. L. Mencken

6. salacious swingers (sə lā´ shəs) These lustful swingers are always leaping from bed to bed. It comes from the Latin, *salacis* = to leap.

> *Sex is nobody's business except the three people involved.*
> —Anonymous

7. sanctimonious hypocrite (sangk´ tə mō´ nē əs) This phony prances around with a hypocritical show of piety. From Latin, *sanctimonia* = holiness.

> *The last Christian died on the cross.*
> —Friedrich Wilhelm Nietzche

8. sanguinary bloodsucker (sang´ gwə ner´ ē) Sanguinary indicates one is attended with blood, so it can denote something positive like "rosy cheeks", but it also can imply one is bloodthirsty. From Latin, *sanguis* = blood.

> *It is better to be wanted for murder than not to be wanted at all.*
> —Marty Winch

9. sarcastic shrew (sär kăs´ tĭk) To be sarcastic is to give sneering, cutting remarks typified by sneering remarks that mean the opposite of what they seem to say. From Greek, *sarkazein* = to rend (flesh) to sneer.

> *If my dog had your face, I'd shave his butt*
> *and teach him to walk backwards.*
> —Jamie Farr

10. sardonic cut-up (sär dŏn´ ĭk) This one disdainfully sneers at others, scornfully and sarcastically mocking them. From Greek, *sardanios* = bitter, scornful.

> *A man who lacks judgment derides his neighbor.*
> —Proverbs 11: 12

Quiz 69

Match the definitions with the words on the left.

Brainy Barbs

__ 1. rumbustious   a. "rosy cheeks", or bloodthirsty
__ 2. saccharine   b. wild, unruly, and boisterous
__ 3. sackless   c. disrespectful to the sacred
__ 4. sacrilegious   d. feeble-minded; lacks energy
__ 5. sadist   e. giving sneering remarks
                        (fits two words)
__ 6. salacious   f. lustful
__ 7. sanctimonious   g. get pleasure from giving pain
__ 8. sanguinary   h. sweet or too sweet
__ 9. sarcastic   i. with a insincere show of piety
__10. sardonic

Basic Barbs

__11. shrew   j. a clumsy idiot
__12. hypocrite   k. a scolding woman
__13. cut-up   l. to speak of God irreverently
__14. blaspheme   m. one easily swindled
__15. patsy   n. clownish to get attention
__16. clodhopper   o. feigns to be virtuous when not

They Have An Attitude

(condescend, disdainful, fastuous, fleer, flippant, flout,)
(ingrate, jeer, patronize, impudent, pettish)

Match.

1. i _ _ _ _ _ _ = one who is ungrateful
2. f _ _ _ _ _ _ _ = scornful contempt, haughty
3. f _ _ _ _ _ _ _ = talkative; disrespectful
4. f _ _ _ r = laugh derisively at
5. f _ _ _ _ = show contempt
6. j _ _ _ = make fun in a rude way
7. p _ _ _ _ _ _ _ _ = treat in a condescending way
8. c _ _ _ _ _ _ _ _ _ = regard as lower the one
                        with whom one is dealing
9. d _ _ _ _ _ _ _ _ _ = look down on, aloof contempt
10. i _ _ _ _ _ _ _ = saucy, impertinent, shameless
11. p _ _ _ _ _ _ = cross, peevish

Do you play Scrabble? Upwords? Boggle? Now is a good time to start. By applying your newfound vocabulary to any word game, you stretch your mind and learn to apply word skills in innovative ways. Try crossword puzzles. Don't sneer. It can make you a better writer and thinker. When you find yourself searching for that right word to say, it will come easier to you if you have been in the habit of playing these word games.

Basic Barbs

➤ **chintzy** = cheap, miserly or gaudy, after chintz, a cotton fabric made in India

➤ **doofus** = slang term for idiot

➤ **dregs** = the particles that drop to the bottom of a liquid; any worthless part, sometimes used in reference to the bottom class in society: the pimps, profligates

➤ **ruttish** = in sexual heat, from Latin, *rugitus*, to roar (like an animal in heat)

Brainy Barbs

1. **saturnine outcasts** (săt´ ər nīn´) Long ago, folks felt Saturn made people melancholic. Hence, to be saturnine is to be sluggish and gloomy. From Old French, *saturnin* = of Saturn; of lead, heavy.

Noble deeds and hot baths are the best cures for depression.
—Dodie Smith

2. **ruttish satyromaniac** (să´ tə rō mā´ nē ăk) A male sexual addict, a satyromaniac is the male counterpart to a nymphomaniac. In Greek mythology, a satyr—an attendant to Bacchus—had horns on his head, the legs of a goat and was given to lechery.

Sex between a man and a woman can be wonderful provided you get between the right man and woman.
—Woody Allen

3. **saucy tease** (sô´ sē) Rude and impudent, this tease likes to strut her stuff. From Latin, *salsus* = salted.

The fastest way to a man's heart is through his chest.
—Roseanne Arnold

4. scabrous guttermouth (skăb´ rəs)   Scabrous means rough; hard to handle; or lewd, indecent and shocking.   From Latin, *scaber* = scurfy (having scales).

When I was growing up, all my friends wanted to have sex
with anything that moved. I told them, "Why limit yourself?"
—Emo Philips

5. scampish squirt (skămp ĭsh)   This mischievous little runt will put frogs down your back, deflate your tires, and stick your underwear on top of the flag pole. From Medieval French, *escamper* = to flee.

A child is a curly, dimpled lunatic. —Emerson

6. scathing satirist (skā´ thing)   This satirist's speech is harsh, and mean-spirited. From Greek, *skethos* = injury.

She doesn't need a steak knife. Rona cuts her steak with her tongue.
—Johnny Carson on Rona Barrett

7. scatological slime bucket (skăt´ ə lŏj´ ĭk)   This one is fixated with excrement or obscenity.   From Greek, *skor* = excrement + *logos* = a word, thought.

<u>Likely comment:</u>
Once there was a lady from Nantucket

<u>Your response:</u>
Who said you're a scatologic slime bucket.

8. sciolistic doofus (sī´ ə lĭs tĭk)   This dope has only a superficial knowledge of the facts. From Late Latin, *sciolus* = one who knows little.

TOMBSTONE EPITAPH:
He tried to balloon
Way up to the moon
But died before noon

9. scrimping dregs (skrĭmp´ ing)   To scrimp is to try to make ends meet. From Danish, *skrumpe* = to shrivel.

Debt is the worst poverty.
—M. G. Lichtwer

10. chintzy <u>scrooge</u> (skrūj)   One who is a scrooge is a cheap, stingy, and mean person.   Ebenezer Scrooge is a character in Dickens' "A Christmas Carol," noted for his miserly behavior.

Who will not feed the cats,
must feed the mice and rats.
—German proverb

Quiz 70

Match the definitions with the words on the left.

Brainy Barbs

__ 1. saturnine   a. a cheap, stingy, mean person
__ 2. satyromaniac   b. a male sexual addict
__ 3. saucy   c. fixated with excrement or obscenity
__ 4. scabrous   d. harsh, and mean-spirited
__ 5. scampish   e. having a superficial knowledge of the facts
__ 6. scathing   f. mischievous
__ 7. scatologic   g. rough; hard to handle; or lewd, indecent and shocking
__ 8. sciolistic   h. rude and impudent
__ 9. scrimp   i. sluggish and gloomy
__10. scrooge   j. to try to make ends meet

Basic Barbs

__11. ruttish   k. in sexual heat
__12. dregs   l. cheap, miserly or gaudy
__13. chintzy   m. the particles that drop to the bottom of a liquid

One Big Zero

(apathetic, automaton, nondescript, stolid, cipher,)
(nebulous, negligible, clone, nonentity)

Unscramble.

1. ondentsricp = having no definite class or type   _____
2. geneliiblg = ignored since it's unimportant   _____
3. bulenous = indistinct   _____
4. utoamanot = like a robot   _____
5. patacheti = not caring   _____
6. ttnnnoeiy = not existing; a person of little or no importance   _____
7. necol = a duplicate produced by genetic engineering   _____
8. rehpic = zero; a person of no importance   _____
9. tosild = impassive, showing no feeling   _____

LE MOT QUOTE 42
Match each quote with the appropriate word.

1. As we must render an account of every idle word, so we must of our idle silence. —Ambrose

2. Great men may jest with saints; 'tis wit in them; but, in the less foul profanation. —Shakespeare

3. He who is in evil, is also in the punishment of evil.
   —Swedenborg

4. Lizzie Borden took an axe
   And gave her mother forty whacks;
   When she saw what she had done,
   She gave her father forty-one! —Anonymous

5. The man who is fond of complaining, likes to remain amid the objects of his vexation. It is at the moment that he declares them insupportable that he will most strongly revolt against every means proposed for his deliverance. This is what suits him. He asks nothing better than to sigh over his position and to remain in it.
   —Guizot

___ a. sanguinary

___ b. repine

___ c. reprobate

___ d. reticent

___ e. ribald

LE MOT QUOTE 43
Circle the word that best matches all three quotes.

1. One is very crazy when in love. —Sigmund Freud

2. The head is always the dupe of the heart.
   —La Rochefoucauld

3. Everybody in love is blind. —Propertius

   a. repine   b. infatuated   c. ribald

LE MOT QUOTE 44

Match each quote with the appropriate word.

1. He that studieth revenge
    keepeth his own wounds green,
    which otherwise would heal and do well. —Bacon

2. Hypocrites do the devil's drudgery in Christ's livery.
    —Matthew Henry

3. Television is a whore:
    Any man who wants her full favors
    can have them in five minutes with a pistol.
    —Hijacker, quoted in <u>Esquire</u>, 1977

4. To save the state the expense of a trial, your honor,
    my client has escaped. —Chon Day

5. Violence in the voice is often only the death rattle
    of reason in the throat. —Boyes

___ a. sanctimonious

___ b. rant

___ c. recidivistic or mizzle

___ d. revanchist

___ e. maleficent

Chapter 15

Speak clearly, if you speak at all;
Carve every word before you let it fall.
—Oliver Wendell Holmes

Grisly List 71

Many of these words are not necessarily disparaging. If you are part of the aristocracy you don't consider aristocracy a pejorative. And likewise, if you are part of some underground seditious movement, you don't feel the words anarchy, nihilist, or seditious are bad. A great deal depends on your point of view. My goal is to give enough people enough verbiage to insult those on the other side of the spectrum. Therefore, just what side are you on? What words fit you? And what words fit the people you dislike?

Basic Barbs

➤ **faction** = a contentious minority within a larger group
➤ **geezer** = a crotchety or eccentric old man
➤ **canaille** (kə nāl) = riffraff, literally in Italian it means "pack of dogs"

Brainy Barbs

1. **sebaceous pus bucket** (sĭ bā´ shəs) This oily creep oozes oil and fat out of every pore. From Latin, *sebum* = tallow, fat.

> *I never eat more than I can lift.*
> —Miss Piggy

2. **sebiferous blimp** (sĭ bĭf´ ər əs) This blimp secretes fat like a link of sausage on a skillet. From Latin, *sebum* = tallow, fat.

> **TOMBSTONE EPITAPH:**
> *They say his heart went kerplop*
> *when second helpings made him drop*

3. **sectarian faction** (sĕk târ´ ē ən) A sectarian group is narrow-minded. It can also be used as a noun; e.g. That dimwitted sectarian. From Latin, *secta* = a path, faction.

> *Beware of the man of one book.*
> —St. Thomas Aquinas

4. sedentary bump on a log (sĕd´ ən ter´ ē)   Anyone sedentary doesn't move, doesn't budge and is always sitting.   From Latin, *sedentarius* = sitting.

A sedentary life is the real sin against the Holy Spirit.
—Nietzche

5. seditious canaille (sĭ dĭsh´ əs)   A seditious group stirs up discontent. From Latin, *sadire* = to go aside; hence, to rebel.

Let the ruling classes tremble at a Communist revolution.
The proletarians have nothing to lose but their chains.
They have a world to win. Working men of all countries, unite!
—Marx and Engels

6. self-adulating jerk (sĕlf ăj´ ə lāt´ ing)   To adulate means to show excessive devotion, flattery or admiration in a servile way.   So, this one praises himself/herself too highly. From Latin, *adulatus* = to fawn upon.

I have nothing to declare except my genius.
—Oscar Wilde,
at New York customs

7. senescent geezer (sə nĕs´ ənt)   Anyone senescent is growing old. From Latin, *senex* = old.

You know you're growing old when everything hurts.
And what doesn't hurt doesn't work.
—Hy Gardner

8. senile nutcase (sē´ nīl)   This one is dumb and weak from old age. From Latin, *senex* = old.

I'm in the prime of my senility.
—Benjamin Franklin

9. sententious smart aleck (sĕn tĕn´ shəs)   A sententious person can be pithy (filled with aphorisms) or is full of pompous moral sayings.   From Latin, *sententia* = way of thinking, opinion.

Platitudes are the Sundays of stupidity.
—Unknown

10. sequacious sheep (sĭ kwā´ shəs)   Lacking self-will, these sheep tend to follow a leader. From Latin, *sequi* = to follow.

People, like sheep, tend to follow a leader
—occasionally in the right direction.
—Alexander Chase

Quiz 71

Match the definitions with the words on the left.

Brainy Barbs

___ 1. sebaceous   a. doesn't move; always sitting
___ 2. sebiferous   b. dumb and weak from old age
___ 3. sectarian   c. growing old
___ 4. sedentary   d. narrow-minded
___ 5. seditious   e. oily and fatty (fits two words)
___ 6. self-adulate   f. full of pompous moral sayings
___ 7. senescent   g. stirring up discontent
___ 8. senile   h. tending to follow
___ 9. sententious   i. show excessive devotion to
___10. sequacious   oneself

Basic Barbs

___11. canaille   j. contentious minority within a
                      larger group
___12. faction   k. crotchety, eccentric old man
___13. geezer   l. riffraff, "pack of dogs"

You Stink

(excrementitious, pedicular, fetid, foul, malodorous,)
(mephitic, noisome, feculent, putrid)

Match.

1. m _ _ _ _ _ _ _ _ _ = bad-smelling
2. p _ _ _ _ _ _ _ _ _ = lousy
3. p _ _ _ _ _ = stinking
4. e _ _ _ _ _ _ _ _ _ _ _ _ _ _ = like feces
5. f _ _ _ _ _ _ _ = have the nature of feces
6. f _ _ _ _ = stinking
7. f _ _ _ = offensive
8. m _ _ _ _ _ _ _ = bad-smelling
9. n _ _ _ _ _ _ = harmful; bad-smelling

Grisly List 72

Malcolm X was stuck in jail for some time. He could have let his mind go to rot, but he didn't: he read! He read and read and read. He even read all the way through the dictionary. Is it any wonder then that he went on to become one of the most powerful and influential speakers of his era. People still debate over what it was that his legacy has left us, but no one can dismiss his power as a speaker to influence people. Which brings us to you. No one can dismiss you either. The rest of your life is an open book. And the key to what may make you a force to be reckoned with, might be the next book you pick up.

Basic Barbs

> ➤ **cabal** = a conspiratorial group of plotters
> ➤ **gimp** = one who walks with a limp
> ➤ **rook** = a gregarious bird; a swindler
> ➤ **sap** = a gullible person
> ➤ **siren** = From Greek mythology, Sirens were sea nymphs, half bird and half woman, who lured sailors to their death by their seductive singing. Now it's used to describe any woman who uses her charms to entice men.

Brainy Barbs

1. **serpentine rook** (sûr´ pən tēn)   To be serpentine is to be like a serpent, especially in terms of movement, winding and sinuous. However, it also connotes being cunning and devious. From Latin, *serpens bestia* = a creeping or gliding beast.

> *The prince of darkness is always a gentleman.*
> —Shakespeare,
> King Lear III. sc. 4

2. **servile gimp** (sur´ vīl, vĭl)   This gimp crawls around on his hands and knees acting like a slave. From Latin, *servus* = a slave.

> *One sheep follows another.*
> —English proverb

3. **sexist pig** (sĕk´ sĭst)   Anyone sexist discriminates against the opposite sex, believing the other sex inferior. From Latin, *secare* = to cut, divide.

> *I don't mate in captivity.*
> —Gloria Steinam,
> on why she has not married and had children

4. simian dork (sĭm´ ē ən)   A simian is an ape or a monkey or something like an ape or a monkey. From Latin, *simia* = an ape.

> *Man is more an ape than many of the apes.*
> —Friedrich Nietzsche

5. slick simoniac (sĭ mō´ nē ăk´)   In Acts 8:18, Simon the magician offers money to the disciples of Jesus Christ in exchange for their spiritual power; hence, a simoniac is anyone trying to buy or sell sacred things for dishonest reasons.

> *What price salvation now?*
> —George Bernard Shaw,
> Major Barbara

6. simpering sap (sĭm´ pər ing)   This sap wears a silly and stupid smile. From Middle Dutch, *simperlijc* = dainty, affected.

> *Whatever it is, wherever he is, whatever he is doing,*
> *he smiles; it is a malady he has.*
> —Gaius Valerius Catullus

7. lazy sinecurist (sī´ nə kyûr´ ĭst)   A sinecure is any job requiring no work yet it pays a salary. A sinecurist is the lazy slob who gets a job like this. From a Latin phrase, *sine cura* = without care.

> *Office hours are from 12 to 1 with an hour off for lunch.*
> —George S. Kaufman,
> speaking of the US Senate

8. sinister cabal (sĭn´ ĭ stər)   Think of the KGB. Anyone sinister is devious and wicked. From Latin, *sinister* = of the left hand.

> *Where trust is greatest, there treason is in its most horrid shape.*
> —Dryden

9. sinuous siren (sĭn´ yū əs)   This one is either gracefully winding or devious. From Latin, *sinuosus* = bending in and out; hence, serpentine.

> *Hell can lie between the eyelashes of a beautiful woman's eyes.*
> —Anonymous

10. Sisyphean workhorse (sĭs´ ə fē´ ən)   Sisyphus was a mythical person whose penalty was to eternally roll a stone up a hill only to have it slip and roll down the hill again. Anything Sisyphean is endlessly difficult.

> *To crush... a man utterly...*
> *one need only give him work of an absolutely,*
> *completely useless and irrational character.*
> —Dostoevsky

Quiz 72

Match the definitions with the words on the left.

Brainy Barbs

___ 1. serpentine
___ 2. servile
___ 3. sexist
___ 4. simian
___ 5. simoniac

___ 6. simper

___ 7. sinecurist
___ 8. sinister
___ 9. sinuous

___10. Sisyphean

a. devious and wicked
b. discriminates against other sex
c. like an ape
d. like a slave
e. one trying to buy or sell sacred things for dishonest reasons
f. one with a job requiring no work yet it pays a high salary
g. pointlessly or endlessly difficult
h. smile in a silly and stupid way
i. winding; devious (fits two words)

Basic Barbs

___11. rook
___12. gimp
___13. sap
___14. siren
___15. cabal
___16. sinecure

j. a gregarious bird; a swindler
k. a gullible person
l. conspiratorial group of plotters
m. a high-paying job with no work
n. one who walks with a limp
o. uses her charms to entice men

Dirty Little Buggers

(Augean, bedraggled, disheveled, dowdy, frowsy,)
(smirchy, grubby, sordid, squalid, unkempt)

Unscramble.

1. debragedgl = wet and dirty _____
2. dirosd = filthy, wretched; mean, greedy _____
3. qusdali = dirty, filthy and wretched _____
4. dsideheelv = not combed, untidy _____
5. pkunemt = not combed; untidy, not neat _____
6. brugby = dirty _____
7. yowdd = shabby _____
8. wsorfy = stinking; dirty, untidy _____
9. geauan = filthy and degraded _____
10. phcrims = dirty _____

In this chapter there are great words that can be used as nouns or verbs. Try mixing your adjectives and nouns around and see just how many combinations you can get. How about a cadging sloven, or a mizzling slattern? Maybe you're fed up with that smarmy cadger who skulks and slavers around town, brownnosing his way into everybody's kitchen.

Basic Barbs

- ➢ **brownnoser** = one who follows or flatters just to gain something
- ➢ **cadge** (kăj) **cadging, cadger** = to get by imposing on another's charity, to beg
- ➢ **dullard** = one who is slow-witted
- ➢ **hypochondriac** = one overly anxious about one's health
- ➢ **mizzler** = one who is clever at affecting his own escape
- ➢ **sow** = an adult female pig
- ➢ **spud** = a potato

Brainy Barbs

1. **skittish hypochondriac** (skĭt´ ĭsh) This one is easily frightened, very fickle, or playfully coy. From Scandinavian, *skite* = to dart about.

We poison our lives with fear of burglary and shipwreck and, ask anyone, the house is never burgled and the ship never goes down.
—Jean Anouilh

2. **skulking creep** (skŭlk´ ing) To skulk is to move about in a sneaking or cowardly way, or to hide and wait for some evil purpose. From Low German, *schulken* = to play truant, or from Dutch, *skulke* = to skulk.

Even though a snake enters a bamboo tube, it still is apt to slither.
—Chinese proverb

3. **slatternly sow** (slăt´ ərn lē) A slattern is either an untidy woman or a harlot; hence, to be slatternly is to be untidy, sloppy or to be sluttish. Possibly from Medieval English, *slatter* = to slash or slit (clothes).

Of all the tame beasts, I hate sluts.
—John Ray

4. **slavering dullard** (slăv´ ər ing) To slaver is to drool, fawn or flatter in a slobbering way. From Icelandic, *slafra* = to slobber.

Flatterers are cats that lick before and scratch behind.
—German proverb

5. **slavish brownnoser** (slā´ vĭsh)   This brownnoser acts like a slave. From Old Bulgarian, *Slovene* = inhabitant name for Slavic populace, so named given that many Slavs were enslaved in the Middle Ages.

> Many men die at twenty-five
> and aren't buried until they are seventy-five.
> —Benjamin Franklin

6. **sleekit mizzler** (slē´ kĭt)   Anyone sleekit is sneaky. From Old English, *slician* = to make smooth.

> The weak in courage is strong in cunning.
> —William Blake

7. **slovenly spud** (slŭv´ ən lē)   A sloven is one who is careless in appearance. One who is slovenly is habitually dirty and untidy. Wear a gas mask before you go near. From Medieval Dutch, *slof* = lax, limp.

> Women were made to give our eyes delight;
> A female sloven is an odious sight.
> —Edward Young

8. **slothful do-nothing** (slôth´ fəl)   A sloth is an animal that moves so slowly it appears to be half-asleep; hence, a slothful person is one who is either slow or lazy. It is also one of the seven deadly sins. From Old English, *slaw* = slow.

> A little sleep, a little slumber,
> a little folding of the hands to rest,
> and poverty will come upon you like a vagabond,
> and want like an armed man.
> —Proverbs 6: 10,11.

9. **smarmy cadger** (smär´ mē)   This one flatters in an oily, insincere way. From English, *smarm* = to smear, gush.

> Learn that every flatterer lives at the flattered listener's cost.
> —La Fontaine

10. **smirchy little rugrat** (smûr´ chē)   This little rugrat is dirty and grimy. Smirchy can also mean dishonored. It is possibly a blend of smutch from Middle High German, *smutz* = to smear and smear from German, *schmer* = grease, OR from Old French, *esmorcher* = to hurt.

> In Koln, a town of monks and bones
> And pavements fanged with murderous stones,
> And rags, and hags, and hideous wenches;
> I counted two and seventy stenches.
> —Unknown

Quiz 73

Match the definitions with the words on the left.

Brainy Barbs

__ 1. skittish
__ 2. skulk
__ 3. slatternly
__ 4. slaver
__ 5. slavish
__ 6. sleekit
__ 7. slovenly
__ 8. slothful
__ 9. smarmy
__10. smirchy

a. careless in appearance, habitually dirty and untidy
b. dirty, and grimy
c. easily frightened, very fickle
d. flatter in an oily, deceitful way
e. like a slave
f. cowardly sneak about
g. slobber, drool and/or fawn
h. slow or lazy
i. sluttish
j. sneaky

Basic Barbs

__11. sow
__12. dullard
__13. brownnoser
__14. mizzler
__15. spud
__16. cadge

k. a potato
l. an adult female pig
m. clever at affecting escape
n. flatters just to gain something
o. impose on other's generosity
p. one who is slow-witted

Toxic Tales

(scurvy, blight, nocuous, noxious, scourge,)
(venomous, virulent, pestiferous)

Match.

1. vi _ _ _ _ _ _ = poisonous
2. v _ _ _ _ _ _ _ _ = poisonous
3. n _ _ _ _ _ _ = causing injury to health or morals
4. b _ _ _ _ _ = a pestilence; any person or thing that withers one's hopes or ambitions
5. n _ _ _ _ _ _ = poisonous, noxious
6. s _ _ _ _ _ _ _ = a whip used to punish; any cause of pervasive affliction
7. p _ _ _ _ _ _ _ _ _ _ = bearing disease; mischievous, annoying
8. s _ _ _ _ _ = a disease caused by the lack of vitamin C; a mean, contemptible person

The word specious an adjective that describes a person, but it is a great way to insult someone's reasoning in a dispute; as in, "That is a specious argument!!" That sounds much better than, "Uh, you are like, totally wrong, dude." In fact, many times when I hear the elite argue, the difference between them and your average Joe Blow on the street is simply their vocabulary. It can be an effective way to win a debate.

Basic Barbs

- ➤ **castaway** = one who has been shipwrecked; an outcast
- ➤ **cur** = a mixed breed dog, a contemptible person
- ➤ **egoist** = a self-centered person
- ➤ **geek** = Originally, a geek was a carnival performer performing grotesque acts for entertainment, such as biting off the heads of chickens etc. Now it is synonymous with nerd, dweeb or fool.
- ➤ **souse** = a drunk

Brainy Barbs

1. **sniveling small fry** (snĭv´ ə ling) Snivel has several meanings: it can mean to whine, or to have snot drip from your nose, or to make an audible sound by drawing up snot into your nose, or to speak while your nose is running, or to pretend you're crying. It is from Old English, *snofl* = mucus.

> *Babies: a loud noise at one end*
> *and no sense of responsibility at the other.*
> —Father Ron Knox

2. **sodden souse** (sŏd´ ən) Anything sodden is soaked with liquid, but it can refer to one soaked in too much liquor. From the past participle of seethe = to boil; to soak, < Old Norse, *sauthr* = a burnt offering.

> *I drink too much.*
> *The last time I gave a urine sample there was an olive in it.*
> —Rodney Dangerfield

3. **solecistic lightweight** (säl´ ə sĭs´ tĭk) This one is characterized by making errors in grammar. From Greek, *soloikos* = speaking incorrectly.

> *A writer who can't write in a grammarly manner better shut up shop.*
> —Artemus Ward

4. **solipsistic egoist** (sŏl´ ĭp sĭs tĭk) This egoist waxes philosophical about how only the self exists. From Latin, *solus* = alone.

> *The more you speak of yourself, the more you are likely to lie.*
> —Zimmerman

5. **sophistical snake** (sō fĭs´ tĭ kəl)   In Ancient Greece, a sophist was a skilled teacher of reasoning, but as time passed, these sophists began to use ingenuity and sly, misleading arguments. Now it signifies one who uses deceptive reasoning. From Greek, *sophistes* = sage, a wise man.

> *Sophistry is like a window curtain:*
> *it pleases as an ornament,*
> *but its true use is to keep out the light.*
> —Burke

6. **sophomoric geek** (sŏf ə môr´ ĭk)   This one is annoyingly immature. From Greek, *sophos* = wise + *moros* = foolish.

> *The highlight of my childhood was making my brother*
> *laugh so hard that food came out of his nose.*
> —Garrison Keillor

7. **soporific poet** (sŏp´ ə rĭf´ ĭk)   Anything soporific induces drowsiness or sleep or it is boring and dull. From Latin, *sopire* = to send to sleep.

> *I never sleep comfortably*
> *except when I am at a sermon or when I pray to God.*
> —Rabelais

8. **sordid castaway** (sôr´ dĭd)   Anything sordid displays the most horrible characteristics of human personality; depravity, avarice, self-centeredness. It can also mean something is filthy and wretched. From Indo-European, *swordo* = black, dirty.

> *Man is god in ruins.*
> —Ralph Waldo Emerson

9. **specious argument** (spē´shəs)   Anything specious looks good, but in actuality is false, deceptive. From Latin, *specios* = fair, beautiful.

> *Some so speak in exaggerations and superlatives*
> *that we need to make a large discount from their statements*
> *before we can come at their real meaning.*
> —Tyron Edwards

10. **splenetic cur** (splĭ nĕt´ ĭk)   Long ago, when doctors still thought using leeches to bleed patients was a good idea, people had the notion that the spleen caused folks to be testy or irritable; hence, to be splenetic is to be irritable, peevish and spiteful. From Latin, *spleen* = spleen.

> *A tart temper never mellows with age.*
> —Washington Irving

Quiz 74

Match the definitions with the words on the left.

Brainy Barbs

___ 1. snivel
___ 2. sodden
___ 3. solecistic
___ 4. solipsistic

___ 5. sophistical
___ 6. sophomoric
___ 7. soporific
___ 8. sordid
___ 9. specious

___10. splenetic

a. believing only the self exists
b. making errors in grammar
c. filthy and wretched
d. with the appearance of being right but actually being wrong
e. immature
f. soaked with liquid; drunk
g. testy, irritable, peevish
h. tending to produce sleep
i. to make an audible sound by drawing up snot into your nose
j. using deceptive reasoning

Basic Barbs

___11. souse
___12. cur
___13. geek
___14. egoist

k. a nerd, dweeb or fool
l. a self-centered person
m. a mixed breed dog
n. a drunk

On Your Nerves

(exacerbate, exasperate, gadfly, galling, intolerable,)
(intrusive, irksome, nettle, pesky, gall)

Match.

1. n _ _ _ _ _ = irritate, annoy
2. g _ _ _ _ _ _ = irritating
3. g _ _ _ _ _ = one who is annoying
4. e _ _ _ _ _ _ _ _ _ = annoying
5. i _ _ _ _ _ _ = tiresome, annoying
6. e _ _ _ _ _ _ _ _ _ = to make a situation worse, irritate
7. i _ _ _ _ _ _ _ _ = intruding, pushy
8. i _ _ _ _ _ _ _ _ _ _ = unbearable
9. p _ _ _ _ = annoying, troublesome
10. g _ _ _ = disrespectful boldness

Spurious is like the word specious in that it's not something you would use to describe a person, but it's another great way to put down someone's argument, or logic or both. When you attack someone's reasoning, they can't keep saying the same argument; they now have to defend the way they come to their conclusions. If the one you're debating can't match your vocabulary, it lends more credence to your own argument. If gaining an advantage in a debate is your goal, then I suggest you go back through this book and circle any words that you think would be helpful in an argument. Then right them on a list to study. Make sure you understand the differences between each word. When you use these words in your next debate, it will unnerve and unravel your opponent if he has to stop and ask you the definitions of the words you're using.

Basic Barbs

> **bedlamite** = a lunatic, Bedlam was a popular name given to the Hospital of St. Mary of Bethlehem in London, at one time an insane asylum; hence, a bedlamite was a resident of Bedlam. Bedlam also means a scene of wild uproar and confusion
> **maggot** = larva found in decaying matter; scum
> **pigsty** = a house for pigs
> **pipsqueak** = a small person
> **spendthrift** = a wasteful spender

Brainy Barbs

1. **spluttering bedlamite** (splŭt´ ər ing) From a blend of splash and sputter, to splutter is to make a spitting sound or speak incoherently or speak incoherently while spitting.

   Great talkers are like leaky pitchers, everything runs out of them.
   —*English proverb*

2. **spoliating burglar** (spō´ lē āt´ ing) To spoliate is to steal, plunder or despoil. From Latin, *spoliare* = to spoil.

   Old burglars never die, they just steal away.
   —*Glen Gilbreath,*
   facing his 13th robbery charge

3. **spurious spinmeister** (spûr´ rē əs) If something is spurious it is false, or deceitfully false. From Latin, *spurius* = illegitimate.

   In much of your talking, thinking is half murdered.
   —*Kahlil Gabran*

4. **squalid pigsty** (skwŏl´ ĭd)   This dump is dirty, filthy and wretched. From Latin, *squalere* = to be foul or filthy.

> I hate housework! You make the bed;, you do the dishes;
> and six months later you have to start all over again.
> —Joan Rivers

5. **squandering spendthrift** (skwŏn´ dər ing)   To squander is to spend wastefully. The derivation of squander is uncertain, but it was popularized after Shakespeare's <u>Merchant of Venice</u>.

> I wasted time, and now doth time waste me. —Shakespeare

6. **squeamish pipsqueak** (skwē´ mĭsh)   Thin-skinned, this one is easily sickened or offended. From Anglo-French, *escoimous* = disdainfully shy.

> He who is afraid of every nettle should not piss in the grass.
> —Thomas Fuller

7. **stagnant sweathog** (stăg´ nənt)   This sluggish person is foul and putrid from not moving. From Latin, *stagnum* = a swamp.

> The only difference between a rut and a grave is the depth.
> — Unknown

8. **steatopygous lardass** (stē´ ə tō pī´ gəs)   One who is steatopygous has an extremely fat butt. From Greek, *stear* = fat + *pyge* = buttocks.

> <u>Likely comment:</u>
> Gentlemen come from miles around just to see me.

> <u>Your response:</u>
> That's because it takes them miles to get around you.

9. **stentorian big mouth** (stĕn tôr´ ē ən)   This one is excessively loud, speaking with a deafening roar. Stentor was a Greek herald in the Trojan War in the Iliad. It is akin to the Greek word, *stenein* = to rumble or roar.

> They that are loudest in their threats are the weakest
> in the execution of them. It is probable that he who is killed
> by lightning hears no noise; but the thunder-clap which follows,
> and which most alarms the ignorant, is the surest proof of their safety.
> —Colton

10. **stigmatized maggot** (stĭg´ mə tīzd)   A stigma was a mark cut or burned into the skin of a criminal or slave.   Hence, stigmatized is to be branded as disgraced. Stigmata refer to the hands and feet of those who, out of religious devotion, bleed like Jesus. From German, *stizein* = to prick.

> One speck of rat's dung spoils a whole pot of rice.
> —Chinese proverb

Quiz 75

Match the definitions with the words on the left.

Brainy Barbs

___ 1. splutter
___ 2. spoliate
___ 3. spurious
___ 4. squalid
___ 5. squander
___ 6. squeamish
___ 7. stagnant
___ 8. steatopygous
___ 9. stentorian
___10. stigmatized

a. dirty, filthy and wretched
b. easily sickened
c. excessively loud
d. false, illegitimate
e. having an extremely fat butt
f. branded as disgraced
g. not moving
h. spend wastefully
i. to speak incoherently
j. to steal, plunder or despoil

Basic Barbs

___11. pigsty
___12. spendthrift
___13. pipsqueak
___14. maggot
___15. bedlamite

k. house for pigs
l. larva found in decaying matter
m. small person
n. wasteful spender
o. lunatic

Erratic Oddballs, Part 1

(discombobulated, capricious, chimerical, ephemeral, erratic, frothy,)
(gadabout, impetuous, vagarious, volatile, whimsical, astigmatic)

Unscramble.

1. pacuricios = erratic, flighty   _____
2. shimwilca = capricious, fanciful; odd, quaint   _____
3. gavasiour = full of odd and eccentric behavior _____
4. lovalite = fickle; unstable; explosive   _____
5. pehelamer = short-lived   _____
6. eticrra = irregular, wandering   _____
7. daabogut = restless seeker after fun   _____
8. micherical = indulging in imaginary fancies,
                      unrealistic   _____
9. thoyrf = foamy; light, worthless   _____
10. petimuous = rash   _____
11. detalubobmocsid = with one's composure upset

                                                                   _____
12. acitamgits = having a skewed view   _____

LE MOT QUOTE 45

Match each quote with the appropriate word.

1. A fixed point of view kills anybody who has one.
   —Brooks Atkinson

2. Fixed like a plant on his peculiar spot
   To draw nutrition, propagate, and rot.
   —Alexander Pope

3. God hates those who praise themselves.
   —St. Clement

4. What an ugly beast is the ape, and how like us.
   —Cicero

5. You can always rely on a society of equals
   taking it out on the woman. —Alan Sillitoe

   __ a. sectarian
   __ b. sedentary
   __ c. self-adulate
   __ d. sexist
   __ e. simian

LE MOT QUOTE 46

Match each quote with the appropriate word.

1. A disagreeable smile distorts the lines of beauty,
   and is more repulsive than a frown. —Lavater

2. A man takes a drink, then the drink takes a drink,
   and the next drink takes a man. —Japanese proverb

3. If you sleep with a dog you will rise full of fleas.
   —Greek proverb

4. When a crook kisses you, count your teeth.
   —Anonymous

   __ a. sinister
   __ b. smirchy
   __ c. sodden
   __ d. simper

LE MOT QUOTE 47
Match each quote with the appropriate word.

1. A sweet disorder in the dress
   Kindles in clothes a wantonness. —Robert Herrick

2. If the chief party, whether it be the people, or the
   army, or the nobility, which you think most useful and
   of most consequence to you for the conservation of
   your dignity, be corrupt, you must follow their humor
   and indulge them, and in that case honesty and virtue
   are pernicious.
   —Machiavelli, <u>The Prince</u>

3. Violence in the voice is often only the death rattle
   of reason in the throat.
   —Boyes

4. We will bury you. —Nikita S. Khrushchev

_ a. stentorian

_ b. machiavellian

_ c. menacious

_ d. slattern

Chapter 16

Satire should, like a polished razor keen,
Wound with a touch that's scarcely felt or seen.
—Lady Mary Wortley Montagu

Grisly List 76

Don't get so lost in all of my suggestions in learning this vocabulary that you end up forgetting the main purpose of this book—to insult people! I want you to enjoy yourself; when the occasion arises, to puff your chest up with pride and spit out some slight that whittles your stultified schlemiel down to size.

Basic Barbs

➤ **chatterbox** = one who talks too much
➤ **killjoy** = one who kills the joy of others
➤ **schlemiel** = from Yiddish, a habitual bungler, derived from Hebrew, *Shelumiel*, a character in the Bible
➤ **schlep** = an ineffectual person
➤ **slumlord** = a landlord of a dilapidated, run-down building
➤ **upstart** = one whose recent wealth or power has led to presumptuous, pretentious behavior

Brainy Barbs

1. **stinting slumlord** (stĭnt´ ing) One who stints is stingy and sparing. From Medieval English, *stinten* = to stint, cease, stop.

> *He's so stingy that if he gave you the measles,*
> *it would be one measle at a time.*
> —Irish proverb

2. **stolid dunderhead** (stŏl´ ĭd) This one is impassive and shows no feeling whatsoever. From Latin, *stolidus* = firm, slow, stupid.

> *I didn't know he was dead; I thought he was British.*
> —Unknown

3. **stringent killjoy** (strĭn´ jənt) A stringent will impose rigorous standards and rigid control. From Latin, *stringere* = to draw tight.

> *I know a man who gave up smoking, drinking, sex, and rich food.*
> *He was healthy right up to the time he killed himself.*
> —Johnny Carson

4. stultified schlemiel (stŭl´ tə fīd´)   To stultify is to make to look foolish or stupid. From Latin, *stultus* = foolish + *facere* = to make.

> *A schlemiel falls on his back and breaks his nose.*
> —Yiddish proverb

5. stunted hillbilly (stŭnt əd)   If something is stunted it has been slowed down in growth or development. From Old English, *stunt* = dull, stupid.

> *You have the brain of a four-year-old,*
> *and I bet he was glad to get rid of it.*
> —Groucho Marx

6. subservient schlep (səb sûr´ vē ənt)   Need a slave? This schlep is totally submissive. From Latin, *sub* = under + *servus* = a slave.

> *It is dangerous to free people who prefer to be slaves.*
> —Mackiavelli

7. sullen wet blanket (sŭl´ ən)   Depressed and morose, this one has seen better days. From Latin, *solus* = alone.

> **TOMBSTONE EPITAPH:**
> *He was so depressed and out of sorts*
> *and thought his life a wreck*
> *He tried to jump off of a bridge*
> *but slipped and broke his neck*

8. supercilious upstart (sū´ pər sĭl´ ē əs)   Arrogantly vain, this brat acts disdainful and haughty. From Latin, *supereciliam* = eyebrow; hence, with one's eyebrows raised.

> *I can't help it. I was born sneering.*
> —Pooh Bah, <u>The Mikado</u>,
> Gilbert and Sullivan

9. superficial phony (sū´ pər fĭsh´ əl)   Shallow!! Whatever you see on the surface, that's it! No depth. From Latin, *superficies* = the fact of being positioned on top, surface < *super* = above, beyond + *ficies* = face.

> *I'm a deeply superficial person.*
> —Andy Warhol

10. superfluous chatterbox (soo pər´ flū əs)   This is what you hear when some loudmouth tells you more than you want to hear. Anything superfluous is excessive and needless to what is required. From Latin, *super* = over + *fluere* = to flow.

> *To go beyond is as wrong as to fall short.*
> —Confucius

Quiz 76

Match the definitions with the words on the left.

Brainy Barbs

__ 1. stinting   a. depressed and morose
__ 2. stolid   b. disdainful and haughty
__ 3. stringent   c. more than what is required
__ 4. stultified   d. hindered in growth
__ 5. stunted   e. impassive, showing no feeling
__ 6. subservient   f. rigidly controlling
__ 7. sullen   g. shallow
__ 8. supercilious   h. stingy and sparing
__ 9. superficial   i. to look foolish or stupid
__10. superfluous   j. totally submissive

Basic Barbs

__11. slumlord   k. a habitual bungler
__12. schlemiel   l. a landlord of a dilapidated,
                                run-down building
__13. schlep   m. an ineffectual person
__14. upstart   n. one who kills the joy of others
__15. killjoy   o. recent wealth has led to
                                pretentious behavior

Erratic Oddballs, Part 2

(dither, frenetic, histrionic, imprudent, mercurial, quixotic, nonplused,)
(dabbler, eccentric, flummoxed, dilettante)

Match.

1. m _ _ _ _ _ _ _ _ = apt to change moods with little cause
2. q _ _ _ _ _ _ _ = extravagantly chivalrous, impractical
3. f _ _ _ _ _ _ _ = typified by moving about excitedly
4. h _ _ _ _ _ _ _ _ _ = overacting
5. d _ _ _ _ _ = move about nervously excited or confused
6. i _ _ _ _ _ _ _ _ = without thought of the consequences, rash
7. e _ _ _ _ _ _ _ _ _ = full of odd behavior
8. d _ _ _ _ _ _ = one who flits from one interest to another
9. d _ _ _ _ _ _ _ _ _ = a dabbler in the arts
10. f _ _ _ _ _ _ _ _ = confused
11. n _ _ _ _ _ _ _ _ = puzzled

Grisly List 77

In the last Chapter I suggested again that you use this book to insult people. Perhaps I should mention some safety tips: Don't insult people who are bigger than you; Don't insult people with guns, knives, or powerful lawyers; Don't insult people who are psychotic, especially those that lead cult groups who have guns, knives and/or powerful lawyers; And remember, many people who don't look psychotic—are psychotic.

Basic Barbs

➢ **aristocracy** = government by the elite or privileged class; the upper class
➢ **earbinder** = one who talks too much
➢ **hotspur** = one with a hot temper
➢ **jawsmith** = slang term for a talker
➢ **milquetoast** = a meek or timid person
➢ **witling** = one with little wit or intelligence

Brainy Barbs

1. **surly swine** (sûr´ lē)   This swine is bad-tempered with a touch of arrogance. From Early English, *sirly* = like a lord.

> *The best time I had with Joan Crawford*
> *is when I pushed her down the stairs.*
> —Bette Davis

2. **surreptitious spy** (sûr´ əp tĭsh´ əs)   This one acts in a secret, stealthy way. From Latin, *surreptitius* = stolen, clandestine.

> *A man chases a woman until she catches him. —Anonymous*

3. **Sybaritic aristocracy** (sĭb´ə rĭ´ tĭk)   They love luxury. Don't we all. But a sybarite loves luxury to the point of self-indulgence. It comes from the name Sybaris, an ancient Greek city noted for its wealth and luxury.

> *On the soft bed of luxury most kingdoms have expired.*
> —Young

4. **lying sycophant** (sĭk´ ə fənt)   A sycophant is a self-seeking flatterer; that flatters just to get something from you. The adjective is sycophantic. From Greek, *sykophant* = informer.

> *Sycophant: One who says things to your face*
> *that he wouldn't say behind your back.*
> —Anonymous

5. **tabescent string bean** (tə bĕs´ ənt)   This poor soul is emaciated, generally as a consequence of a persistent illness. From Latin, *tabescent* = dwindling.

His eyes were like the eyes of a fish not in the best of health.
—*P. G. Wodehouse*

6. **taciturn milquetoast** (tăs´ ĭ tûrn´)   One who is taciturn is almost always silent. From Latin, *tacere* = to be silent.

Silence is argument carried on by other means.
—*Ernesto "Che" Guevara*

7. **tactless witling** (tăkt´ ləs)   This witling lacks the delicate perception to know when to not say something because it might be offensive.   To have tact is just the opposite: you have a keen sense of what to say or do in difficult situations. From Latin, *tactus* = sense of touch + less.

<u>Likely comment:</u>
(shouting at a VIP party)
Hey, how's the diarrhea?
<u>Your response:</u>
Fine. How's the impotence?

8. **tangential jawsmith** (tăn jĕn´ shəl)   A tangent is a line that connects to but doesn't cross or intersect another line. To be tangential is to stray off the topic of discussion on a subject matter only slightly related but not germane to the conversation. From Latin, *tangere* = to touch.

The tongue of a fool carves a piece of his heart to all that sit near him.
—*English proverb*

9. **taurine hotspur** (tôr´ īn)   Anyone taurine is like a bull. Taurine is also a crystalline by-product of cysteine. From Latin, *taurus* = a bull.

Don't help a bull out of a ditch,
for when he's out he'll butt.
—*Malagasy proverb*

10. **tautological earbinder** (tŏt´ ə lŏj´ ĭ kəl)   Redundant, this one needlessly repeats an idea using different words.   From Greek, *tauto* = same + *logos* = a word.

TOMBSTONE EPITAPH
While on earth his tongue never ceased
Now that he's dead, WE can rest in peace.

Quiz 77

Match the definitions with the words on the left.

Brainy Barbs

___ 1. surly   a. almost always silent
___ 2. surreptitious   b. bad-tempered; arrogant
___ 3. Sybaritic   c. emaciated
___ 4. sycophant   d. like a bull
___ 5. tabescent   e. loves luxury self-indulgently
___ 6. taciturn   f. needlessly repeating an idea
                                using different words
___ 7. tactless   g. secretive, stealthy
___ 8. tangential   h. self-seeking flatterer
___ 9. taurine   i. straying off the topic of on a
                                topic not germane to the
                                conversation
___10. tautological   j. without sense or care of what
                                to say without hurting others

Basic Barbs

___11. aristocracy   k. a meek or timid person
___12. milquetoast   l. the elite, privileged class
___13. witling   m. one who talks too much
___14. jawsmith   n. one with little wit
___15. hotspur   o. one with a hot temper

Don't Meet Them In A Dark Alley, Part 1

(mob, rabble, riffraff, canaille, vermin, quisling)

Match.

1. r _ _ _ _ _ = a wild mob; the lower class
2. r _ _ _ _ _ _ _ = worthless, disreputable persons
3. m _ _ = a lawless and disorderly crowd
4. v _ _ _ _ _ = any annoying, harmful animal or insect;
                any contemptible person
5. c _ _ _ _ _ _ _ = riffraff, literally in Italian it means "pack of dogs"
6. q _ _ _ _ _ _ _ = traitor

Grisly List 78

I knew a waiter years ago. A dropout. He hadn't achieved anything in life and didn't have any plans to achieve anything. So he became a waiter. And he soon realized the more he knew about the wine he served the more tips he made. Plus, he liked wine. So he begin to ask more questions from the bartender, and when that was not enough, he read books, and when that fell short, he began to vacation in the wine country, visiting as many wineries as he could. Today, he is a connoisseur of wines and he makes a hefty salary tasting wines. That can be true for you when it comes to words. Maybe you shouldn't stop here. You never know where the road will lead.

Basic Barbs

➤ **gasbag** = slang, one who is full of hot air
➤ **live wire** = an excitable person
➤ **relic** = something old that has survived decay
➤ **scamp** = a rascal; a mischievous child
➤ **trollop** = a shabby, loose woman, a prostitute
➤ **twit** = a fool, nerd etc.

Brainy Barbs

1. **tawdry trollop** (tô´ drē)   One who is tawdry is cheap, showy and sleazy. It comes from a blending of St. Audry, where at the St. Audrey's fair in Norwich, England, cheap, showy neckpieces were sold.

> *A lot of women are getting tattoos. Don't do it. That's sick.*
> *That butterfly looks great on your breast when you're 20, 30.*
> *When you get to be 70, 80, it stretches into a condor.*
> —*Billy Elmer*

2. **temerarious half-wit** (tem´ ə rär´ ē əs)   Some people are bold and some people are foolishly bold. This half-wit might try to ski down Mt. Everest. From Latin, *temere* = rashly, blindly.

> *Always goes as if he had a spare neck in his pocket.*
> —*R. S. Surtees.*

3. **tempestuous wildcat** (tĕm pĕs chū əs)   If you marry one, you'll reap the whirlwind. This one is violent and stormy. From Latin, *tempestes* = calamity, storm.

> *Of all the wild beasts of land or sea, the wildest is woman.*
> —*Menander*

4. **tendentious twit** (tĕn dĕn´ shəs) With a tendency for a specific way, this one is biased, overly opinionated. From Latin, *tendens* = to extend.

Everyone has a right to my opinion.
—Madonna

5. **teratoid horror** (ter´ ə toid) Yikes! Cover your face. This horror resembles a monster. From Greek, *teras* = a monster, wonder.

Her face was her chaperone.
—Rupert Hughes

6. **tergiversating scamp** (tûr´ jĭv ər sā´ ting) To tergiversate is to desert a cause or a party, to be a traitor; or tergiversate can mean to equivocate or use evasions to hide the truth. From Latin, *tergiversari* = to turn one's back, decline.

False in one thing, false in everything.
—Law Maxim

7. **plug-ugly termagant** (tûr´ mə gənt) In Medieval Times, Christians believed (wrongly) a Termagant was a Moslem deity. Christians introduced it into their morality plays as a violent, overbearing person in long robes. It now signifies a scolding, quarrelsome woman.

My wife was too beautiful for words, but not for arguments.
—John Barrymore

8. **testy relic** (tĕs´ tē) A testy person is too irritably impatient and touchy. From Old French, *teste* = the head.

Why be disagreeable, when with a little effort you can be impossible?
—Douglas Woodruff

9. **tetched live wire** (tĕcht) This one is a tad demented, a little crazy. From Late Medieval English, *teche* = a mark.

If a patient is poor he is committed to a public hospital as a "psychotic."
If he can afford a sanatorium, the diagnosis is "neurasthenia."
If he is wealthy enough to be in his own home under the constant watch of nurses and physicians, he is simply "an indisposed eccentric."
—Pierre Janet

10. **thrasonical gasbag** (thrā sŏn´ ĭ kəl) This one likes to brag. From Greek, *thrasos* = too bold > Thrason, a braggart in Terrence's play, Eunuch.

<u>Likely comment:</u>
I have five sport cars.

<u>Your response:</u>
Then get in one and drive away.

Quiz 78

Match the definitions with the words on the right.

Brainy Barbs

___ 1. tawdry	a. a little crazy
___ 2. temerarious	b. a quarrelsome woman
___ 3. tempestuous	c. bragging
___ 4. tendentious	d. cheap, showy and sleazy
___ 5. teratoid	e. desert a cause or a party; or be evasive
___ 6. tergiversate	f. foolishly bold
___ 7. termagant	g. irritably impatient
___ 8. testy	h. overly opinionated
___ 9. tetched	i. resembling a monster
___10. thrasonical	j. violent and stormy

Basic Barbs

___11. gasbag	k. a fool, nerd etc.
___12. relic	l. a mischievous child
___13. twit	m. a shabby, loose woman
___14. scamp	n. slang, one that is full of hot air
___15. trollop	o. old item that has endured rot

Don't Meet Them In A Dark Alley, Part 2

(fiend, hellion, perpetrator, rogue)

Match.

1. p _ _ _ _ _ _ _ _ _ _ = the doer of the crime
2. h _ _ _ _ _ _ = one fond of devilry or mischief
3. r _ _ _ _ = a rascal
4. f _ _ _ _ = an evil spirit; a wicked, cruel person

(racketeer, scoundrel, varmint, thug)

Unscramble.

5. tarvmin = a troublesome person or animal   _____
6. kertaecer = obtains money illegally by bootlegging or extortion   _____
7. drelnuocs = a villain   _____
8. guth = a rough, brutal hoodlum   _____

Grisly List 79

I've suggested your love of language should go beyond this book. It never hurts to pick up another vocabulary book and whisk through it. Then one wordbook makes the other easier and so on. Soon you'll make yourself a word sleuth. The easier each book becomes, the less frustrating it is to study. In time you end up perusing the pages to see if there is anything you don't already know.

Basic Barbs

➢ **belauder** (bǐ lôd ər) = one who praises excessively, especially sarcastically
➢ **lunk** = slang for a big, clumsy idiot
➢ **submoronic** = below the level of a moron
➢ **tenderfoot** = an inexperienced beginner not used to hardships
➢ **tinhorn** = one who pretends to be an expert but actually has little experience or ability. Once, this was primarily used for an inexperienced gambler, but it now describes any beginner.

Brainy Barbs

1. **timorous tenderfoot** (tĭm´ ər əs) To be timorous is to tremble, to be fearful, to be tentative. From Latin, *timor* = fear.

> TOMBSTONE EPITAPH:
> *His ticker stopped ticking*
> *and gave up the fight*
> *When kittens so tiny*
> *mewled in the night.*

2. **torpid vegetable** (tôr´ pĭd) This one is sluggish and/or apathetic. From Latin, *torpere* = to be numb or sluggish.

> *The biggest sin is sitting on your ass.*
> *—Florynce Kennedy*

3. **traducing pile of rubbish** (trə dōōs´ ing) To traduce is to slander, to make a mockery of others. From Latin, *traducere* = to exhibit as a spectacle.

> *Alas they had been friends in youth;*
> *but whispering tongues can poison truth.*
> *—Samuel T. Coleridge*

4. **treacly belauder** (trē´ klē)   A treacly person is given to overly sweet talk or sentiment. Treacle was a concoction used as an remedy for poison. In the 17th century when molasses was added to many remedies, treacle took on the overly sweet connotation. From Latin, *theriaca* = antidote for poison.

> *Honeyed speech often conceals poison and gall.*
> —Danish proverb

5. **tremulous tinhorn** (trĕm´ yə ləs)   Trembling with fear or anxiety, this one shakes like a bowl of Jell-O. From Latin, *tremere* = tremble.

> *I was so timid I was beaten up by Quakers.*
> —Woody Allen

6. **submoronic troglodyte** (trŏg´ lə dīt)   This one lives in a cave, chiefly a prehistoric one. From Greek, *troglodytes* = one who creeps into holes.

> *Man is the missing link between the ape and the human being.*
> —Anonymous

7. **truckling dipwad** (trŭk´ ling)   A truckle is a small wheel, but because of its low place it can imply one is servile, cringing or obsequious. From Greek, *trokhos* = a wheel.

> *Servitude debases men to the point where they end up liking it.*
> —Vauvenargues

8. **truculent lunk** (trŭk´ yə lənt)   This savage brute is vicious in both manner and speech. From Latin, *truculentus* = ferocious, cruel.

> *Man is still a savage to the extent*
> *that he has little respect*
> *for anything that cannot hurt him.*
> —Edgar Watson Howe

9. **turgid motor-mouth** (tûr´ jĭd)   Turgid means swollen and can also refer to someone's speech as being "swollen," i.e. bombastic and pompous . From Latin, *turgere* = to swell.

> *If only I had a little humility, I would be perfect.*
> —allegedly Ted Turner

10. **tongue-tied tyro** (tī´ rō)   A tyro is a rank beginner, one who is just starting to learn something. From Latin, *tiro* = a young soldier.

> *A good man is always a beginner.*
> —Martial

Quiz 79

Match the definitions with the words on the right.

Brainy Barbs

__	1. timorous	a.	a beginner
__	2. torpid	b.	a caveman
__	3. traduce	c.	a small wheel; servile, cringing or obsequious
__	4. treacly	d.	overly sweet in speech
__	5. tremulous	e.	savage, vicious
__	6. troglodyte	f.	slander, make a mockery
__	7. truckling	g.	sluggish and apathetic
__	8. truculent	h.	swollen; pompous
__	9. turgid	i.	trembling (fits two words)
__	10. tyro		

Basic Barbs

__	11. lunk	j.	an inexperienced beginner not used to hardships
__	12. submoronic	k.	below level of a moron
__	13. tinhorn	l.	praises excessively and sarcastically
__	14. belauder	m.	pretends to be an expert but has little experience
__	15. tenderfoot	n.	slang for a big, clumsy idiot

Two Left Feet

(bungler, flounder, gangling, incompetent,)
(inept, klutz, maladroit, ungainly)

Match.

1. m _ _ _ _ _ _ _ _ = clumsy or blundering
2. i _ _ _ _ = unfit; awkward; inefficient
3. u _ _ _ _ _ _ _ _ = clumsy; not attractive
4. i _ _ _ _ _ _ _ _ _ _ = inept
5. g _ _ _ _ _ _ _ = thin, tall and awkward
6. f _ _ _ _ _ _ _ _ = move, speak or act in a awkward and confused way
7. k _ _ _ _ = any clumsy stupid person
8. b _ _ _ _ _ _ = one who is clumsy and unsuccessful

There are two words in this list that need clarification. The word ulterior is not in and of itself, a disparaging term. If something is ulterior it is more than what is being said, but you always hear it used as a pejorative term when coupled with the word motive, and it is always used in that context, "He has ulterior motives." So I've included it in this list. You will often hear the phrase, "Don't take umbrage," but you probably have never heard the adjective, umbrageous, and that's the beauty of it.

Basic Barbs

➤ **battle-ax** = a heavy ax used as a weapon; a bossy woman
➤ **Delilah** = biblical character who used her seductive charms to enslave Samson; a seductress
➤ **heckler** = one who annoys a speaker by shouting out objections or abuse
➤ **novice** = one on probation in a religious order before taking vows; a beginner
➤ **perpetrator** = the doer of a crime
➤ **powder keg** = anything or anyone that can explode at any time

Brainy Barbs

1. **ugsome perpetrator** (ŭg´ səm) Anyone ugsome is loathsome and horrid. From Medieval English, *uggen* = to fear, cause loathing.

> *I have found little that is good about human beings.*
> *In my experience most of them are trash.*
> —Sigmund Freud

2. **ulterior motive** (əl tēr´ ē ər) Anything ulterior is undisclosed, hidden. When one has an ulterior motive, he or she is concealing his or her true motive. Beware! From Latin, *ultra* = beyond.

> *He can best avoid a snare that knows how to set one.*
> —Publilius Syrus

3. **umbrageous powder keg** (ŭm brā´ jəs) To be umbrageous is to take offense too easily. From French, *ombrageux* = shy, suspecting.

> TOMBSTONE EPITAPH:
> *A little too touchy.*
> *A little too hurt*
> *Now he won't take offense.*
> *Under six feet of dirt*

4. unbitted Delilah (ŭn bĭt´ əd)   A bit is the metal mouthpiece used for controlling the horse; hence, to be unbitted is to be wild and uncontrolled. From Old English, un = not + *bitan* = bite.

Give a woman an inch and she'll park her car on it.
—*E. P. B. White*

5. unbridled battle-ax (ŭn brĭd´ əld)   A bridle is the harness used to control a horse. To be unbridled is to be unrestrained. From Old English, un = not + *bregdan* = to pull, turn.

When passion is on the throne, reason is out of doors.
—*M. Henry*

6. unconscionable worm (ŭn kŏn´shə nə bəl)   This one has no morals, no conscience. From Latin, un = without + *conscientia* = moral sense.

Pity was invented by the weak.
—*Mendele Mocher Serforim*

7. uncouth animal (ŭn kūth´)   This one is strange, clumsy and crude. From Old English, *uncuth* = unknown.

There is a vast difference between the savage and the civilized man,
but it is never apparent to their wives until after breakfast.
—*Helen Rowland*

8. unctuous manipulator (ungk´ chū əs)   This oily person is smooth and deceitful. From Latin, *unctum* = ointment.

In the mouths of many men soft words are like roses
that soldiers put into the muzzles of their muskets on holidays.
—*Longfellow*

9. undermining heckler (ŭn´ dər mīn´ ing)   This one digs underneath you, wearing away at your base, or weakens you by some insidious means. From Old Icelandic, *undir* = under + Gaelic, *mein* = ore, mineral.

Why do you heckle me? For all you know, I'm your father.
—*Jack White*

10. unfledged novice (ŭn flĕjd´)   An unfledged novice is immature and untried. From Medieval English, *un* = not + *flegge* = ready to fly.

Youth is a disease that only time can cure.
—*P. Snurd*

Quiz 80

Match the definitions with the words on the right.

Brainy Barbs

___ 1. ugsome
___ 2. ulterior
___ 3. umbrageous
___ 4. unbitted
___ 5. unbridled
___ 6. unconscionable
___ 7. uncouth
___ 8. unctuous

___ 9. undermine
___10. unfledged

a. deceptively concealing something
b. horrid, and loathsome
c. immature and untried
d. smooth and deceitful
e. strange, clumsy and crude
f. take offense too easily
g. weaken insidiously
h. wild, unrestrained (fits two words)
i. with no conscience

Basic Barbs

___11. novice
___12. heckler
___13. powder keg
___14. battle-ax

___15. Delilah
___16. perpetrator

j. a heavy ax used as a weapon; a domineering woman
k. can explode anytime
l. a seductress
m. annoys a speaker by shouting out objections or abuse
n. the doer of a crime
o. a beginner

Diehards

(*dogged, indurate, inexorable, mulish, obdurate,*)
(*pertinacious, precipitous, willful*)

Match.

1. d _ _ _ _ _ = stubborn
2. w _ _ _ _ _ _ = stubborn
3. i _ _ _ _ _ _ _ = hardened; stubborn
4. o _ _ _ _ _ _ _ = hardhearted; stubborn
5. m _ _ _ _ _ = stubborn
6. i _ _ _ _ _ _ _ _ _ = unyielding
7. p _ _ _ _ _ _ _ _ _ _ = steep; headlong in disposition
8. p _ _ _ _ _ _ _ _ _ _ _ = stubborn

LE MOT QUOTE 48
Match each quote with the appropriate word.

1. If you sleep with a dog you will rise full of fleas.
   —Greek proverb

2. He is looking for the donkey while sitting on it.
   —Armenian proverb

3. The larger the income, the harder it is to live within it.
   —Whately

4. Without tact you can learn nothing. —Disraeli

___ a. stultified

___ b. Sybaritic

___ c. smirchy

___ d. tactless

LE MOT QUOTE 49
Match each quote with the appropriate word.

1. Behind every great fortune there is a crime. —Balzac

2. While you're saving your face you're losing your ass.
   —Lyndon B. Johnson

3. Three may keep a secret, if two of them are dead.
   —Franklin

4. Some men, like dogs,
   will only fawn the more when repulsed,
   but will pay little heed to a friendly caress.
   —Abd-el-Kader

5. The bigger the man's head, the worse his headache.
   —Persian Proverb

___ a. truckling

___ b. arriviste

___ c. timorous

___ d. surreptitious

___ e. supercilious

LE MOT QUOTE 50
Match each quote with the appropriate word.

1. By means of a whorish woman
   a man is brought to a piece of bread. —Proverbs 6: 26

2. With audacity one can undertake anything,
   but not do everything. —Napoleon I

3. Wind puffs up empty bladders; opinion, fools.
   —Socrates

4. We must interpret a bad temper
   as a sign of an inferiority complex. —Dr. Alfred Adler

5. They brag most that do the least. —English proverb

___ a. treacly

___ b. thrasonical

___ c. testy

___ d. tendentious

___ e. temerarious

___ f. Delilah

Chapter 17

A healthy ear can stand hearing sick words.
—Senegalese proverb

Grisly List 81

As you near the end of this book, I suggest you look again at the list of synonyms. Now is an excellent time to emphasize this section. This will help greatly expand your choice of words. Soon, the word senile will at once bring to mind senescent, anachronistic, preadamic.

Basic Barbs

➤ **loan shark** = one who lends money at exorbitant rates of interest
➤ **ruck** = a mass of common people
➤ **tool** = one used as a tool for someone else's shenanigans
➤ **warmonger** = one who wants war
➤ **welsh (or welch)** (wĕlsh´, wĕlch´) = To welsh is to cheat by failing to pay a debt. A welsher is one who welshes.

Brainy Barbs

1. **ungainly stumblebum** (ŭn gān´ lē) This one is uncoordinated and unattractive. From Old Norse, un = not + gegn = straight, fit.

> He had a profile like a flight of steps.
> —Kipling,
> of King Edward VII

2. **unkempt mutt** (ŭn kĕmpt´) Uncombed and untidy, this mutt looks shabby. From Middle English, un + kembe = to comb.

> There was a young belle of old Natchez
> Whose garments were always in patchez.
> When comment arose
> On the state of her clothes,
> She drawled, When Ah itchez, Ah scratches.
> —Ogden Nash

3. **unmitigated cuckoo** (ŭn mĭt´ ə gā´ tĭd) Anything unmitigated is absolute or not lessened (e.g. unmitigated gall = complete impudence, rudeness) Combined with cuckoo it describes an out-and-out lunatic. From Middle English, un = not, the opposite of + mitigare = to make mild.

> TOMBSTONE EPITAPH:
> Get me out of here!!

4. unregenerate ruck (ŭn´ rĭ jĕn´ ər ĭt) Literally, unregenerate means not born again, but now it signifies an obstinate, recalcitrant, profane or heathen person. From Latin, *in* = not + *re* = again + *generare* = to create.

> *I'm a born-again atheist.*
> —Gore Vidal

5. unsavory welsher (ŭn sā´ və rē) To be unsavory is to have a bad taste or odor, but it can also mean to be morally bad. From Old French, *un* + *savourer* = to taste.

> *Why do Kennedy men cry during sex? Mace!*
> —Anonymous

6. unscrupulous warmonger (ŭn skrū´ pyə ləs) This one is without morals or conscience. From Latin, *in* = without + *scrupus* = a sharp pebble or stone.

> *I propose getting rid of conventional armaments*
> *and replacing them with reasonably priced hydrogen bombs*
> *that would be distributed equally throughout the world.*
> —Idi Amin

7. unseemly sleazebag (ŭn sēm´ lē) To be unseemly is to be rude, indecent, improper. From Medieval English, *un* = not + *semlich* = fitting.

> *Want of decency is want of sense.*
> —Wentworth Dillon

8. untoward remark (ŭn tōrd´) This can mean an unfortunate remark or more likely, an unseemly remark. From Old English, *un* = not + *toweard* = in the direction of, facing.

> *I've been around so long, I knew Doris Day before she was a virgin.*
> —Groucho Marx

9. unwitting tool (ŭn wĭt´ ing) Completely unaware, this tool could end up being the unintentionally accomplice of others. From Old English, *un* = not + *witan* = to know.

> *Ignorance, when voluntary is criminal.*
> —Samuel Johnson

10. usurious loan shark (yū zhŏŏr´ ē əs) Don't borrow money from this jerk; anyone usurious lends money at exorbitant high interest. From Latin, *uti* = to use.

> *A legal thief, a bloodless murderer,*
> *A fiend incarnate, a false usurer.*
> —Joseph Hall

Quiz 81

Match the definitions with the words on the right.

Brainy Barbs

___ 1. ungainly
___ 2. unkempt
___ 3. unmitigated
___ 4. unregenerate
___ 5. unsavory
___ 6. unscrupulous
___ 7. unseemly
___ 8. untoward
___ 9. unwitting
___10. usurious

a. absolute or not lessened
b. completely unaware
c. indecent (fits two words)
d. uncoordinated; unattractive
e. lends money at high interest
f. profane, heathen, obstinate
g. tastes bad
h. uncombed and untidy, shabby
i. without morals or conscience

Basic Barbs

___11. loan shark
___12. tool
___13. warmonger
___14. ruck

j. mass of common people
k. lends money at inflated rates of interest
l. one who wants war
m. slang, one used unwittingly by another

Wet Behind The Ears, Part 1

(sophomoric, novice, greenhorn, neophyte, tyke, tenderfoot,)
(puerile, callow, tinhorn, stray, gamine, whelp)

Match.

1. n _ _ _ _ _ = one on probation in a religious order before taking vows; a beginner
2. n _ _ _ _ _ _ _ = a recent convert; a beginner
3. t _ _ _ = a small child
4. t _ _ _ _ _ _ = one who pretends to be an expert, once meant for gamblers
5. t _ _ _ _ _ _ _ _ _ = inexperienced beginner
6. g _ _ _ _ _ _ _ _ = an inexperienced person
7. p _ _ _ _ _ _ = juvenile, childish
8. c _ _ _ _ _ = immature
9. s _ _ _ _ _ _ _ _ _ = immature
10. s _ _ _ _ = a homeless child
11. w _ _ _ _ = young offspring of a dog or wolf; or an impudent youth
12. g _ _ _ _ _ = a neglected kid; a roguish girl

Grisly List 82

When you need to memorize a phone number you listen to it; repeat it; then write it down. As you use it over and over it sinks into your long-term memory. It is there, sitting in your brain, ready to be used when needed. That sums up about half the suggestions I've given you for this book. If you follow those suggestions, you will surely be the local wit!

Basic Barbs

- ➤ **comatose** = in a coma: dull, torpid
- ➤ **cretin** = an idiot, Cretin comes from the Swiss French, *crestin*, literally meaning Christian. Originally, it was not a slur but was used to describe the mentally retarded as human —not animals. It is now known Cretinism is caused by a thyroid condition.
- ➤ **dunce** = an idiot, after John Duns Scotus, 1265-1308, a writer ridiculed in the 16th century; his followers were called dunsmen
- ➤ **eccentric** = one full of odd behavior, deviating from the norm
- ➤ **pixilated** = eccentric, daft, nutty. Altered from of pixy-led, one carried away or affected by pixies; hence, mentally unstable.
- ➤ **pooh bah** = a pompous official capable of being bribed. From a fictitious person, Pooh Bah, in Gilbert and Sullivan's, The Mikado,
- ➤ **socialite** = one who is prominent in the "in" crowd, often valuing status above depth

Brainy Barbs

1. **uxorious dunce** (ŭk sôr´ ē əs) Yuck! This sheepish one is excessively, submissively devoted to his wife. From Latin, *uxor* = wife.

A husband is what's left of a man after the nerve has been extracted.
—Helen Rowland

2. **vacuous cretin** (văk´ yū əs) Anyone vacuous is empty, lacking intelligence. From Latin, *uacare* = to be empty.

I locked my keys in the car
and had to break the windshield to get my wife out.
—Red Skelton

3. **pixilated vagabond** (văg´ ə bŏnd) Moving from place to place, a vagabond is a hobo. From Latin, *vagari* = to wander.

I'm dating a homeless woman.
It was easier to talk her into staying over.
—Garry Shandling

4. **vagarious eccentric** (və gâr´ ē əs)   A vagarious person is full of odd and eccentric behavior. From Latin, *vagari* = to wander.

> *Shirley Maclaine could go to group therapy all by herself.*
> —Cynthia Nelms

5. **comatose vagrant** (vā´ grənt)   This hobo wanders from place to place. From Latin, *vagari* = to wander.

> *They say the homeless are homeless by choice. That's true.*
> *I was walking down Bleaker Street at two in the morning,*
> *and I just had that burning desire to go to sleep right there.*
> —Scott Blakeman

6. **vainglorious show-off** (vān glôr´ ē əs)   This high and mighty one is boastfully conceited. From Latin, *vana gloria* = empty boasting.

> *Who knows himself a braggart, let him fear this;*
> *for it shall come to pass that every braggart shall be found an ass.*
> —Shakespeare
> All's Well That Ends Well

7. **vapid socialite** (văp´ ĭd, vā´ pĭd)   To be vapid is to be dull and/or tasteless. From Latin, *vapidus* = stale, insipid.

> *Being popular is important. Otherwise, people might not like you.*
> —Mimi Pond

8. **self-vaunting know-it-all** (vôn´ ting)   To vaunt is to boast, to brag about one's success. From Latin, *vanus* = empty, vain.

> *Self-praise smells bad.*
> —Swedish proverb

9. **venal pooh bah** (vēn´ əl)   Anyone venal is capable of being bribed or corrupted. From Latin, *venalis* = for sale.

> *A conscience, which has been bought once, will be bought twice.*
> —Norbert Wiener

10. **venerious player** (věn ər´ ē əs)   Venery has two meanings: from Latin, venery comes from *Venus* = goddess of love; hence, it means lustful. It also comes from *venari*, = to hunt. So it can depicts one given to hunting or one on the hunt for sex.

> *He said he got the misery, but he had a lot of fun.*
> —Little Richard

Quiz 82

Match the definitions with the words on the right.

Brainy Barbs

___ 1. uxorious
___ 2. vacuous
___ 3. vagabond
___ 4. vagarious
___ 5. vagrant
___ 6. vainglorious
___ 7. vapid
___ 8. vaunt
___ 9. venal
___10. venerious

a. a hobo (fits two words)
b. boastfully conceited
c. capable of being bribed
d. dull and/or tasteless
e. empty
f. overly devoted to one's wife
g. full of eccentric behavior
h. lustful; given to hunting
i. to boast

Basic Barbs

___11. pixilated
___12. dunce
___13. cretin
___14. comatose

___15. eccentric
___16. socialite
___17. pooh bah

j. a pompous official capable of being bribed
k. idiot (fits two words)
l. in a coma; unconscious
m. one full of odd behavior, daft, nutty (fits two words)
n. is prominent in the "in" crowd

Wet Behind The Ears, Part 2

(bantling, delinquent, whippersnapper,)
(scamp, unfledged, fledgling)

Unscramble.

1. psmca = a rascal; a mischievous child _____
2. bltgnina = a brat _____
3. dtenuqniel = failing to do one's duty; a young troublemaker _____
4. glefdglin = a young bird just ready for flight; an inexperienced person _____
5. funedledg = immature, not developed, untried _____
6. reppihwseranpp = a young insignificant, pretentious person _____

Grisly List 83

Let's say you have a favorite beach that you visit. Whenever you have the time you go there. You swim in the ocean, climb along the rocks, run along the sand. You know that beach backwards and forwards, every nook and cranny, where to park, how to leave, when it's busy, when it's not etc. You've never studied the beach; you've simply been there and enjoyed it. The more you use this book as a pleasant pastime the more you will retain the information without any effort.

Basic Barbs

➤ **lamia** = From Greek mythology, a Lamia was a half-snake/half-woman monster who fed on humans and sucked the blood of infants. It can also signify a female vampire.

➤ **varmint** = a troublesome person or animal

➤ **voyeur** = one who derives sexual pleasure from peeping at others disrobed or in intimate relations

➤ **Xanthippe** = Xanthippe was the wife of Socrates. Socrates once said, "If you don't have a good wife, there's always philosophy." So, I guess we have her nagging to thank for his legacy. It is now used as a pejorative for any quarrelsome, nagging wife.

➤ **yenta** = a Yiddish slang term for an annoying, gossipy woman

Brainy Barbs

1. **vengeful Xanthippe** (vĕnj´ fəl) This witch wants revenge, full of venge, which is an archaic word meaning avenge. From Old French, *venger* = to avenge.

> *Revenge is sweet and not fattening.*
> —Alfred Hitchcock

2. **venomous villain** (vĕn´ ə məs) This villain is poisonous, full of venom, the toxic liquid created by an animal to stop prey or defend itself. It can also describe one who is spiteful. From Latin, *venenum* = a poison.

> *The man recovered of the bite.*
> *The dog it was that died.*
> —Goldsmith

3. **verbose yenta** (vər bōs´) This yenta simply uses too many words. From Latin, *verbum* = word.

> *Open your mouth only to change feet.*
> —Stanley Ralph Ross

4. **vexatious in-laws** (vĕk sā´ shəs)   Anyone vexatious is annoying. From French, *vexer* = to torment < Latin, *vexare* = to shake, agitate.

> People who think they know everything
> are very irritating to those of us that do.
> —Anonymous

5. **vicarious voyeur** (vī kâr´ ē əs)   This one is thrilled by imagined participation watching another's experience, as when a fan gets a thrill watching a sports team win a game. From Latin, *vicarius* = substituting.

> An orgy looks particularly alluring
> seen through the mists of righteous indignation.
> —Malcolm Muggeridge

6. **vilipending snitch** (vĭl´ ə pĕnd´ ing)   This one treats others with low regard or speaks slanders about them. From Latin, *vili* = cheap.

> Accuse. To affirm another's guilt or unworthiness;
> most commonly as a justification of ourselves of having wronged him.
> —Ambrose Bierce

7. **villainous mugger** (vĭl´ ə nəs)   Anyone villainous is criminal, wicked. From Vulgar Latin, *villanus* = a farm worker.

> A man cannot become perfect in a hundred years;
> but he may become corrupt in less than one day.
> —Chinese proverb

8. **vindictive viper** (vĭn dĭk´ tĭv)   Watch your back! This fiend wants revenge. From Latin, *vindicare* = avenge, to claim.

> She always tells stories in the present vindictive.
> —Tom Peace

9. **virulent lamia** (vĭr´ yə lənt)   This one is poisonous, infectious. Virulent can also be used to describe one who is spiteful. From Latin, *virulentus* = full of poison.

> What does not poison fattens.
> —Italian proverb

10. **vitiated varmint** (vĭsh´ ē āt´ əd)   Literally, vitiated means spoiled, but it can also describe one who has been weakened morally. From Latin, *vitiare* = to spoil.

> Corruption is like a ball of snow:
> whence once set a-rolling it must increase.
> —Charles Caleb Colton

Quiz 83

Match the definitions with the words on the right.

Brainy Barbs

___ 1. vengeful
___ 2. venomous
___ 3. verbose

___ 4. vexatious
___ 5. vicarious
___ 6. vilipend
___ 7. villainous
___ 8. vindictive
___ 9. virulent
___10. vitiated

a. annoying
b. criminal, wicked
c. experienced through another person via imagination
d. poisonous (fits two words)
e. spoiled; weakened morally
f. to slander
g. using too many words
h. revengeful (fits two words)

Basic Barbs

___11. varmint

___12. lamia
___13. yenta
___14. Xanthippe

i. half-snake/half-woman monster who fed on humans
j. a troublesome person or animal
k. an annoying, gossipy woman
l. a quarrelsome, nagging wife

Old And In The Way, Part 1

(rugose, has-been, obsolete, relic, anachronistic, decrepit,)
(antiquated, fusty, senile, senescent, doddering)

Match.

1. h _ _ - _ _ _ _ = no longer famous
2. r _ _ _ _ = a thing old that has survived decay
3. a _ _ _ _ _ _ _ _ _ _ _ _ _ = out of proper time
4. a _ _ _ _ _ _ _ _ _ = old and in the way
5. d _ _ _ _ _ _ _ = worn out by old age
6. d _ _ _ _ _ _ _ _ = trembling from old age
7. f _ _ _ _ = stale; old-fashioned
8. s _ _ _ _ _ = growing dumb from old age
9. s _ _ _ _ _ _ _ _ _ = aging, growing old
10. o _ _ _ _ _ _ _ = being out of use or fashion
11. r _ _ _ _ _ = wrinkled

You're almost finished, but your journey has just begun. Set the book down for a month or two. Then read it again. You'll get much more than you did the first time around. That's the way memory works. Reviewing information is always ten times more important than the initial study time.

Basic Barbs

> **opportunist** = one who adapts one's actions to take advantage of the immediate situation without regard to anyone else
> **vamp** = derived from vampire, it now describes a woman who uses her charms to seduce men
> **vermin** = any annoying, destructive animal or insect; any contemptible person or persons
> **vile** = evil, repulsive
> **vixen** = a female fox or a shrewish woman
> **wimp** = a weakling

Brainy Barbs

1. **vitriolic tongue-lasher** (vĭ´ trē ŏl´ ĭk) Anyone vitriolic is sharp, bitter and biting. The oil of vitriol is sulfuric acid. From Latin, *vitreus* = glassy because of the oil's glassy appearance

Any fool can criticize, and many of them do.
—C. Garbett

2. **vituperative vermin** (vī tū´ pə rā´ tĭv) Hurling abuse, this vermin spits accusations out, ranting and raving. From Latin, *vituperare* = to blame.

By blackening another you do not whiten yourself.
—Rumanian proverb

3. **vociferous griper** (vō sĭf´ ər əs) To be vociferous is to shout to be loud, clamorous. From Latin, *vociferare* = to shout, to cry out noisily.

What he lacks in substance he makes up for in volume.
—Unknown

4. **volatile vixen** (vŏl´ ə tĭl) Volatile has several meanings: able to fly; vaporizing quickly; or fickle, unstable, and explosive. If you're a volatile person you're likely to explode at any time. From Latin, *volare* = to fly.

Do we know much about women? Do we? We don't.
We know when they're happy, we know when they're crying,
we know when they're pissed off. We just don't know
what order those are gonna come at us.
—Evan Davis

5. **voracious vamp** (vō rā´ shəs)　Voracious usually means to eat with greediness, as in "a voracious appetite"; but it also signifies one who is immoderate, as in, "His voracious lust for power was his undoing". From Latin, *vorare* = to devour.

> *Big mouthfuls often choke.*
> *—Italian proverb*

6. **vile vulgarian** (vŭl gâr´ ē ən)　Plug your children's' ears. A vulgarian is given to coarse tastes. He's indecent, crude, and shows a lack of good breeding. From Latin, *vulgus* = the general public.

> *Maintain your rank, vulgarity despise.*
> *To swear is neither brave, polite, nor wise.*
> *—Cowper*

7. **vulpine opportunist** (vul´ pīn)　Vulpine means like a fox. So a vulpine opportunist is a crafty fellow who sees a chance to get ahead and takes it. From Latin, *vulpes* = fox.

> *The fox changes his skin but not his habits.*
> *—Suetonius*

8. **waffling wimp** (wăf´ ling)　This wimp speaks in an indecisive way or perhaps in a purposely vague way in order to equivocate. Probably from wave which is from Indo-European, *webh* = to fluctuate.

> *His indecision is final.*
> *—Anonymous*

9. **waggish clown** (wăg´ ĭsh)　In British slang a wag is one given to droll, roguish humor. Imagine the humor a pirate might have. The origin of wag is uncertain, but it may come from Middle English, *wag-halter*, a gallows bird. A gallows bird was anyone who deserves hanging. To call someone a wag-halter is synonymous with rogue, joker.

> *A hooker told me she'd do anything I wanted for fifty bucks.*
> *I said, "Paint my house."*
> *—Henny Youngman*

10. **wanton womanizer** (wŏn´ tən)　Wanton can mean unmanageable; as in, "The wanton brat tossed the cake out the window"; or sexually loose; as in, "The wanton woman leered provocatively at the shy stranger"; or senseless; as in, "His wanton act of violence left the city in shock." Take your pick. From Medieval English, *wantowen* = undisciplined

> *Don't accept rides from strange men,*
> *and remember that all men are strange.*
> *—Robin Morgan*

Quiz 84

Match the definitions with the words on the right.

Brainy Barbs

__ 1. vitriolic   a. able to fly; vaporizing quickly; or fickle, unstable, explosive
__ 2. vituperative   b. eating with greediness
__ 3. vociferous   c. given to droll, roguish humor
__ 4. volatile   d. hurling abuse, ranting
__ 5. voracious   e. like a fox
__ 6. vulgarian   f. loud, clamorous
__ 7. vulpine   g. one given to coarse tastes
__ 8. waffle   h. sharp, bitter and biting
__ 9. waggish   i. speak in purposely vague way
__10. wanton   j. unmanageable; sexually loose

Basic Barbs

__11. opportunist   k. female fox; a shrewish woman
__12. vile   l. a weakling
__13. vamp   m. a woman who uses her charms to seduce men
__14. vixen   n. adapts one's actions to take advantage of the situation
__15. vermin   o. evil, repulsive
__16. wimp   p. annoying, destructive animal

Old And In The Way, Part 2

(antediluvian, geezer, gammer, dotard,)
(gaffer, preadamic, Noachian)

Unscramble.

1. adapremic = existing before Adam   _____
2. achianon = of Noah's age   _____
3. teandivulian = before the flood, old   _____
4. zeeger = a crotchety or eccentric old man   _____
5. mmerag = an elderly woman   _____
6. tadord = one who is weak and child-like due to old age   _____
7. ferafg = an old man, used contemptuously or humorously   _____

You have come to the end. You should feel a sense of pride of accomplishment. Refer back to this book from time to time when you feel the need. Always remember: the more you use these words again and again, the more they will work for you.

Basic Barbs

- ➤ **bigot** = one who blindly holds to attitudes of intolerance and prejudice; from Old French, an insult used by the Normans, possibly meaning, "by god"
- ➤ **buttery** = as slang, oily, slippery
- ➤ **dabbler** = one who flits from interest to interest
- ➤ **racist** = one who hates other races out of prejudice and ignorance
- ➤ **simp** = slang for a simpleton, an idiot
- ➤ **stray** = to stray is to wander away from the group; as a noun, it is one who has wandered away, a homeless child
- ➤ **wit** = humor, or a person who can make lively, clever remarks

Brainy Barbs

1. **wretched wastrel** (wā´ strəl) This poor wretch has wasted away his money, life and essence. From Latin, *vastus* = empty, waste.

> *The greater cantle of the world is lost with very ignorance,*
> *we have kissed away kingdoms and provinces.*
> —Shakespeare
> Anthony and Cleopatra

2. **buttery wheedler** (bŭt´ ə rē) To wheedle is to try to influence by flattery or guile. From German, *wedein* = to wag a fan or tail; thus, to flatter < *wedel* = a fan or tail.

> *He who knows how to flatter*
> *also knows how to slander.*
> —Napoleon

3. **whimsical dabbler** (hwĭm´ zĭ kəl) This one's capricious, fanciful, odd . Possibly from Old Norse, *hvima* = to let one's eyes wander.

> *Some have at first for wits,*
> *then poets passed;*
> *turned critics next,*
> *and proved plain fools at last.*
> —Pope

4. **willful bigot** (wĭl´ fəl)   Willful can mean two things: it can mean voluntary; or it can mean one is unreasonable, stubborn to the bitter end. From Indo-European, *wel* = to wish, to choose.

> O sir, to willful men, the injuries that they themselves procure
> must be their schoolmasters.
> —Shakespeare, King Lear

5. **wily coyote** (wī´ lē)   Think of the roadrunner cartoon, only not so unlucky. This critter is crafty and sly. From Old English, *wicca* = witchcraft.

> In order to be the master, the politician poses as the servant.
> —Charles de Gaulle

6. **wincing simp** (wĭns´ ing)   To wince is to shrink back involuntarily, from pain or fear. From Medieval English, *wincen* = to kick.

> Hollow men, like horses hot at hand,
> make gallant show and promise of their mettle;
> but when they should endure the bloody spur,
> they fall their crests, and like deceitful jades sink in the trial.
> —Shakespeare, Julius Caesar

7. **wizened old leper** (wĭz´ ənd)   This one is shriveled, dried up withered. From Icelandic, *visna* = to wither.

> I prefer old age to the alternative.
> —Maurice Chevalier

8. **woebegone stray** (wō´ bĭ gôn)   This wretched one is filled with sorrow. From Middle English, *wo* = great sorrow + *begon* = to go around.

> Man's grandeur stems from his knowledge of his own misery.
> A tree does not know itself to be miserable.
> —Pascal

9. **wry wit** (rī)   Some people's humor is a little twisted, a little perverse. From Old English, *writhan* = to twist.

> Wit is educated insolence.
> —Aristotle

10. **xenophobic racist** (zĕn´ ə fō´ bĭk)   Xenophobes are fearful of strangers or contamination from the outside, or they may blame problems on foreigners. From Greek, *xeno* = stranger, foreign + *phobos* = a fear.

> Likely comment:
> You from 'round here?
>
> Your response:
> Why yes! I'm your mother.

Quiz 85

Match the definitions with the words on the right.

Brainy Barbs

___ 1. wastrel
___ 2. wheedle
___ 3. whimsical
___ 4. willful
___ 5. wily
___ 6. wince
___ 7. wizened

___ 8. woebegone
___ 9. wry
___10. xenophobic

a. capricious, fanciful, odd
b. crafty and sly
c. dried up, shriveled, withered
d. fearful of strangers, foreigners
e. filled with woe, wretched
f. shrink back involuntarily
g. one who has wasted away his money, life and essence
h. stubborn, unreasonable
i. to influence by flattery or guile
j. twisted, perverse

Basic Barbs

___11. racist
___12. wit
___13. stray
___14. simp

___15. bigot

___16. dabble
___17. buttery

k. a homeless child
l. as slang, oily, slippery
m. makes lively, clever remarks
n. one who hates other races out of prejudice and ignorance
o. one who blindly holds views of intolerance and prejudice
p. slang for a simpleton, an idiot
q. to flit from interest to interest

Old And In The Way, Part 3

(primordial, sackless, grimalkin, crone, codger, fogy, biddy)

Unscramble.

1. malirgkin = an old female cat; a shrewish old woman   _____
2. onerc = an ugly, withered old woman   _____
3. dgecor = an eccentric old man   _____
4. yogf = one who is old-fashioned   _____
5. ddybi = a fussbudget or fussy old woman   _____
6. mopirdiral = existing from the beginning, primitive   _____
7. skalcess = feebleminded, lacking energy   _____

LE MOT QUOTE 51

Match each quote with the appropriate word.

1. One should forgive one's enemies,
   but not before they are hanged. —Heinrich Heine

2. Hunger is a slut hound on a fresh track. —Josh Billings

3. Some guy hit my fender the other day,
   and I said unto him, "Be fruitful and multiply."
   but not in those words. —Woody Allen

4. We love a joke that hands us a pat on the back
   while it kicks the other fellow down stairs. —Edson

5. To lead an uninstructed people to war
   is to throw them away. —Confucius

6. You play the spaniel,
   and think with the wagging of your tongue
   to win me. —Shakespeare

7. Man is not man, but a wolf,
   to those he does not know. —Plautus

___ a. voracious

___ b. vengeful

___ c. xenophobic

___ d. wheedle

___ e. warmonger

___ f. wag

___ g. vulgarian

LE MOT QUOTE 52
Match each quote with the appropriate word.

1. A creditor is worse than a master; for a master owns only your person. A creditor owns your dignity and can belabor that.   —Victor Hugo, Les Miserables

2. She has a whim of iron. —Oliver Herford

3. A bribe will enter without knocking. —English proverb

4. Words are like leaves; and where they most abound, much fruit of sense beneath is rarely found. —Pope

5. Lilies that fester smell far worse than weeds.
                                                 —Shakespeare

6. The weak in courage is strong in cunning.
                                                 —William Blake

___ a. vagarious

___ b. venal

___ c. usurious

___ d. verbose

___ e. wily

___ f. vitiated

LE MOT QUOTE 53
Circle the word that best matches the quote.

To the last I stab at thee; from hell's heart I stab at thee; for hate's sake I spit my last breath at thee.
                                                 —Melville
                                                 Moby Dick

a. vitiate   b. vindictive   c. verbose

Final Synonym Slurs

Little Hitlers

(Gestapo, megalomaniac, martinet, fascist, demagogue, imperialist)

Unscramble.

1. scafist = a member of a party that believes
    in a brutal form of dictatorship _____

2. gamelocaniam = a person deluded
    with grandeur, power _____

3. maretint = bossy, disciplinarian _____

4. magodegue = a leader who uses prejudice
    to stir up the mobs _____

5. pimeriatisl = ominates the political affairs
    of weaker governments _____

6. tagespo = the ruthless, secret police force
    of Nazi Germany _____

(autocrat, despot, mogul, taskmaster, tyrant)

Match.

7. d _ _ _ _ _ = an absolute ruler, tyrant
8. t _ _ _ _ _ = a cruel, oppressive ruler
9. t _ _ _ _ _ _ _ _ _ = a demanding person who assigns
    tasks for others
10. m _ _ _ _ = a Mongolian; a powerful person in a autocratic position
11. a _ _ _ _ _ _ _ = one with unlimited power

(authoritarian, autocratic, cashier, coercive, dictatorial, draconian,)
(exacting, exigent, imperious, procrustean, stringent)

Match.

12. d _ _ _ _ _ _ _ _ = extremely cruel
13. d _ _ _ _ _ _ _ _ _ _ = tyrannical
14. c _ _ _ _ _ _ = to dismiss in dishonor
15. a _ _ _ _ _ _ _ _ _ = typified by ruling with absolute power
16. a _ _ _ _ _ _ _ _ _ _ _ _ = enforces obedience,
17. i _ _ _ _ _ _ _ _ = bossy
18. e _ _ _ _ _ _ = urgent; demanding
19. e _ _ _ _ _ _ _ = demanding
20. c _ _ _ _ _ _ _ = using force to control
21. s _ _ _ _ _ _ _ _ = rigidly controlling
22. p _ _ _ _ _ _ _ _ _ = ruthlessly forcing control

So Much Hot Air

(bovarist, complacent, highbrow, pompous, pretentious, solipsistic,)
(supercilious, braggart, fanfaron, rodomontade, thrasonical,)
(turgid, vainglorious, vaunting, wisenheimer)
(rhetorical, adulate, sententious, bombastic, braggadocio)

Unscramble.

1. teprensiotu = affectedly superior _____
2. popomus = full of self-importance _____
3. vaborist = one with an exaggerated view
of oneself _____
4. ocitslipsis = believes only the self exists _____
5. hhbigrow = one excessively pretentious
about status _____
6. peruscisiolu = haughty _____
7. placomcent = self-satisfied, smug _____
8. seniwreheim = a smart aleck _____
9. fonafarn = one who brags too much,
a braggart _____
10. dorodeatmon = arrogant boasting _____
11. traggarb = one who brags _____
12. gnitnuav = boastful _____
13. gloinriavous = boastful conceit _____
14. sonicatharl = boastful _____
15. giturd = swollen; bombastic _____
16. tenuoissent = full of moral sayings _____
17. calirother = effective use of words or artificial,
showy language _____
18. tedaual = praise too highly _____
19. oicodaggarb = someone who brags _____
20. ticasbbom = speaking with high-sounding
but meaningless words _____

(euphuistic, fustian, grandiloquent, grandiose,)
(magniloquent, pontificate)

And match.

21. e _ _ _ _ _ _ _ _ _ = affected, bombastic
22. p _ _ _ _ _ _ _ _ _ _ = to speak in a pompous or dogmatic way
23. m _ _ _ _ _ _ _ _ _ _ _ = pompous; boastful
24. g _ _ _ _ _ _ _ _ = impressive; trying to seem impressive
25. g _ _ _ _ _ _ _ _ _ _ _ _ = bombastic speech
26. f _ _ _ _ _ _ = bombastic, pompous

Take The Money And Run

(felonious, filch, larcenous, mercenary, peculate)

Unscramble.

1. meryracen = influenced by desire for gain;
   a hired gun _____
2. latepuce = steal money entrusted
   to one's care _____
3. suonecral = theft _____
4. chilf = steal _____
5. onifelous = wicked, criminal _____

(abscond, arrogate, defalcate, despoiler, embezzle)

Match.

6. d _ _ _ _ _ _ _ _ = steal entrusted funds
7. a _ _ _ _ _ _ _ = to seize without right
8. a _ _ _ _ _ _ = run away
9. e _ _ _ _ _ _ _ = steal entrusted money
10. d _ _ _ _ _ _ _ _ = one who robs, plunders

(depredatory, pilfer, pillage, plagiarize,)

(purloin, spoliate, usurious, venal)

Match.

11. p _ _ _ _ _ = steal
12. d _ _ _ _ _ _ _ _ _ _ = plundering
13. v _ _ _ _ = capable of being bribed or corrupted
14. u _ _ _ _ _ _ _ = lending money at high interest
15. s _ _ _ _ _ _ _ _ = rob
16. p u _ _ _ _ _ = steal
17. p _ _ _ _ _ _ _ _ _ _ = take other's ideas and pass them off
   as one's own
18. p _ _ _ _ _ _ = to strip property or money by violence

Stingy Buggers

(parsimonious, pelting, penurious, scrooge, cheeseparing,)
(chary, stinting, begrudging)

Unscramble.

1. nueriposu = stingy; poor   _____
2. rasipumoonis = excessive stinginess   _____
3. cheapsering = stingy   _____
4. yarch = careful; stingy   _____
5. grubindgeg = to give with reluctance   _____
6. nittsing = stingy or sparing   _____
7. oscrego = one who is cheap, stingy, mean   _____
8. gelpnit = mean, miserly   _____

(cheap-skate, chintzy, miser, niggardly, skinflint, spendthrift, tightwad)

Match.

9. n _ _ _ _ _ _ _ _ = stingy
10. s _ _ _ _ _ _ _ _ _ = a miser, a stingy person
11. c _ _ _ _ _ _ = cheap, miserly or gaudy
12. s _ _ _ _ _ _ _ _ _ _ = wasteful spender
13. t _ _ _ _ _ _ _ = a stingy person
14. c _ _ _ _ - _ _ _ _ _ = a miser
15. m _ _ _ _ = a stingy person

Off Track

(desultory, digressive, discursive, tangential)

Unscramble.

1. cisurdsive =   wandering from one topic
      to another   _____
2. gidesvresi = wanders from the main point   _____
3. sudelotry = random, disconnected, aimless   _____
4. gantentlia =   typified by straying off the
      topic of discussion on a topic
      not germane to the discussion

      _____

Fat, Skinny Or Plug-Ugly

(blowsy, cacopygian, corpulent, emaciated, gaunt, obese, rotund,)
(sebaceous, sebiferous, steatopygous)

Unscramble.

1. tnuag = thin and bony; grim   _____
2. emadectia = abnormally lean   _____
3. esebo = fat   _____
4. pucorlent = fat   _____
5. paccogyian = having ugly buttocks   _____
6. torund = plump, rounded   _____
7. besiferous = secreting fat   _____
8. besacesou = fatty   _____
9. sgeapotytous = characterized by extremely
                   fat buttocks   _____
10. blysow = fat and coarse looking; untidy   _____

(cadaverous, teratoid, rebarbative, slovenly, grotesque, pockmarked)

Match.

11. s _ _ _ _ _ _ _ = dirty, untidy
12. r _ _ _ _ _ _ _ _ _ _ = unattractive, grim
13. t _ _ _ _ _ _ _ = resembling a monster
14. p _ _ _ _ _ _ _ _ _ = scarred and pitted left from pimples
15. c _ _ _ _ _ _ _ _ _ = like a dead body, pale, ghastly
16. g _ _ _ _ _ _ _ _ = bizarre

Wash Your Mouth Out!

(scatological, wry, ribald, crass, uncouth)

Match.

1. r _ _ _ _ _ = given to vulgar joking
2. c _ _ _ _ = without refinement; gross, stupid
3. u _ _ _ _ _ _ = strange; clumsy; crude
4. w _ _ = twisted; perverse
5. s _ _ _ _ _ _ _ _ _ _ _ _ = given to vulgar language or obsessed
                                with obscenity or excrement

Just Plain Dull

(banal, bland, hackneyed, innocuous, insipid, monotonous,)
(mundane, pedestrian, perfunctory, prosaic)

Match.

1. i _ _ _ _ _ _ = tasteless, dull
2. i _ _ _ _ _ _ _ _ = harmless; dull
3. h _ _ _ _ _ _ _ _ = commonplace by overuse
4. b _ _ _ _ = pleasantly smooth; tasteless, dull
5. b _ _ _ _ = dull
6. p _ _ _ _ _ _ _ _ _ _ = done without care, routine
7. p _ _ _ _ _ _ = like prose rather than poetry; dull, commonplace
8. p _ _ _ _ _ _ _ _ _ = ordinary
9. m _ _ _ _ _ _ = of the world; ordinary
10. m _ _ _ _ _ _ _ _ _ = tiresome since it doesn't vary

(interminable, jejune, ponderous, prosy, provincial)

Match.

11. j _ _ _ _ _ = barren, dull
12. p _ _ _ _ = dull, tedious; resembling prose
13. i _ _ _ _ _ _ _ _ _ _ _ = without end, seeming to last forever
14. p _ _ _ _ _ _ _ _ _ = heavy and bulky; labored and dull
15. p _ _ _ _ _ _ _ _ _ _ = like a province; rustic, devoid of culture;
    narrow, unsophisticated

It's Showtime

(ostentatious, tawdry, garish, gaudy)

1. t _ _ _ _ _ = cheap and showy, sleazy
2. g _ _ _ _ = showy but lacking in good taste
3. g _ _ _ _ _ = showy
4. o _ _ _ _ _ _ _ _ _ _ _ = pretentiously displaying wealth,
    showy,

Revenge

(revanchist, vindictive, vengeful)

Unscramble.

1. nevulgef = seeking revenge   _____
2. dinivectiv = revengeful   _____
3. tshcnvreai = vengeful   _____

Stormy

(rampageous, tempestuous, blusterous, rabid)

Match.

1. r _ _ _ _ _ _ _ _ _ = raging, on a rampage
2. r _ _ _ _ = violent; foaming at the mouth
3. t _ _ _ _ _ _ _ _ _ _ = violent, stormy
4. b _ _ _ _ _ _ _ _ _ = stormy, swaggering

You Could Have Said Please

(brusque, gruff, curt, boorish)

Unscramble.

1. qsrbuue = rough in manner or speech, curt   _____
2. frufg = rough in manner or speech, surly, brusquely rude   _____
3. truc = short in speech to point of rudeness   _____
4. sobihor = rude, ill-mannered   _____

Little Devils

(imp, puck, scamp)

Unscramble.

1. pmi = a young demon; mischievous child   _____
2. kcup = a mischievous sprite or elf   _____
3. mpacs = a mischievous rascal   _____

Salty

(brackish, briny)

Match.

1. b _ _ _ _ _ _ _ = salty
2. b _ _ _ _ = salty, crusty

In The Dark

(benighted, Cimmerian)

Match.

1. C _ _ _ _ _ _ _ _ = living in darkness
2. b _ _ _ _ _ _ _ _ = in the dark, ignorant

Answer Key For Surly Synonyms

Page 3

Men Your Mother
Warned You About,
Part 1

1. lecher
2. deadbeat
3. Peeping Tom
4. fop

Page 6

Men Your Mother
Warned You About,
Part 2

1. misogynous
2. Pavlovian dog
3. Cad
4. gigalo
5. chauvinist
6. priapic
7. sexist
8. Casanova

Page 9

Men Your Mother
Warned You About,
Part 3

1. Don Juan
2. rake
3. Lothario
4. satyromaniac
5. philanderer
6. lecherous
7. ithyphallic
8. dandy

Page 12

Women Your Mother
Warned You About,
Part 1

1. tart
2. trollop
3. virago
4. Circean
5. lamia
6. strumpet

Page 15

Women Your Mother
Warned You About,
Part 2

1. shrew
2. fury
3. Jezebel
4. nymphomaniac
5. harpy
6. femme fatale
7. siren
8. malapert

Page 20

Women Your Mother
Warned You About,
Part 3

1. wench
2. coquette
3. prima donna
4. Delilah
5. battle-ax
6. harridan
7. skank
8. hussy
9. beldam

Page 23

Women Your Mother
Warned You About,
Part 4

1. vixen
2. termagant
3. trull
4. gold digger
5. xanthippe
6. spitfire
7. minx
8. demirep
9. Circe

Page 26

If You Don't Have
Something Nice To
Say, Part 1

1. acerbic
2. acidulous
3. scathing
4. scabrous
5. sardonic
6. sarcastic
7. grizzle
8. maundering

Page 29

If You Don't Have
Something Nice To
Say, Part 2

1. derogatory
2. censorious
3. deride
4. deprecate
5. disparage
6. chastise
7. objurgate
8. belittle
9. berate
10. badger
11. Momus

Page 32

If You Don't Have
Something Nice To
Say, Part 3

1. recriminate
2. lambaste
3. querulous
4. defamatory
5. vituperative
6. pejorative
7. malign
8. derisive
9. grouse
10. denigrate

Page 37

Them's Fightin'
Words, Part 1

1. beetling
2. bellicose
3. belligerent
4. bilious
5. fistic
6. martial
7. dentigerous
8. bestial
9. pugilistic
10. litigious
11. jingo
12. defenestrate

Page 40

Them's Fightin'
Words, Part 2

1. fustigate
2. oppugnant
3. predatory
4. truculent
5. pugnacious
6. jugulate
7. minatory
8. militant

Page 43

Has It Come To
This? Part 1

1. abased
2. mortified
3. ignominious
4. moribund
5. retrogressive
6. recidivistic
7. demeaned
8. debilitated
9. debased
10. peon
11. freeloader

Page 46

Has It Come To
This? Part 2

1. impoverished
2. indigent
3. impecunious
4. destitute
5. derelict
6. leech
7. opprobrious
8. abject
9. pathetic
10. pariah
11. wretch

Page 49

Has It Come To
This? Part 3

1. pauper
2. serf
3. recluse
4. wastrel
5. vagrant
6. vagabond
7. squander
8. mendicant
9. insolvent

Page 54

Has It Come To
This? Part 4

1. scrimp
2. degrade
3. disenfranchised
4. importune
5. necessitous
6. hapless
7. abysmal
8. woebegone
9. nugatory
10. cadge

Page 57

Pride Comes Before
The Fall, Part 1

1. Adonis
2. temerarious
3. audacious
4. arrogant
5. preen
6. narcissistic
7. egotist
8. egocentric
9. flaunty
10. bumptious
11. brash

Page 60

Pride Comes Before
The Fall, Part 2

1. peevish
2. malapert
3. flaunt
4. pert
5. clique
6. presumptuous
7. cavalier
8. flounce
9. petulant
10. impertinent
11. aloof

Page 63
Liar, Liar, Pants On
Fire, Part 1
1. changeling
2. charlatan
3. mountebank
4. fabulist
5. pseudologist
6. equivocal
7. pettifogger
8. Janus-faced

Page 66
Liar, Liar, Pants On
Fire, Part 2
1. renege
2. fabricate
3. mendacious
4. dissemble
5. perjure
6. prevaricate
7. sophistical

Page 71
Liar, Liar, Pants On
Fire, Part 3
1. farcical
2. fallacious
3. dissimulate
4. disingenuous
5. welsher
6. quibble

Page 74
Something Wicked
This Way Comes,
Part 1
1. facinorous
2. flagitious
3. deplorable
4. deleterious
5. despicable
6. execrative
7. execrable
8. diabolical

Page 77
Something Wicked
This Way Comes,
Part 2
1. vile
2. egregious
3. perfidious
4. malevolent
5. nefarious
6. miscreant
7. malignant
8. malefactor

Page 80
Something Wicked
This Way Comes,
Part 3
1. profane
2. hypocrite
3. Simoniac
4. sanctimonious
5. iniquitous
6. impenitent
7. blaspheme
8. sacrilegious
9. peccable

Page 83
Yiddish Schmidish
1. nebbish
2. schlemiel
3. schnook
4. schlep
5. schmuck
6. kvetch
7. yenta
8. nudnik

Page 88
It Takes A Sneak,
Part 1
1. wily
2. calculating
3. Machiavellian
4. devious
5. circuitous
6. collusive
7. surreptitious
8. sinister
9. sinuous
10. serpentine
11. cabal

Page 91
It Takes A Sneak,
Part 2
1. deceptive
2. guileful
3. Byzantine
4. conniving
5. cagey
6. tergiversate
7. casuistic
8. cunning
9. duplicitous
10. fob

Page 94
Say What?
1. babble
2. blither
3. brabble
4. drivel
5. gabble
6. garble
7. gibber
8. inarticulate
9. incoherent
10. jabber
11. splutter
12. maunder

Page 97
You're Such An Animal
1. limacine
2. bovine
3. hircine
4. piscine
5. lupine
6. taurine
7. porcine
8. simian
9. ovine
10. ophidian
11. vulpine

Page 100
Nothing Succeeds Like Excess
1. superfluous
2. cloy
3. saccharine
4. fulsome
5. cachinnate
6. extraneous
7. treacly

Page 105
Get A Spine, Part 1
1. wince
2. poltroon
3. repine
4. fretful
5. snivel
6. cower
7. feckless
8. xenophobic
9. tremulous
10. patsy
11. emasculated
12. milquetoast

Page 108
Get A Spine, Part 2
1. inhibited
2. diffident
3. skittish
4. grovel
5. quail
6. niddering
7. cringe
8. skulk
9. recreant
10. dastardly
11. cark
12. lily-livered
13. wimp

Page 111
Get A Spine, Part 3
1. cosset
2. impotent
3. enervate
4. cocker
5. timorous
6. squeamish
7. quiver
8. quaver
9. pusillanimous
10. craven

Page 114
Class And No Class, Part 1
1. plutocracy
2. fascist
3. aristocracy
4. meritocracy
5. mobocracy
6. masses
7. intelligentsia
8. plebeian
9. blue blood
10. anarchist

Page 117
Class And No Class, Part 2
1. ochlocratic
2. elitist
3. dregs
4. ruck
5. booboisie
6. hoi polloi
7. arriviste
8. preppy
9. upstart
10. reactionary

Page 122
A Real Drag
1. abrasive
2. buttinski
3. insufferable
4. interloper
5. officious
6. onerous
7. proleptic
8. umbrageous
9. vexatious
10. obtrusive

Page 125
Hard To Control, Part 1
1. militate
2. factious
3. mutinous
4. instigating
5. incendiary
6. foment
7. fractious
8. forward
9. refractory
10. contumacious
11. restive
12. seditious
13. saboteur

Page 128
Hard To Control, Part 2
1. incorrigible
2. indocile
3. inbridled
4. unbitted
5. feral
6. recalcitrant
7. insolent
8. insubordinate
9. iconoclast
10. obstreperous
11. intransigent
12. intractable

Page 131
Bad To The Bone, Part 1
1. malicious
2. lapidate
3. ominous
4. remorseless
5. invidious
6. hycra
7. culpable
8. reprehensible
9. ugsome
10. nocent
11. abhorrent
12. be]te noire
13. baneful

Page 134
Bad To The Bone, Part 2
1. baleful
2. minacious
3. unscrupulous
4. unconscionable
5. repugnant
6. culprit
7. pernicious
8. insidious
9. reprobate

Page 139
Bad To The Bone, Part 3
1. homicidal
2. imbruted
3. mortiferous
4. internecine
5. nonfeasant
6. maleficent
7. undermine
8. ignoble
9. misfeasor
10. infernal
11. sanguinary

Page 142
Bad To The Bone, Part 4
1. sadistic
2. tactless
3. callous
4. loathsome
5. odious
6. nemesis
7. contemptible
8. unregenerate
9. villainous

Page 145
Down In The Goondocks
1. moron
2. ignoramus
3. gormless
4. gullible
5. fatuous
6. credulous
7. inane
8. imbecile
9. addlebrained
10. simper

Page 148
Stupid Is As Stupid Does
1. nincompoop
2. unwitting
3. troglodyte
4. Neanderthal
5. stunted
6. opaque
7. asinine
8. obtuse
9. nescient
10. naïve

Page 151

An Idiot By Any Other Name Would Be As Dumb

1. vacuous
2. stultified
3. vapid
4. infatuated
5. cretin
6. insensate
7. distrait
8. impolitic
9. insipient
10. myopic
11. sciolistic

Page 156

To All The Idiots I've Loved Before

1. gawk
2. acephales
3. solecistic
4. dummkkopf
5. grobian
6. hebetate
7. dunce
8. numskull
9. witling

Page 159

Lust In the Dust, Part 1

1. salacious
2. libidinous
3. lewd
4. amoral
5. lascivious
6. libertine
7. unsavory
8. sybaritic
9. vulgarian
10. precocious
11. brazen
12. slatternly
13. meretricious

Page 162

Lust In the Dust, Part 2

1. prurient
2. perverse
3. vitiated
4. wanton
5. pander
6. naughty
7. lubricious
8. licentious
9. bawdy
10. deviate
11. unseemly
12. carnal
13. concupiscent

Page 165

Lust In the Dust, Part 3

1. raffish
2. rakish
3. venerious
4. scatological
5. voyeur
6. ruttish
7. hedonist
8. epicurean
9. profligate
10. jaded

Page 168

Woke Up On The Wrong Side Of The Bed, Part 1

1. inimical
2. irascible
3. irate
4. indignant
5. splenetic
6. testy
7. choleric
8. crusty
9. crabbed
10. crotchety
11. disgruntled
12. curmudgeon

Page 173

Woke Up On The Wrong Side Of The Bed, Part 2

1. dyspeptic
2. divisive
3. dissident
4. cantankerous
5. contentious
6. churlish
7. surly
8. malcontent
9. glower
10. disputatious

Page 176

Ninety-Nine Bottles Of Beer On The Wall

1. dissolute
2. dissipated
3. depraved
4. degenerate
5. decadent
6. deviant
7. debauched
8. bibulous
9. bacchanalian

Page 179

Put A Cork In It

1. lush
2. potvaliant
3. barfly
4. crapulous
5. dipsomaniac
6. sodden
7. souse
8. inebriated
9. intemperate

Page 182

Party Hard

1. roguish
2. Rabelaisian
3. raucous
4. rambunctious
5. rumbustious
6. waggish
7. roisterous

Page 185

Followers and
Brownnosers, Part 1

1. brownnoser
2. beadle
3. underling
4. slavish
5. malleable
6. minions
7. ingratiate
8. ductile
9. docile
10. compliant
11. complaisant
12. belaud
13. truckle

Page 190

Followers and
Brownnosers, Part 2

1. doting
2. gnathonic
3. biddable
4. subservient
5. uxorious
6. servile
7. sequacious
8. claqueur
9. obsequious
10. fawn
11. castrated
12. stooge
13. helot
14. thrall
15. smarmy

Page 193

Followers and
Brownnosers, Part 3

1. Barmicidal
2. wheedle
3. unctuous
4. sycophant
5. oleaginous
6. bathetic
7. toad
8. lackey
9. drudge
10. parasite
11. bootlicker

Page 196

A Tad Pessimistic

1. misanthrope
2. fatalist
3. dystopia
4. misoneist
5. misologist
6. dour
7. funereal
8. misandrist
9. obscurant

Page 199

Cry Me A River

1. distraught
2. disconsolate
3. despondent
4. dejected
5. sullen
6. dolorous
7. saturnine
8. morose
9. melancholy
10. maudlin
11. mawkish
12. lugubrious
13. lachrymose

Page 202

Lazy Good-For-
Nothings, Part 1

1. dawdle
2. dilatory
3. procrastinate
4. bootless
5. fainéant
6. indolent
7. laggard
8. lackadaisical
9. languid
10. lassitude

Page 207

Lazy Good-For-
Nothings, Part 2

1. lethargic
2. listless
3. malinger
4. phlegmatic
5. sedentary
6. torpid
7. slothful
8. stagnant
9. boondoggle
10. otiose

Page 210
Lazy Good-For-
Nothings, Part 3
1. soporific
2. oscitant
3. goldbricker
4. cunctative
5. idler
6. sloth
7. drone
8. slugabed
9. sluggard
10. slouch
11. lollygag
12. loafer

Page 213
A Little Too Tight,
Part 1
1. Lilliputian
2. pedant
3. pedantic
4. pedagogue
5. picayunish
6. priggish
7. bureaucrat
8. tendentious
9. ethnocentric
10. schoolmarm
11. prig

Page 216
A Little Too Tight,
Part 2
1. punctilious
2. fastidious
3. prude
4. sectarian
5. obstipated
6. constrict
7. bluenose
8. dogmatic
9. doctrinaire
10. persnickety
11. didactic
12. inculcate
13. functionary

Page 219
Countrified
1. Philistine
2. agrestic
3. bumpkin
4. hick
5. yahoo
6. galoot
7. Boeotian
8. rude
9. boor
10. churl
11. provincial

Page 224
Out There
1. blatant
2. categorical
3. arrant
4. abysmal
5. flagrant
6. rank
7. abominable
8. unmitigated
9. notorious
10. infamous

Page 227
They're Coming To
Take Me Away, Ha
Ha
1. confabulate
2. demented
3. deranged
4. irrational
5. pathological
6. paranoid
7. bedlamite
8. psychopath
9. lunatic
10. maniac
11. daft

Page 230
Greed Is Good
1. gluttonous
2. esurient
3. voracious
4. rapacious
5. edacious
6. avaricious
7. gulositous
8. insatiable
9. glutton

Page 233
They Have An
Attitude
1. ingrate
2. fastuous
3. flippant
4. fleer
5. flout
6. jeer
7. patronize
8. condescend
9. disdainful
10. impudent
11. pettish

Page 236
One Big Zero
1. nondescript
2. negligible
3. nebulous
4. automaton
5. apathetic
6. nonentity
7. clone
8. cipher
9. stolid

Page 241
You Stink
1. malodorous
2. pedicular
3. putrid
4. excrementitious
5. feculent
6. fetid
7. foul
8. mephitic
9. noisome

Page 244
Dirty Little Buggers
1. bedraggled
2. sordid
3. squalid
4. disheveled
5. unkempt
6. grubby
7. dowdy
8. frowsy
9. Augean
10. smirchy

Page 247
Toxic Tales
1. virulent
2. venomous
3. noxious
4. blight
5. nocuous
6. scourge
7. pestiferous
8. scurvy

Page 250
On Your Nerves
1. nettle
2. galling
3. gadfly
4. exasperate
5. irksome
6. exacerbate
7. intrusive
8. intolerable
9. pesky
10. gall

Page 253
Erratic Oddballs,
Part 1
1. capricious
2. whimsical
3. vagarious
4. volatile
5. ephemeral
6. erratic
7. gadabout
8. chimerical
9. frothy
10. impetuous
11. discombobulate
12. astigmatic

Page 258
Erratic Oddballs,
Part 2
1. mercurial
2. quixotic
3. frenetic
4. histrionic
5. dither
6. imprudent
7. eccentric
8. dabbler
9. dilettante
10. flummoxed
11. nonplused

Page 261
Don't Meet Them In
A Dark Alley, Part 1
1. rabble
2. riffraff
3. mob
4. vermin
5. canaille
6. quisling

Page 264
Don't Meet Them In
A Dark Alley, Part 2
1. perpetrator
2. hellion
3. rogue
4. fiend
5. varmint
6. racketeer
7. scoundrel
8. thug

Page 267

Two Left Feet
1. maladroit
2. inept
3. ungainly
4. incompetent
5. gangling
6. flounder
7. klutz
8. bungler

Page 270

Diehards
1. dogged
2. willful
3. indurate
4. obdurate
5. mulish
6. inexorable
7. precipitous
8. pertinacious

Page 275

Wet Behind The
Ears, Part 1
1. novice
2. neophyte
3. tyke
4. tinhorn
5. tenderfoot
6. greenhorn
7. puerile
8. callow
9. sophomoric
10. stray
11. whelp
12. gamine

Page 278

Wet Behind The
Ears, Part 2
1. scamp
2. bantling
3. delinquent
4. fledgling
5. unfledged
6. whippersnapper

Page 281

Old And In The
Way, Part 1
1. has-been
2. relic
3. anachronistic
4. antiquated
5. decrepit
6. doddering
7. fusty
8. senile
9. senescent
10. obsolete
11. rugose

Page 284

Old And In The
Way, Part 2
1. preadamic
2. Noachian
3. antediluvian
4. geezer
5. gammer
6. dotard
7. gaffer

Page 287

Old And In The
Way, Part 3
1. grimalkin
2. crone
3. codger
4. fogy
5. biddy
6. primordial
7. sackless

Page 290

Little Hitlers
1. fascist
2. megalomaniac
3. martinet
4. demagogue
5. imperialist
6. Gestapo
7. despot
8. tyrant
9. taskmaster
10. mogul
11. autocrat
12. draconian
13. dictatorial
14. cashier
15. autocratic
16. authoritarian
17. imperious
18. exigent
19. exacting
20. coercive
21. stringent
22. procrustean

Page 291
So Much Hot Air
1. pretentious
2. pompous
3. bovarist
4. solipsistic
5. highbrow
6. supercilious
7. complacent
8. wisenheimer
9. fanfaron
10. rodomaontade
11. braggart
12. vaunting
13. vainglorious
14. thrasonical
15. turgid
16. sententious
17. rhetorical
18. adulate
19. braggadocio
20. bombastic
21. euphuistic
22. pontificate
23. magniloquent
24. grandiose
25. grandiloquent
26. fustian

Page 292
Take The Money...
1. mercenary
2. peculate
3. larcenous
4. filch
5. felonious
6. defalcate
7. arrogate
8. abscond
9. embezzle
10. despoiler
11. pilfer
12. depredatory
13. venal
14. usurious
15. spoliate
16. purloin
17. plagiarize
18. pillage

Page 293
Stingy Buggers
1. penurious
2. parsimonious
3. cheeseparing
4. chary
5. begrudging
6. stinting
7. scrooge
8. pelting
9. niggardly
10. skinflint
11. chintzy
12. spendthrift
13. tightwad
14. cheap-skate
15. miser

Off Track
1. discursive
2. digressive
3. desultory
4. tangential

Page 294
Fat, Skinny Or...
1. gaunt
2. emaciated
3. obese
4. corpulent
5. cacopygian
6. rotund
7. sebiferous
8. sebaceous
9. steatopygous
10. blowsy
11. slovenly
12. rebarbative
13. teratoid
14. pockmarked
15. cadaverous
16. grotesque

Wash Your Mouth...
1. ribald
2. crass
3. uncouth
4. wry
5. scatological

Page 295
Just Plain Dull
1. insipid
2. innocuous
3. hackneyed
4. bland
5. banal
6. perfunctory
7. prosaic
8. pedestrian
9. mundane
10. monotonous
11. jejune
12. prosy
13. interminable
14. ponderous
15. provincial

**Page 295
(cont.)**

It's Showtime

1. tawdry
2. gaudy
3. garish
4. ostentacious

Page 296

Revenge Is Sweet

1. vengeful
2. vindictive
3. revanchist

Stormy

1. rampageous
2. rapid
3. tempestuous
4. blusterous

You Could Have
Said Please

1. brusque
2. gruff
3. curt
4. boorish

Little Devils

1. imp
2. puck
3. scamp

Page 297

In The Dark

1. Cimmerian
3. benighted

Salty

1. brackish
2. briny

Le Mot Quote Answer Key

Le Mot Quote 1

a. 3
b. 2
c. 1
d. 4

Le Mot Quote 2

a. 1
b. 3
c. 2

Le Mot Quote 3

a. 2
b. 3
c. 1

Le Mot Quote 4

a. 2
b. 3
c. 1
d. 4

Le Mot Quote 5

a. 4
b. 3
c. 2
d. 1

Le Mot Quote 6

a. 2
b. 1
c. 3
d. 4
e. 6
f. 5

Le Mot Quote 7

a. 4
b. 2
c. 3
d. 1

Le Mot Quote 8

a. 4
b. 5
c. 3
d. 1
e. 2

Le Mot Quote 9

a. 2
b. 1
c. 4
d. 3

Le Mot Quote 10

a. 1
b. 3
c. 4
d. 2

Le Mot Quote 11

a. 5
b. 1
c. 3
d. 2
e. 4

Le Mot Quote 12

a. 5
b. 4
c. 3
d. 2
e. 1

Le Mot Quote 13

B

Le Mot Quote 14

a. 2
b. 3
c. 1

Le Mot Quote 15

a. 3
b. 4
c. 1
d. 2

Le Mot Quote 16

a. 3
b. 1
c. 4
d. 2

Le Mot Quote 17

a. 4
b. 1
c. 2
d. 3

Le Mot Quote 18

a. 4
b. 3
c. 1
d. 2
e. 5

Le Mot Quote 19

a. 5
b. 2
c. 3
d. 1
e. 4

Le Mot Quote 20

a. 3
b. 2
c. 4
d. 2

Le Mot Quote 21

a. 2
b. 1
c. 3
d. 4

Le Mot Quote 22

a. 4
b. 1
c. 2
d. 3

Le Mot Quote 23

a. 3
b. 4
c. 5
d. 2
e. 1

Le Mot Quote 24

a. 3
b. 1
c. 2

Le Mot Quote 25

a. 2
b. 4
c. 3
d. 1

Le Mot Quote 26

a. 4
b. 3
c. 2
d. 1

Le Mot Quote 27

a. 4
b. 3
c. 2
d. 5
e. 1

Le Mot Quote 28

a. 4
b. 5
c. 1
d. 3
e. 2

Le Mot Quote 29

a. 2
b. 1
c. 3
d. 4
e. 5

Le Mot Quote 30

a. 1
b. 2
c. 3
d. 4

Le Mot Quote 31

a. 4
b. 1
c. 2
d. 3

Le Mot Quote 32

a. 4
b. 2
c. 3
d. 1

Le Mot Quote 33

a. 2
b. 1
c. 3
d. 4

Le Mot Quote 34

a. 3
b. 1
c. 2
d. 4

Le Mot Quote 35

a. 4
b. 3
c. 5
d. 2
e. 1

Le Mot Quote 36

B

Le Mot Quote 37

a. 3
b. 2
c. 5
d. 6
e. 4
f. 1

Le Mot Quote 38

a. 2
b. 3
c. 1
d. 4

Le Mot Quote 39

a. 3
b. 1
c. 4
d. 2

Le Mot Quote 40

C

Le Mot Quote 41

a. 2
b. 1
c. 3

Le Mot Quote 43

B

Le Mot Quote 44

a. 2
b. 4
c. 1
d. 3

Le Mot Quote 45

a. 1
b. 2
c. 3
d. 5
e. 4

Le Mot Quote 46

a. 4
b. 3
c. 2
d. 1

Le Mot Quote 47

a. 3
b. 2
c. 4
d. 1

Le Mot Quote 48

a. 2
b. 3
c. 1
d. 4

Le Mot Quote 49

a. 4
b. 1
c. 2
d. 3
e. 5

Le Mot Quote 50

a. 1
b. 5
c. 4
d. 3
e. 2

Le Mot Quote 51

a. 2
b. 1
c. 7
d. 6
e. 5
f. 4
g. 3

Le Mot Quote 52

a. 2
b. 3
c. 1
d. 4
e. 6
f. 5

Le Mot Quote 53

B

Answer Key For Quizzes

Quiz 1
1. B
2. A
3. B
4. A
5. C
6. E
7. B
8. D
9. D
10. F
11. G
12. J
13. H
14. I

Quiz 3
1. B
2. I
3. B
4. A
5. D
6. G
7. C
8. E
9. F
10. H
11. L
12. L
13. J
14. K

Quiz 5
1. A
2. B
3. F
4. B
5. H
6. E
7. D
8. I
9. G
10. C
11. K
12. J
13. M
14. N

Quiz 7
1. F
2. E
3. G
4. H
5. C
6. D
7. B
8. A
9. I
10. J
11. M
12. K
13. N
14. L
15. O

Quiz 9
1. I
2. D
3. E
4. G
5. B
6. H
7. A
8. C
9. J
10. F
11. P
12. Q
13. M
14. K
15. N
16. L
17. O

Quiz 2
1. C
2. C
3. D
4. B
5. H
6. E
7. A
8. F
9. I
10. G
11. O
12. J
13. M
14. Q
15. P
16. N
17. K
18. L

Quiz 4
1. F
2. A
3. G
4. H
5. E
6. D
7. B
8. I
9. J
10. C
11. M
12. L
13. K

Quiz 6
1. E
2. C
3. A
4. D
5. G
6. B
7. F
8. H
9. I
10. E
11. K
12. L
13. J

Quiz 8
1. E
2. F
3. D
4. C
5. B
6. G
7. A
8. J
9. I
10. H
11. N
12. M
13. L
14. K
15. P
16. O
17. Q

Quiz 10
1. G
2. B
3. F
4. D
5. J
6. A
7. E
8. C
9. H
10. I
11. M
12. O
13. P
14. K
15. L
16. N

Quiz 11	Quiz 13	Quiz 15	Quiz 17	Quiz 19
1. H	1. A	1. B	1. H	1. A
2. I	2. E	2. J	2. G	2. F
3. J	3. C	3. C	3. I	3. J
4. B	4. G	4. D	4. F	4. E
5. C	5. H	5. I	5. E	5. D
6. D	6. D	6. E	6. C	6. G
7. G	7. B	7. G	7. B	7. I
8. E	8. F	8. H	8. A	8. B
9. A	9. G	9. A	9. E	9. H
10. F	10. L	10. F	10. D	10. C
11. L	11. M	11. L	11. O	11. L
12. K	12. J	12. M	12. L	12. P
	13. K	13. N	13. N	13. M
		14. O	14. M	14. N
		15. P	15. Q	15. Q
		16. Q	16. P	16. K
		17. K	17. K	

Quiz 12	Quiz 14	Quiz 16	Quiz 18	Quiz 20
1. C	1. E	1. F	1. G	1. D
2. F	2. G	2. G	2. A	2. I
3. G	3. H	3. I	3. D	3. G
4. H	4. D	4. H	4. H	4. B
5. D	5. I	5. E	5. B	5. A
6. B	6. J	6. C	6. C	6. I
7. I	7. F	7. J	7. E	7. E
8. E	8. C	8. D	8. F	8. C
9. A	9. B	9. B	9. F	9. H
10. J	10. A	10. A	10. G	10. F
11. N	11. K	11. M	11. L	11. K
12. M	12. O	12. O	12. M	12. J
13. L	13. M	13. K	13. N	13. L
14. K	14. N	14. K	14. I	14. M
15. O	15. L	15. L	15. J	15. O
			16. K	16. N

Quiz 21	Quiz 23	Quiz 25	Quiz 27	Quiz 29
1. I	1. E	1. H	1. I	1. C
2. B	2. A	2. J	2. E	2. J
3. F	3. I	3. E	3. G	3. A
4. E	4. H	4. D	4. F	4. I
5. D	5. D	5. A	5. B	5. F
6. A	6. J	6. F	6. H	6. G
7. G	7. B	7. C	7. C	7. D
8. A	8. C	8. I	8. D	8. B
9. C	9. G	9. B	9. A	9. H
10. C	10. F	10. G	10. J	10. E
11. J	11. M	11. L	11. L	11. N
12. I	12. N	12. K	12. O	12. Q
13. K	13. L	13. M	13. M	13. L
14. L	14. K		14. N	14. P
			15. P	15. O
			16. K	16. K
			17. Q	17. M

Quiz 22	Quiz 24	Quiz 26	Quiz 28	Quiz 30
1. A	1. J	1. B	1. G	1. C
2. I	2. D	2. E	2. D	2. F
3. E	3. H	3. G	3. B	3. J
4. C	4. G	4. A	4. H	4. E
5. D	5. F	5. I	5. C	5. A
6. B	6. E	6. C	6. F	6. H
7. H	7. I	7. H	7. E	7. I
8. G	8. B	8. F	8. A	8. G
9. B	9. A	9. D	9. I	9. B
10. F	10. C	10. D	10. J	10. D
11. J	11. K	11. N	11. O	11. K
12. Q	12. M	12. J	12. M	12. M
13. L	13. N	13. K	13. N	13. O
14. P	14. P	14. M	14. L	14. L
15. N	15. N	15. L	15. K	15. P
16. O	16. L			16. N
17. M				
18. K				

Quiz 31	Quiz 33	Quiz 35	Quiz 37	Quiz 39
1. J	1. J	1. B	1. G	1. C
2. E	2. I	2. G	2. E	2. H
3. F	3. H	3. D	3. B	3. J
4. H	4. F	4. I	4. C	4. A
5. D	5. B	5. H	5. G	5. F
6. A	6. C	6. F	6. D	6. B
7. C	7. G	7. E	7. A	7. I
8. G	8. E	8. C	8. F	8. G
9. B	9. D	9. A	9. H	9. E
10. I	10. A	10. J	10. F	10. D
11. L	11. M	11. K	11. M	11. L
12. K	12. L	12. M	12. J	12. N
13. M	13. O	13. L	13. K	13. M
	14. Q	14. N	14. I	14. K
	15. N		15. L	
	16. K			
	17. P			

Quiz 32	Quiz 34	Quiz 36	Quiz 38	Quiz 40
1. D	1. A	1. C	1. F	1. H
2. G	2. G	2. A	2. C	2. D
3. C	3. C	3. D	3. J	3. B
4. A	4. F	4. B	4. E	4. I
5. E	5. H	5. I	5. I	5. C
6. H	6. D	6. J	6. A	6. D
7. I	7. I	7. E	7. G	7. E
8. B	8. E	8. H	8. H	8. A
9. F	9. B	9. G	9. D	9. G
10. I	10. J	10. F	10. B	10. F
11. N	11. L	11. M	11. N	11. M
12. M	12. K	12. L	12. L	12. L
13. J	13. O	13. N	13. M	13. J
14. K	14. N	14. K	14. K	14. K
15. L	15. M	15. O	15. O	15. J

Quiz 41

1. F
2. I
3. H
4. A
5. D
6. I
7. E
8. C
9. G
10. B
11. M
12. J
13. K
14. L

Quiz 43

1. E
2. J
3. A
4. D
5. B
6. I
7. G
8. F
9. C
10. H
11. L
12. M
13. O
14. N
15. K

Quiz 45

1. D
2. D
3. G
4. C
5. B
6. E
7. I
8. A
9. F
10. H
11. J
12. P
13. M
14. L
15. O
16. N
17. K

Quiz 47

1. J
2. F
3. D
4. H
5. G
6. C
7. A
8. B
9. E
10. I
11. M
12. O
13. K
14. L
15. N

Quiz 49

1. I
2. H
3. G
4. G
5. C
6. F
7. A
8. B
9. E
10. D
11. N
12. M
13. K
14. J
15. L
16. O

Quiz 42

1. G
2. C
3. A
4. I
5. E
6. F
7. H
8. D
9. J
10. B
11. N
12. M
13. A
14. K

Quiz 44

1. D
2. F
3. E
4. B
5. G
6. B
7. A
8. H
9. B
10. C
11. I
12. L
13. K
14. N
15. K
16. M
17. J

Quiz 46

1. C
2. E
3. H
4. F
5. D
6. B
7. A
8. G
9. G
10. G
11. J
12. M
13. I
14. L
15. K

Quiz 48

1. H
2. G
3. C
4. E
5. A
6. J
7. F
8. B
9. D
10. I
11. L
12. N
13. O
14. K
15. P
16. M

Quiz 50

1. E
2. H
3. I
4. I
5. C
6. G
7. B
8. D
9. A
10. F
11. O
12. N
13. L
14. K
15. J
16. M

Quiz 51	Quiz 53	Quiz 55	Quiz 57	Quiz 59
1. G	1. D	1. E	1. G	1. K
2. D	2. D	2. B	2. A	2. I
3. H	3. E	3. C	3. C	3. A
4. E	4. G	4. F	4. H	4. D
5. B	5. B	5. H	5. E	5. B
6. C	6. A	6. J	6. I	6. C
7. A	7. C	7. A	7. B	7. C
8. I	8. D	8. D	8. J	8. F
9. F	9. F	9. G	9. F	9. E
10. J	10. H	10. I	10. D	10. G
11. K	11. N	11. M	11. K	11. K
12. Q	12. M	12. N	12. N	12. J
13. L	13. J	13. K	13. M	13. N
14. O	14. L	14. L	14. O	14. M
15. M	15. I	15. O	15. P	15. L
16. N	16. K		16. L	
17. K				

Quiz 52	Quiz 54	Quiz 56	Quiz 58	Quiz 60
1. C	1. B	1. E	1. I	1. J
2. G	2. C	2. C	2. B	2. F
3. I	3. A	3. I	3. G	3. C
4. E	4. J	4. F	4. H	4. E
5. F	5. H	5. G	5. J	5. I
6. H	6. G	6. J	6. E	6. H
7. J	7. F	7. B	7. F	7. G
8. B	8. E	8. H	8. D	8. B
9. A	9. D	9. A	9. C	9. A
10. D	10. I	10. D	10. A	10. D
11. N	11. K	11. N	11. M	11. O
12. M	12. O	12. K	12. N	12. N
13. K	13. N	13. M	13. L	13. L
14. L	14. L	14. L	14. K	14. M
15. O	15. M			15. K
				16. P

Quiz 61	Quiz 63	Quiz 65	Quiz 67	Quiz 69
1. C	1. I	1. D	1. H	1. B
2. F	2. B	2. B	2. D	2. H
3. D	3. B	3. C	3. C	3. D
4. A	4. G	4. I	4. I	4. C
5. E	5. D	5. E	5. A	5. G
6. H	6. F	6. F	6. G	6. F
7. G	7. E	7. A	7. J	7. I
8. B	8. H	8. H	8. E	8. A
9. J	9. A	9. G	9. B	9. E
10. I	10. C	10. J	10. F	10. E
11. N	11. K	11. M	11. K	11. K
12. M	12. J	12. N	12. P	12. O
13. L	13. L	13. K	13. L	13. N
14. P		14. L	14. M	14. L
15. K		15. O	15. O	15. M
16. O		16. P	16. N	16. J

Quiz 62	Quiz 64	Quiz 66	Quiz 68	Quiz 70
1. A	1. A	1. J	1. E	1. I
2. H	2. E	2. H	2. F	2. B
3. E	3. D	3. I	3. I	3. H
4. C	4. H	4. F	4. B	4. G
5. I	5. C	5. C	5. D	5. F
6. F	6. G	6. G	6. A	6. D
7. J	7. I	7. E	7. C	7. C
8. G	8. F	8. B	8. G	8. E
9. D	9. J	9. D	9. H	9. J
10. B	10. B	10. A	10. J	10. A
11. L	11. N	11. M	11. K	11. K
12. M	12. O	12. K	12. O	12. M
13. K	13. M	13. N	13. M	13. L
14. N	14. L	14. L	14. L	
	15. K	15. O	15. N	

Quiz 71	Quiz 73	Quiz 75	Quiz 77	Quiz 79
1. E	1. C	1. I	1. B	1. I
2. E	2. F	2. J	2. G	2. G
3. D	3. I	3. D	3. E	3. F
4. A	4. G	4. A	4. H	4. D
5. G	5. E	5. H	5. C	5. I
6. I	6. J	6. B	6. A	6. B
7. C	7. A	7. G	7. J	7. C
8. B	8. H	8. E	8. I	8. E
9. F	9. D	9. C	9. D	9. H
10. H	10. B	10. F	10. F	10. A
11. L	11. L	11. K	11. L	11. N
12. J	12. P	12. N	12. K	12. K
13. K	13. N	13. M	13. N	13. M
	14. M	14. L	14. M	14. L
	15. K	15. O	15. P	15. J
	16. O		16. O	

Quiz 72	Quiz 74	Quiz 76	Quiz 78	Quiz 80
1. I	1. I	1. H	1. D	1. B
2. D	2. F	2. E	2. F	2. A
3. B	3. B	3. F	3. J	3. F
4. C	4. A	4. I	4. H	4. H
5. E	5. J	5. D	5. I	5. H
6. H	6. E	6. J	6. E	6. I
7. F	7. H	7. A	7. B	7. E
8. A	8. C	8. B	8. G	8. D
9. I	9. D	9. G	9. A	9. G
10. G	10. G	10. C	10. C	10. C
11. J	11. N	11. L	11. N	11. O
12. N	12. M	12. K	12. O	12. M
13. K	13. K	13. N	13. K	13. K
14. O	14. L	14. M	14. L	14. J
15. L		15. O	15. M	15. L
16. M				16. N

Quiz 81	Quiz 82	Quiz 83	Quiz 84	Quiz 85
1. D	1. F	1. H	1. H	1. G
2. H	2. E	2. D	2. D	2. I
3. A	3. A	3. G	3. F	3. A
4. F	4. G	4. A	4. A	4. H
5. G	5. A	5. C	5. B	5. B
6. I	6. B	6. F	6. G	6. F
7. C	7. D	7. B	7. E	7. C
8. C	8. I	8. H	8. I	8. E
9. B	9. C	9. D	9. C	9. J
10. E	10. H	10. E	10. J	10. D
11. K	11. M	11. J	11. N	11. N
12. M	12. K	12. I	12. O	12. M
13. L	13. K	13. K	13. M	13. K
14. J	14. L	14. L	14. K	14. P
	15. M		15. P	15. O
	16. N		16. L	16. Q
	17. J			17. L

Index for Basic Words

parasite G. L. 58
partisan G. L. 60
party-pooper G. L. 23
parvenu G. L. 25
patsy G. L. 69
pauper G. L. 37
pawn G. L. 54
peacock G. L. 61
pedant G. L. 64
Peeping Tom G. L. 45
penny pincher G. L. 56
peon G. L. 14
perpetrator G. L. 80
Philistine G. L. 63
pig-headed G. L. 21
pigsty G. L. 75
pipsqueak G. L. 75
pixilated G. L. 82
plebeian G. L. 51
plodder G. L. 61
plutocracy G. L. 58
pooh bah G. L. 82
poseurs G. L. 9
prattler G. L. 63
preppy G. L. 24
prig G. L. 57
priggish G. L. 57
prima donna G. L. 58
provocateur G. L. 42
prude G. L. 28
psychopath G. L. 2
pulpit drone G. L. 20
puppet G. L. 57
quack G. L. 15
rabble G. L. 55
rabble-rouser G. L. 27
racist G. L. 85
racketeer G. L. 67
ragamuffin G. L. 17
ragtag and bobtail
G. L. 52
rapscallion G. L. 14
rat race G. L. 13
reactionary G. L. 66
rebel G. L. 14
relic G. L. 78
renegade G. L. 59
riffraff G. L. 65
rogue G. L. 59
rook G. L. 72
roundheel G. L. 42
rube G. L. 2
ruck G. L. 81
rummy G. L. 32

runagate G. L. 41
runt G. L. 24
ruthless G. L. 19
ruttish G. L. 70
saboteur G. L. 68
sap G. L. 72
scag G. L. 37
scamp G. L. 78
schemer G. L. 46
schlemiel G. L. 76
schlep G. L. 76
schmuck G. L. 18
schnook G. L. 51
schoolmarm G. L. 19
scofflaw G..L. 36
scoffer G. L. 6
scoundrel G. L. 51
scourge G. L. 6
scruff G. L. 38
scullion G. L. 29
scumbag G. L. 44
scurvy G. L. 9
sea wolf G. L.
sell-out G. L. 55
serf G. L. 40
shcmo G. L. 7
shrew G. L. 69
shyster G. L. 45
simp G. L. 85
siren G. L. 72
skank G. L. 40
skinflint G. L. 12
slacker G. L. 7
sloth G. L. 38
slouch G. L. 43
slugabed G. L. 45
sluggard G. L. 44
slumlord G. L. 59
snitch G. L. 55
snoop G. L. 55
snoot G. L. 28
snot G. L. 59
soc G. L. 76
social climber G. L. 30
socialite G. L. 82
sot G. L. 57
sourpuss G. L. 1
souse G. L. 74
sow G. L. 73
space cadet G. L. 30
spastic G. L. 29
spendthrift G. L. 75
spieler G. L. 33
spitfire G. L. 37

sponge G. L. 60
spud G. L. 7
swine G..L. 44
stick-in-the-mud G. L. 50
stickler G. L. 41
stiff G. L. 54
stooge G. L. 12
stray G. L. 85
stripling G. L. 31
strumpet G. L. 18
stuffed shirt G. L. 2
stupe G. L. 20
submoronic G. L. 79
swine G. L. 44
syndicate G. L. 9
tart G. L. 48
taskmaster G. L. 10
tease G. L. 70
tenderfoot G. L. 79
thrall G. L. 40
throwback G. L. 3
thug G. L. 56
tightwad G. L. 76
tinhorn G. L. 79
toad G. L. 7
tool G. L. 81
trendoid G. L. 25
tripe G. L. 64
trollop G. L. 78
trull G. L. 2
turncoat G. L. 16
turpitude G. L. 24
twerp G. L. 37
twit G. L. 78
tyke G. L. 67
tyrant G. L. 4
underhanded G. L. 49
underling G. L. 33
upstart G. L. 76
vamp G. L. 84
vandal G. L. 38
varmint G. L. 83
vermin G. L. 84
vile G. L. 84
virago G. L. 42
vixen G. L. 84
voyeur G. L. 83
waif G. L. 33
wall flower G. L. 20
wanna be G. L. 53
warlord G. L. 46
warmonger G. L. 81
washout G. L. 19
Weasel G. L. 16